THE WRITINGS OF PHILLIS WHEATLEY PETERS

Published according to Act of Parliament, Sept.ʳ 1, 1773 by Arch.ᵈ Bell.
Bookseller Nᵒ 8 near the Saracens Head Aldgate.

Poems on various subjects, religious and moral | By Phillis Wheatley, Negro servant to Mr. John Wheatley, of Boston, in New England.

P O E M S

O N

VARIOUS SUBJECTS,

RELIGIOUS AND MORAL.

BY

PHILLIS WHEATLEY,

NEGRO SERVANT to Mr. JOHN WHEATLEY,
of BOSTON, in NEW ENGLAND.

L O N D O N:
Printed for A. BELL, Bookseller, Aldgate; and sold by
Meſſrs. COX and BERRY, King-Street, *BOSTON.*

M DCC LXXIII.

Vincent Carretta, Professor Emeritus of English at the University of Maryland, specializes in eighteenth-century transatlantic historical and literary studies. In addition to more than one hundred articles and reviews on a range of eighteenth-century subjects, Carretta has published two books on verbal and visual Anglophone political satire between 1660 and 1820, as well as authoritative editions of the works of Olaudah Equiano, Quobna Ottobah Cugoano, and other eighteenth-century transatlantic authors of African descent. Carretta's most recent books are *Equiano, the African: Biography of a Self-Made Man* (2022); *The Life and Letters of Philip Quaque, The First African Anglican Missionary* (2010), co-edited with Ty M. Reese; and *Phillis Wheatley: Biography of a Genius in Bondage* (2011). He is also the editor of *Letters of the Late Ignatius Sancho, an African* (2015).

THE WRITINGS OF

Phillis Wheatley Peters

EDITED BY

VINCENT CARRETTA

OXFORD
UNIVERSITY PRESS

OXFORD
UNIVERSITY PRESS

Great Clarendon Street, Oxford, OX2 6DP,
United Kingdom

Oxford University Press is a department of the University of Oxford.
It furthers the University's objective of excellence in research, scholarship,
and education by publishing worldwide. Oxford is a registered trade mark of
Oxford University Press in the UK and in certain other countries

Introduction and Editorial Material © Vincent Carretta 2019

The moral rights of the author have been asserted

First published 2019

First published in paperback 2024

Published in the United States of America by Oxford University Press
198 Madison Avenue, New York, NY 10016, United States of America

British Library Cataloguing in Publication Data
Data available

Library of Congress Control Number: 2023951851

ISBN 9780198834991

ISBN 9780192885296 (pbk.)

DOI: 10.1093/oso/9780198834991.001.0001

Printed and bound by
CPI Group (UK) Ltd, Croydon, CR0 4YY

MIX
Paper | Supporting
responsible forestry
FSC
www.fsc.org   FSC® C013604

For Pat

PREFACE TO THE PAPERBACK EDITION

As the title of *The Writings of Phillis Wheatley Peters* indicates, it is not simply a paperback reprint of the hardback *The Writings of Phillis Wheatley* originally published by Oxford University Press in 2019. This revised edition includes significant additions and some corrections in several sections of the earlier version, made in light of my own further research, as well as that of others. Given my arguments that Phillis Wheatley demonstrated as much control over her life as was possible during the eighteenth century for a woman of her age, race, and status, as well as that since the nineteenth century John Peters has probably been wrongly maligned as being overambitious for a person of African descent, the title *The Writings of Phillis Wheatley Peters* reflects how I believe we should refer to the author best known today as *Phillis Wheatley*.[1] I hope that my revised title will help readers better appreciate the opportunities as well as the precarity that aspiring women authors faced, even someone as extraordinarily talented and ingenious as Phillis Wheatley.

Others have also recently made compelling arguments that the author of my edition should be referred to as either *Phillis Peters* or *Phillis Wheatley Peters*.[2] I have chosen to use the latter because it combines the surname still most familiar to readers, with the surname most appropriate for her own ultimate self-identification. By marrying John Peters, Phillis Wheatley chose to discard her enslaved surname to embrace the name he had created for himself after he had gained his own freedom. Hence, Phillis Wheatley's decision to marry the self-made man John Peters may be seen as one of her most significant acts of self-fashioning, rather than as the disastrous mistake her earlier biographers would have us believe it was.

Phillis spent more than half her non-enslaved life surnamed *Peters*, not *Wheatley*. She was *Peters*, rather than *Wheatley*, for over 25% of the time she lived in America. Although she published forty-two poems under the name *Wheatley*, she intended to publish the thirty-three poems and eleven letters in her proposed second volume as *Phillis Peters*, the name she used as well with the three poems she published in 1784. As Hutchins notes, "To say her name, the one name she chose—Peters—is to honor her agency."[3]

[1] See my *Phillis Wheatley Peters: Biography of a Genius in Bondage* (Athens, Georgia: University of Georgia Press, 2023).

[2] Honorée Fannone Jeffers, *The Age of Phillis* (Middletown, Connecticut: Wesleyan University Press, 2020); Zachary McCleod Hutchins, "'Add New Glories to Her Name,'" *Early American Literature* 56:3 (2021), 663-667.

[3] Hutchins, 666.

CONTENTS

ACKNOWLEDGMENTS

This edition is greatly indebted to the staffs and collections of the following institutions. In the United States: the American Antiquarian Society; the American Philosophical Society; the Boston Public Library; the Church of Latter Day Saints' Family History Library; the College of Physicians of Philadelphia Historical Library and Wood Institute; the Connecticut Historical Society; the Dartmouth College Library; Emory University; the Folger Shakespeare Library; Harvard University, the Widener and Houghton Libraries; the Haverford College Library; the Historical Society of Pennsylvania; the Howard University Library; the John Carter Brown Library; the Library of Congress; the Library Company of Philadelphia; the Massachusetts Archives; the Massachusetts Historical Society; the New England Historic Genealogical Society; the Newport Historical Society; the Rhode Island Historical Society; the Wilmington Historical Commission; the University of Maryland, McKeldin Library; the University of Pennsylvania, Van Pelt Library. In the United Kingdom: the British Library; the Cheshunt Foundation; the Dr. Williams's Library; the National Archives (Kew); the London Metropolitan Archive; the National Records of Scotland; the Staffordshire Record Office.

For advice, assistance, encouragement, and support in my research and writing I thank Valerie Andrews, William L. Andrews, Paula Backscheider, J.L. Bell, Anne E. Bentley, Elizabeth Bouvier, Randall K. Burkett, Tara Bynum, Patricia Carretta, Sean P. Casey, Ashley Cataldo, Betsy Cazden, Philander D. Chase, Katherine Chiles, Patrick Collins, William W. Cook, Philip N. Cronenwett, Susan Danforth, Cornelia H. Dayton, Karen DePauw, Jeremy Dibbell, Peter Drummey, Norman Fiering, Samuel Forman, Henry Louis Gates Jr., Jordan Goffin, James N. Green, Elaine Grublin, Carole Holden, Andrea Houser, Maurice Jackson, Judi Jennings, Jane Kamensky, Phil Lapsansky, Bertram Lippincott III, Judy Lucey, Terry McDermott, Joseph F. Marcy, Jr., Julian D. Mason, Jr., Steve Mentz, Sylvia Miller, Margot Minardi, Philip D. Morgan, Kimberly Nusco, Felicity Nussbaum, Leslie Tobias Olsen, Adele Passmore, Zachary Petrea, John Pollack, Tracy Potter, David Powell, Kim Reynolds, Pat Rogers Anna Russo, Boyd Stanley Schlenther, Chernoh Sesay, David S. Shields, John C. Shields, Garry Shutak, Eric Slauter, Russell Stoermer, John Wood Sweet, Kirsten Sword, Lee Teverow, Margaret Thompson, Jennifer J. Thorn, Laurel Thatcher Ulrich, Ruth Holmes Whitehead, Edward L. Widmer, Conrad E. Wright, David L. Wykes.

My greatest debts are to the textual work and research of the excellent editors William H. Robinson and Julian D. Mason, Jr., who preceded me in working from Wheatley's manuscript and contemporaneous printed copies. The present edition has profited as well from the insights of John C. Shields and many other literary critics.

I am very grateful to Professor Julian D. Mason for his generous advice and encouragement and for bringing to my attention the recently discovered "Hymn to Humanity" variant at Emory University; to Joseph F. Marcy, Jr., for telling me of the new Wheatley variant poems at Dartmouth College; to William W. Cook for information about the Dartmouth variants; to Randall K. Burkett and Philip N. Cronenwett for conversations and correspondence regarding Wheatley variants at, respectively, Emory University and Dartmouth College; to Ruth Holmes Whitehead and Garry Shutak for, respectively, making known and available to me the references to Phillis Wheatley in the *Nova Scotia Gazette and the Weekly Chronicle* in the collections of the Nova Scotia Archives and Records Management.

I thank Brendan O'Neill, Eleanor Collins, Jacqueline Norton, Tara Werger, Jonathan Rowley, and Hannah Doyle at Oxford University Press for their encouragement and support in making possible this edition of Phillis Wheatley Peters's writings. I am grateful as well to my copy-editor, Monica Kendall, and proofreader Hayley Buckley.

I am particularly grateful to the following people and institutions for permission to reproduce transcriptions of Phillis Wheatley's manuscripts and published poems used in this edition:

"To the University of Cambridge, Wrote in 1767" and "On the Death of the Rev'd Dr. Sewall. 1769" (MSS Misc. Boxes W Phillis Wheatley Poems [manuscript], 1767; 1769), Courtesy, American Antiquarian Society.

Wheatley's 6 May 1774 letter to Samuel Hopkins (Chamberlin Collection, Ch A.6.20). Courtesy of Boston Public Library/Rare Books.

"[On the Capture of General Lee]." Bowdoin Family Collection (M15.2.3, box 1, folder 84a). Courtesy of the George J. Mitchell Department of Special Collections & Archives, Bowdoin College Library, Brunswick, Maine.

"On the Decease of the Rev'd Dr. Sewell" (A3/1/29); Wheatley's 25 October 1770 (A3/5/1), 27 June 1773 (A3/5/4), and 17 July 1773 (A3/5/5) letters to the Countess of Huntingdon, in the Papers of the Countess of Huntingdon. Courtesy of the Cheshunt Foundation, Westminster College, Cambridge, United Kingdom.

"To the Rev. Mr. Pitkin, on the Death of his Lady" and "On the Death of Dr. Samuel Marshall." (MS 09172, Phillis Wheatley poems). Courtesy of The Connecticut Historical Society.

"On the Decease of the Revd Doctr Sewall" and "A Poem on the death of Charles Eliot aged 12 months" (Rauner Ticknor 7669940.2; Rauner Ticknor 772501.1). Courtesy of the Rauner Special Collections Library, Dartmouth College.

Wheatley's 19 May 1772 manuscript letter to Arbour Tanner (Quaker and Special Collections, Charles Roberts Autograph Collection, American Poets 110). By permission of the Haverford College Library.

Wheatley's manuscript 9 February 1774 letter to Samuel Hopkins (Simon Gratz Collection, Box 7/Case 10, folder 36), and Wheatley's manuscript poem "To the King's Most Excellent Majesty" (Simon Gratz Collection, Case 6, folder 40). By permission of The Historical Society of Pennsylvania.

"A Poem on the Death of Charles Eliot" (Autograph File W: Phillis Wheatley, 1). Courtesy of the Houghton Library, Harvard University.

"On Friendship" (Thomas Montgomery Gregory Papers Collection, Box 37-12/folder 362). By permission of Howard University.

Poems on Various Subjects, Religious and Moral (London, 1773), and 28 February 1776 letter from George Washington to Phillis Wheatley. Courtesy, Library of Congress.

"Deism" (Pierre Eugène du Simitière Collection, Series X. Miscellaneous Papers from du Simitière [Scraps], 1740–83, Box 6/Folder 42); "On the Death of Mr. Snider" (Pierre Eugène du Simitière Collection, Series X. Miscellaneous Papers from du Simitière [Scraps], 1740–83, Box 6/Folder 44); "America," "Atheism," "To the Hon.ble Commodore Hood" (Rush Family Papers, Series IV. Miscellaneous Documents, Box 14/Folder 27). By permission of The Library Company of Philadelphia.

Untitled MS in Reverend Jeremy Belknap's 1773 diary; "An Address to the Atheist"; "An Address to the Deist"; "Atheism"; "A Poem on the Death of Charles Eliot"; and "An Elegy Sacred to the Memory of the Revd. Samuel Cooper D.D."; as well as Wheatley's manuscript 18 October 1773 letter to David Worcester [Wooster]; her 15 July letter to Mary Wooster; and Wheatley's 19 July 1772, 30 October 1773, 21 March 1774, 6 May 1774, 29 May 1778, and 10 May 1779 letters to Obour (Arbour) Tanner; and the 17 November 1774 letter from Thomas Wallcut to Phillis Wheatley. By permission of the Massachusetts Historical Society.

"Ocean." Courtesy of The Mark E. Mitchell Collection of African American History.

Wheatley's 21 April 1772 (GD26/13/663/2), 1 December 1773 (GD26/13/663/4), 29 March 1774 (GD26/13/663/5), and 30 October 1770 [1774] (GD26/13/663/6), Thornton to Wheatley, c.February 1774 (GD26/13/663/7) correspondence in the National Records of Scotland

(GD26/13/663), Edinburgh. By permission of the Earl of Leven and Melville.

"To the Right Honl. William Earl of Dartmouth," and Wheatley's 10 October 1772 letter to Lord Dartmouth (D(W)1778/I/ii/835), the Staffordshire & Stoke on Trent Archive Service, Staffordshire Record Office, Stafford, United Kingdom. By permission from the Trustees of the Dartmouth Heirloom Trust.

Wheatley's manuscript 14 February 1776 letter to Obour Tanner. By permission of the private owner.

For generous financial support for the research that underlies this edition I am indebted to the University of Maryland, the National Endowment for the Humanities, the John Carter Brown Library, the Massachusetts Historical Society, the American Society for Eighteenth-Century Studies, the Library Company of Philadelphia, Queen Mary University of London, and the John Simon Guggenheim Foundation. I am very grateful to my former dean, James Harris, and to my former department chair, Kent Cartwright, for having granted me leaves to pursue my research.

I thank the University of Georgia Press for permission to include in this edition's Textual and Explanatory Notes versions of sections from my *Phillis Wheatley: Biography of a Genius in Bondage* (2014).

Every effort has been made to trace and contact copyright holders prior to publication. If notified, the publisher will be pleased to rectify any errors or omissions at the earliest opportunity.

CHRONOLOGY

1753?	Future Phillis Wheatley Peters (PWP) born in Africa, probably south of Senegambia region.
25 October 1760	George III becomes King of Great Britain and Ireland.
11 July 1761	PW brought to Boston aboard *Phillis*.
July 1761	PW bought from slave dealer John Avery by Susanna (1709–74) and John (1703–78) Wheatley, King Street, parents of 18-year-old twins Mary (1743–78) and Nathaniel (1743–83), John, Susanna, and Sarah (d. 11 May 1752, aged 7 years, 9 months, 18 days). Wheatley family belongs to New South Congregational Church.
10 February 1763	Treaty of Paris ends Seven Years' War, known in North America as French and Indian War.
22 March 1765	Stamp Act passed in Britain.
After 11 July 1765	PW's first surviving MS poem, a brief elegy on deaths of Sarah and Oxenbridge Thacher, Jr. PW reportedly "wrote a Letter to the Rev. Mr. [Samson] Occom, the *Indian* Minister, while in *England*."
18 March 1766	Stamp Act repealed.
21 December 1767	"On Messrs. Hussey and Coffin" published in *Newport Mercury*.
1768	MS poem "To The King's Most Excellent Majesty on His Repealing the American Stamp Act," subsequently revised and published in *Poems on Various Subjects, Religious and Moral* (1773).
Late February–early March 1770	Unpublished MS elegy "On the Death of Mr Snider Murder'd by Richardson."
5 March 1770	"Boston Massacre."
1770	Now-lost PW MS poem "On the Affray in King-Street, on the Evening of the 5th of March."
October 1770	Broadside *An Elegiac Poem, On the Death of that Celebrated Divine, and Eminent Servant of Jesus Christ, the Late Reverend, and Pious George Whitefield, Chaplain to the Right Honourable the Countess of Huntingdon, &c &c.* (Boston) brings PW transatlantic fame.
June 1771	Broadside elegy *To Mrs. Leonard, on the Death of her Husband* (Boston).

18 August 1771	PW baptized at Old South Church by Rev. Samuel Cooper, of Brattle Street Church.
7 October 1771	"On the Death of Doctor Samuel Marshall" published in *Boston Evening-Post*.
29 February 1772	Proposal to publish a volume of PW's poems in Boston.
March 1772	"On Recollection" published in *London Magazine: or, Gentleman's Monthly Intelligencer* (London).
16 June 1772	Broadside elegy *To the Rev. Mr. Pitkin, on the Death of his Lady* (Boston).
22 June 1772	Widely reported Mansfield ruling in London that no enslaved person brought to England could legally be forced to return to the colonies as a slave.
10 October 1772	PW writes to the Earl of Dartmouth, enclosing MS poem "To the Right Honourable WILLIAM, Earl of Dartmouth, His Majesty's Principal Secretary of State for North America, &c. &c. &c.," subsequently revised version published in *Poems on Various Subjects, Religious and Moral* (1773).
Early 1773	Broadside elegy *To the Hon'ble Thomas Hubbard, Esq: on the Death of Mrs. Thankfull Leonard* (Boston).
8 May 1773	PW leaves Boston aboard the *London*, Capt. Calef.
10 May 1773	*Boston Post-Boy* publishes "To the Empire of America, beneath the Western Hemisphere. Farewell to America. To Mrs. S.W."
3 June 1773	*New-York Journal* publishes variant of PW's 1772 MS poem to Lord Dartmouth.
17 June 1773	PW reaches London.
26 July 1773	PW leaves London aboard the *London*, Capt. Calef, to return to Boston.
Early September 1773	*Poems on Various Subjects, Religious and Moral* (London: Archibald Bell, 1773) published in London while PW at sea.
September 1773	Unpublished MS poem "Ocean."
13 September 1773	PW arrives at Boston.
18 October 1773	PW tells David Wooster that she has gained her freedom since returning to Boston from London.
16 December 1773	Boston Tea Party delays until late January 1774 the unloading and distribution in Boston of first edition of PW's *Poems on Various Subjects, Religious and Moral*.

3 March 1774	Susanna Wheatley dies.
11 March 1774	*Connecticut Gazette; and the Universal Intelligencer* (New London) publishes extract of PW's 11 February 1774 letter to Rev. Samson Occom.
26 April 1774	300 copies of 2nd edition of PW's *Poems* arrive at Boston from London.
December 1774– January 1775	*Royal American Magazine, or Universal Repository of Instruction and Amusement* (Boston) publishes PW's "To a Gentleman of the Navy"; "The Answer" [By the "Gentleman of the Navy"]; and "Philis's [*sic*] Reply to the Answer in our last by the Gentleman in the Navy."
19 April 1775	Battles of Lexington and Concord.
19 April 1775–17 March 1776	British occupation of Boston, during which PW accompanies Rev. John Lathrop and Mary Wheatley Lathrop in exile in Providence, Rhode Island.
16 June 1775	Continental Congress appoints George Washington commander-in-chief of Continental Army.
26 October 1775	PW writes to George Washington, enclosing panegyric.
28 February 1776	George Washington responds to PW.
April 1776	*Pennsylvania Magazine* (Philadelphia) publishes PW's 26 October 1775 poem to George Washington.
4 July 1776	Declaration of Independence.
30 December 1776	PW sends James Bowdoin unpublished MS poem "On the Capture of General Lee."
12 March 1778	John Wheatley dies, leaving PW nothing in his will.
1 April 1778	PW intended marriage to John Peters announced. Tax assessment records describe Peters variously as a trader, shopkeeper, pintlesmith, physician, lawyer, gentleman.
29 May 1778	PW asks Obour Tanner, in Worcester, to write to her c/o John Peters, Queen Street, Boston.
15 July 1778	PW writes to Mary Clap Wooster, enclosing unpublished MS elegy "On the Death of General Wooster."
24 September 1778	Mary Wheatley Lathrop dies of "a tedious Bilious & nervous complaint," aged 35.
26 November 1778	Rev. Lathrop performs marriage of John Peters and Phillis Wheatley, "Free Negroes," in combined New Brick and Old North Church, Boston.

30 October 1779	Phillis Peters's "Proposal" for 2nd volume, containing new poems and correspondence, to be dedicated to Benjamin Franklin.
July 1780	John Peters loses large lawsuit brought against him by Susannah Child Sheaffe.
Mid-1780–4	John and Phillis Wheatley Peters (PWP) disappear from public prints while living in Middleton, Massachusetts, before returning to Boston.
18 October 1781	British forces surrender at Yorktown, Virginia, ending military hostilities in American Revolution.
3 September 1783	Treaty of Paris formally concludes American Revolution.
January or October? 1784	*Liberty and Peace, a Poem. By Phillis Peters* (Boston).
January 1784	*An Elegy, Sacred to the Memory of that Great Divine, the Reverend and Learned Dr. Samuel Cooper* (Boston).
28 July 1784	John Peters, "Shopkeeper," petitions for a license to "Retail Spirits & at his shop, and thereby be upon a footing with other shop-keepers in his way of Trade."
1 September 1784	John Peters imprisoned for debt.
September 1784	PWP's final proposal for 2nd volume published in *Boston Magazine*, includes "To Mr. and Mrs.,—on the Death of their Infant Son."
5 December 1784	PWP dies. Death announced in *Boston Independent Chronicle and Universal Advertiser*, 9 December 1784.
10 February 1785	*Boston Independent Chronicle and Universal Advertiser*: "The person who borrowed a volume of manuscript poems && of Phillis Peters, formerly Phillis Wheatley, deceased, would very much oblige her husband, John Peters, by returning it immediately, as the whole of her works are intended to be published." Manuscript remains undiscovered.
1786	First American publication of *Poems on Various Subjects, Religious and Moral*, in Philadelphia.
9–12 March 1801	*Independent Chronicle and Advertiser* (Boston) announces, "At Charlestown [just north of Boston], Dr. *John Peters*, aged 55."
2 June 1801	Administration of "John Peters late of Charlestown negro & physician, deceased, intestate." Debts far exceed his personal worth. Assets sold at auction.

INTRODUCTION

Phillis Wheatley Peters's life

Phillis Wheatley Peters (1753?–1784), as she is now known, was born around 1753 in West Africa, probably somewhere between present-day Gambia and Ghana.[1] She was forced to endure the Middle Passage from Africa to America in 1761, when she was about seven or eight years old. She was brought to Boston, where the transatlantic merchant John Wheatley (1703–78) purchased her to be a domestic servant for his wife, Susanna, née Wheeler (1709–74), and their eighteen-year-old twins, Mary (1743–78) and Nathaniel (1743–83). The Wheatleys renamed her Phillis, after the slave ship that had brought her from Africa.

Encouraged by her owners, Phillis Wheatley quickly became literate. Notwithstanding contemporaneous prejudices against her race, social status, gender, and age, Wheatley became the first published woman of sub-Saharan African descent when a Rhode Island newspaper printed one of her poems in 1767. The publication in Boston and London in 1770 of her funeral elegy on the death of the English evangelist George Whitefield (1714–70) gained Wheatley transatlantic recognition. She addressed the poem to Whitefield's patron, Selina Shirley Hastings, Countess of Huntingdon (1707–91).

Phillis Wheatley had written enough poems by 1772 to justify her attempt to capitalize on her growing transatlantic reputation with a book of her new, as well as previously printed works. Whether by necessity or choice, or a combination of both, her book was not published in Boston. Accompanying her master's son, Nathaniel, Phillis Wheatley sailed to London in late spring 1773 to arrange for the promotion and publication of her book. Her *Poems on Various Subjects, Religious and Moral*, dedicated to the Countess of Huntingdon, was published in London in September 1773. Wheatley was on her way back to Boston before her book appeared. She quickly took charge of promoting, distributing, and selling her book once it became available in Boston during the winter of 1773–4.

Phillis Wheatley's six-week stay in London was a turning point in her personal and professional lives. Having gone to England as an enslaved

---

[1] On Wheatley's life and times, see Vincent Carretta, *Phillis Wheatley Peters: Biography of a Genius in Bondage* (Athens, GA: University of Georgia Press, 2023).

African Briton, she returned to the colonies prepared to embrace the free African American identity that the American Revolution would soon make available to her. The network of associations that she established in London included many of the militarily, politically, religiously, and socially most important people in North America and Britain. Phillis probably agreed to return to Boston only if John and Susanna Wheatley promised to free her, as she told a correspondent, "at the desire of [her] friends in England."

One of those "friends" was Phillis's principal tour guide in London, Granville Sharp (1735–1813). Sharp had procured a ruling from the King's Bench in 1772 that no slave brought to England from its colonies could legally be forced to return to them as a slave. The ruling and its implications had been well publicized in Boston before Wheatley's departure to London. Sharp and Phillis probably discussed his judicial triumph the preceding year in extending British liberty to enslaved people of African descent. Sharp considered himself ethically and morally bound to help people in Wheatley's condition: "the glorious system of the gospel destroys all *narrow, national partiality*; and makes us *citizens of the world*, by obliging us to profess *universal benevolence*: but more especially are we bound, as Christians, to commiserate and assist to the utmost of our power all persons in *distress*, or *captivity*."[2] Nothing would demonstrate the significance of the Mansfield ruling more than the emancipation of the most celebrated enslaved person of African descent in the British Empire.

Rather than passively receiving the promise of freedom from her master "at the desire of my friends in England," Phillis Wheatley probably compelled Nathaniel Wheatley to agree to manumit her in exchange for her promise to return to Boston: one promise for another. As a businessman engaged in transatlantic commerce, Nathaniel Wheatley's word was his bond. In this negotiation, Phillis Wheatley had the stronger hand. In England the year after *Somerset*, and in the presence of Sharp and other "friends in England," to whom she could attribute the idea for her emancipation, and in front of whom she could insist that her master's son give his word that she would be freed if she returned, Phillis Wheatley could not legally be forced back to the colonies. In effect, the choice of freedom, the terms, and the place were hers to make. Phillis Wheatley's owners freed her sometime between her return to Boston on 13 September, and 18 October 1773, when she told a correspondent that she had been freed.

Although Phillis continued to live with her former owners until John Wheatley's death in March 1778 (Susanna Wheatley died in March 1774),

---

[2] Granville Sharp, *An Essay on Slavery* (Burlington, VT: Printed and Sold by Isaac Collins, 1773), 22–3. Emphases in original.

the practical effects of her liberation were immediate. Manumission gave Wheatley agency, the ability to act on her own behalf. But emancipation also gave her new responsibilities. She was now in the vulnerable situation of being a free woman of African descent in a world with very limited economic opportunities for any woman. Life was especially precarious for anyone trying to live by his or her pen during the eighteenth century. She overestimated by a few months how soon copies of her book would be sent from London to Boston. Her concern for protecting its profits reveals a young woman of extraordinary business acumen. Her decision to autograph copies shows that she anticipated that pirated editions would demonstrate the popularity of her work, but would cost her profits. Wheatley's surviving letters display a familiarity with the business of bookselling and the need for authentication that demonstrate how actively she marketed her works.

Wheatley's public anti-slavery stance became far more overt once she was free than it had been while she was enslaved. Her letter to the Indian Presbyterian minister Samson Occom (1723–92) denouncing slave owners as "Modern Egyptians" was widely reprinted in newspapers in March 1774 throughout British North America, including Canada. Wheatley increasingly came to believe that the colonial struggle for freedom from Britain would lead to the end of slavery in the former colonies. In her poem "To His Excellency General Washington" Wheatley endorses the revolutionary cause in late 1775. In her poem "On the Death of General Wooster," included in a letter to Wooster's widow, Mary, on 15 July 1778, Wheatley exclaims, "But how, presumptuous shall we hope to find | Divine acceptance with th' Almighty mind— | While yet (O deed ungenerous!) they disgrace | And hold in bondage Afric's blameless race?"

Much about Phillis Wheatley's life between 1776 and her death in 1784 remains a mystery. She probably returned with John and Mary Wheatley Lathrop in 1776 to Boston from their self-imposed exile in Providence, Rhode Island, during the British occupation of Boston. She probably lived again with John Wheatley. And she probably remained a member of Reverend Lathrop's congregation when they accepted the invitation from Reverend Ebenezer Pemberton (1704–77) to join with members of the New Brick Church to re-form the Second Church. (The British had destroyed Lathrop's Old North Meeting House during their 1775–6 occupation of Boston.)

Phillis Wheatley married John Peters (1746?–1801), a free black, on Thanksgiving Day, 1778, eight months after John Wheatley's death on 12 March.[3] She and Peters apparently shared the same address soon after

---

[3] Fortunately for Phillis Wheatley's biographer, there are few men named *John Peters* in relevant Boston records, and Phillis's husband can usually be distinguished from them by

John Wheatley died. Phillis Wheatley was optimistic in 1778 about the future. She continued to write and manage her own business affairs until she married. John Peters, like many of his contemporaries in the post-war United States, juggled several occupations to try to remain out of debt. He practiced law, as well as medicine, and styled himself a gentle-man. Phillis Wheatley Peters appeared to be on the verge of an *annus mirabilis* in 1780 equivalent to that of 1773, the year that saw the publi-cation of her *Poems*, and that brought her freedom. She sought subscrip-tions for a new book in 1779, and she and her husband were seemingly relatively prosperous.

In April 1780 John and Phillis Wheatley Peters moved to Middleton, Massachusetts, where John had been enslaved to John and Naomi Wilkins. After her husband's death, the widow Wilkins invited Peters to take pos-session of her house and land in exchange for satisfactorily providing for her and her daughter's needs for the rest of their lives. The agreement unfortunately soon began to unravel, leading to a series of lawsuits that eventuated in the ejection of Peters from Middleton. He and Phillis were back in Boston by the beginning of 1784. Phillis published no poems while living in Middleton, and none of her correspondence from that period survives. John and Phillis Wheatley Peters fell victim to the general eco-nomic depression that followed the war. John Peters, repeatedly incarcer-ated for debt, was probably in jail when Phillis died on 5 December 1784. She was about thirty-one years old. Her cause of death is unknown, but may have been related to the "Asthmatic complaint" that had afflicted her during previous winters. No records have been found of any births, bap-tisms, or burials of children of Phillis and John Peters. John Peters failed to publish Phillis's proposed second volume before he died in Charlestown, Massachusetts, just north of Boston, in March 1801.

Phillis Wheatley Peters's writings

Phillis Wheatley Peters began to compose verse while still a child. Her first known piece of writing is the recently discovered four-line elegy on the deaths of Sarah (d. 1764) and Oxenbridge Thacher, Jr. (1719–65). Congregationalist Reverend Jeremy Belknap (1744–98) transcribed the poem on the last page of his 1773 diary, which is interleaved in *Bickerstaff's*

comparing contemporaneous records. For example, Phillis's husband was certainly neither the *John Peters* listed in *The Boston Directory* (Boston: John West, June 1796) as "Peters John, labourer, Short street," nor the *John Peters*, probably the same person, listed in *The Boston Directory* (Boston: John West, 1800) as "Peters John, labourer, Belknap's lane." Tax assess-ment records prove that Phillis's widower lived in a different ward.

Boston Almanack. For the Year of Our Lord, 1773 (Boston, [1772]). Belknap identifies the poem as "Phillis Wheatley's first Effort_____A.D. 1765. AE 11."[4] Belknap transcribes the text twice, first in three lines, then in four. He may have been unsure whether it was prose or poetry.

Poems that Wheatley composed in 1766 and 1767 demonstrate how extraordinarily rapidly her poetic abilities developed. Her use of blank verse and enjambment in "On Virtue," dated 1766 in her 1772 "Proposals" for the publication of a book of her poems, reveals a level of skill and control that almost seems impossible for the author of the clumsy verses on the deaths of the Thachers. Some of that improved skill and control is no doubt due to Wheatley's practice of revising her compositions before publication. Her surviving manuscript variants of subsequently published poems show how dedicated she was to her craft. Their existence also demonstrates that at least some of her poems circulated in manuscript before publication.

Two of Wheatley's early poems that exist only in various manuscript versions enable us to follow her developing skill. "An Address to the Atheist, by P. Wheatley at the Age of 14 Years—1767—" is a revision of an earlier draft entitled "Atheism." Two versions of another of Wheatley's unpublished early poems, "Deism" and "An Address to the Deist— 1767—," are at least as philosophically and theologically sophisticated as "An Address to the Atheist." Comparison of the initial verse paragraph in "To the University of Cambridge, Wrote in 1767—," to the corresponding paragraph in the revised "To the University of Cambridge, in New-England" published in her *Poems on Various Subjects, Religious and Moral* shows how carefully and rapidly Wheatley improved her craft. The differences between the two versions in versification, diction, concision, and specificity of metaphors are striking.

Phillis Wheatley's poetry brought her recognition far beyond Boston while she was still an adolescent. Her first published work, "On Messrs. Hussey and Coffin," appeared in Rhode Island in the 14–21 December 1767 issue of the *Newport Mercury* through the support and contacts of Susanna Wheatley. It is undoubtedly a version of the poem "On two friends, who were cast away" that was promised and misdated 1766 in Wheatley's 1772 "Proposals." The heavily end-stopped couplets in "On Messrs. Hussey and Coffin" reflect the author's youth and inexperience. Its combination of Christian piety and classical allusions anticipates the themes found in many of Wheatley's later poems. The poem was never published again.

---

[4] Massachusetts Historical Society: Jeremy Belknap Papers, MS N-1827, Diaries 1770–5.

Phillis was already commenting on transatlantic economic and political subjects by the time she was about fifteen years old. She effectively claimed to be a proto-national American muse. The growing tension between Britain and its colonies occasioned several poetic responses from Wheatley, only one of which was published during her lifetime.[5] Wheatley commemorated the Stamp Act crisis of 1765–6 with "To the King's Most Excellent Majesty on His Repealing the American Stamp Act 1768." It is a draft of her "On the King" listed in the 1772 "Proposals," and was ultimately published in *Poems on Various Subjects, Religious and Moral* as "To the King's Most Excellent Majesty. 1768." Another of Wheatley's surviving poems on the Stamp Act crisis and Britain's other efforts to tax the colonies is more subversive than her published work on the same subjects. The allegorical "America" is a draft version of "On America, 1768," listed in her 1772 "Proposals," but never published.

The continuing unrest in Boston led the British government in 1768 to send Royal Governor Francis Bernard (1712–79) the four thousand troops he requested to try to keep the peace. Their presence had the opposite effect, however, because the residents of Boston were forced to house them. The occupation appeared to confirm fears of a design to impose tyrannical rule

[5] Wheatley's relationship to Revolutionary events has been frequently noted, for example: James A. Rawley, "The World of Phillis Wheatley," *New England Quarterly* 50 (December 1977), 657–77; John C. Shields, *Phillis Wheatley's Poetics of Liberation: Backgrounds and Contexts* (Knoxville: University of Tennessee Press, 2008); Betsy Erkkila, "Phillis Wheatley and the Black American Revolution," in *A Mixed Race: Ethnicity in Early America*, ed. Frank Shuffleton (New York: Oxford University Press, 1993), 225–40; Daniel J. Ennis, "Poetry and American Revolutionary Identity: The Case of Phillis Wheatley and John Paul Jones," *Studies in Eighteenth-Century Culture* 31 (2002), 85–98; Peter Coviello, "Agonizing Affection: Affect and Nation in Early America," *Early American Literature* 37:3 (Fall 2002), 439–68; Eric Slauter, "Neoclassical Culture in a Society with Slaves: Race and Rights in the Age of Wheatley," *Early American Studies* (Spring 2004), 81–122; Slauter, *The State as a Work of Art: The Cultural Origins of the Constitution* (Chicago: University of Chicago Press, 2011), 169–214; Phillip M. Richards, "Phillis Wheatley and Literary Americanization," *American Quarterly* 44:2 (June 1992), 163–91; Richards, "Phillis Wheatley, Americanization, the Sublime, and the Romance of America," *Style* 27:2 (Summer 1993), 194–221; Dickson D. Bruce, Jr., *The Origins of African American Literature, 1680–1865* (Charlottesville: University Press of Virginia, 2001), 39–91; Charles W. Akers, " 'Our Modern Egyptians': Phillis Wheatley and the Whig Campaign against Slavery in Revolutionary Boston," *Journal of Negro History* 60:3 (1975), 397–410; Helen Burke, "Problematizing American Dissent: The Subject of Phillis Wheatley," in *Cohesion and Dissent in America*, ed. Carol Colatrella and Joseph Alkana (Albany: State University of New York Press, 1994), 193–209; Sidney Kaplan and Emma Nogrady Kaplan, *The Black Presence in the Era of the American Revolution, 1777–1800*, rev. ed. (Amherst: University of Massachusetts Press, 1989); T.H. Breen, "Making History: The Force of Public Opinion and the Last Years of Slavery in Revolutionary Massachusetts," in *Through a Glass Darkly: Reflections on Personal Identity in Early America*, ed. Ronald Hoffman, Mechal Sobel, and Fredrika J. Teute (Chapel Hill: Published for the Omohundro Institute of Early American History & Culture, Williamsburg, Virginia, by the University of North Carolina Press, 1997), 67–95.

on the colonies. The formation of the self-described "Sons of Liberty" and subsequent acts of resistance in turn appeared to confirm British fears of a colonial rebellion. Harassment of the occupying forces soon led to the death of eleven-year-old Christopher Snider (sometimes spelled Seider). He was only about two years younger than Wheatley when she commemorated him as "the first martyr for the [colonial] cause" (l. 2) in her never-published "On the Death of Mr. Snider Murder'd by Richardson." The Boston Massacre was the subject of Wheatley's now-lost "On the Affray in King-Street, on the Evening of the 5th of March" advertised in her 1772 "Proposals."

Wheatley also continued to write non-political occasional poems in response to current events: "On the Death of a Young Lady of Five Years of Age," dated 1770 in Wheatley's 1772 "Proposals," was probably circulated in manuscript before being first published in her 1773 *Poems*. Wheatley's conflation of religious and political themes in her unpublished eulogies for Reverend Joseph Sewall in 1769, and for the little-known Snider in 1770 anticipated the first poem that she published in Boston, the poem that arguably eventually led to her freedom. The announcement in October 1770 of Wheatley's illustrated broadside elegy occasioned by the recent death of George Whitefield was more appropriate for an established poet than for a seventeen-year-old enslaved girl. Wheatley closes *An Elegiac Poem, On the Death of that Celebrated Divine, and Eminent Servant of Jesus Christ, the Late Reverend, and Pious George Whitefield, Chaplain to the Right Honourable the Countess of Huntingdon, &c &c.* with a direct address to Whitefield's patron, as if Wheatley, too, is bidding for the Countess of Huntingdon's patronage.

The widespread distribution, and enthusiastic reception of Phillis's elegy inaugurated the most productive period of her life. She quickly followed that elegy with others on locally eminent people known to the Wheatley family. Her *To Mrs. Leonard, on the Death of her Husband* was published in Boston as a broadside shortly after the death of Dr. Thomas Leonard (1744–71) on 21 June. His widow, to whom he had been married for less than nine months, was Thankfull Leonard (1745–72), daughter of Thomas Hubbard (1702–73). She would become the subject of Wheatley's Boston broadside *To the Hon'ble Thomas Hubbard, Esq; On the Death of Mrs. Thankfull Leonard* at the beginning of 1773. Phillis knew the Hubbard family because they had been neighbors of the Wheatleys on King Street. Samuel Marshall (1735–71), a relative of Susanna Wheatley, was the subject of Phillis's "On the Death of Doctor SAMUEL MARSHALL," which appeared unsigned in the *Boston Evening-Post* on 7 October 1771.

During 1772 Wheatley wrote more occasional poems on Christian consolation, offering the familiar admonition to appreciate the loss of this world as the means to gain a greater. She assumes a position of moral and religious authority in these elegies more insistently than she had ever done before in her published works. In "To the University of Cambridge," written five years earlier, she had audaciously called on "the muses" to "assist" her in warning and advising prospective ministers. In *To the Rev. Mr. Pitkin, on the DEATH of his LADY*, published as a broadside on 16 June 1772, Wheatley adopts the persona of "the Muse" herself. Consolation is also the theme of "A Poem on the Death of *Charles Eliot*, Aged 12 Months," which Wheatley sent to the child's father, Samuel Eliot (1739–1820), on 1 September 1772. Wheatley distributed the poem in manuscript before she revised and published it in her *Poems* the following year.

Phillis Wheatley and her owners confidently announced in the *Boston Censor* on 29 February, 14 March, and 18 April 1772 the "Proposals for Printing by Subscription" a rather expensive book. It was to include Phillis's new as well as previously published poems. The Wheatleys probably turned to Ezekiel Russell (1743–96) to produce the book because he had been one of the publishers of Phillis's Whitefield elegy. We do not know who wrote the "Proposals," but as an editor of Wheatley's writings observes, she very likely was its author: "Certainly she cooperated in [its] conception and contents."[6] Readers of the *Boston Censor* must have been startled by the elaborate advertisement for a book of poetry by an enslaved adolescent girl. Publication of the "Proposals" in the *Boston Censor* was apparently part of a sophisticated transatlantic publicity campaign. The "Poetical Essays" section in the March 1772 issue of the prestigious *London Magazine: Or, Gentleman's Monthly Intelligencer* included Wheatley's most belletristic, or literary, poem to date. It was titled "On Recollection" when it was republished in her *Poems on Various Subjects, Religious and Moral* in London in 1773.

Why Wheatley's *Poems on Various Subjects, Religious and Moral* was not published in Boston is unclear. John Andrews (1743–1822), a Boston lawyer, offers two very different explanations. On the one hand, Andrews complained on 29 May 1772 to his brother-in-law, William Barrell, a merchant in Philadelphia, "Its above two months since I subscribed for Phillis's poems, which I expected to have sent you long ago, but the want of Spirit to carry on any thing of the kind here has prevented it, as they are

---

[6] Julian D. Mason, Jr., ed., *The Poems of Phillis Wheatley: Revised and Enlarged Edition with an Additional Poem* (Chapel Hill: University of North Carolina Press, 1966; rev. ed. 1989), 35.

not yet publish'd."[7] In other words, Andrews says that despite the seem-ingly coordinated transatlantic effort to elicit support, Wheatley failed to obtain the three hundred subscribers in Boston that Ezekiel Russell thought he needed to make the risk of publishing her book of poems worth taking.

On the other hand, Andrews told his brother-in-law on 24 February 1773 that Phillis participated in the decision to withdraw the manuscript of her book from Russell in Boston, and that she played a very active role in marketing it to a London publisher instead:

In regard to Phillis's poems they will originate from a London press, as she was blam'd by her friends for print^g them here & made to expect a large emolument if she sent ye copy home [i.e., London] which induced her to remand it of ye printers & dld [delivered] it [to] Capt Calef who could not sell it by reason of their not crediting ye performance to be by a Negro, since which she has had a paper Drawn up & signed by the Gov. Councils, Ministers & most of ye people of note in this place, certifying the authenticity of it, which Capt Calef carried last fall, therfore [sic] we may expect it in print by the spring ships, it is supposed the Coppy [sic] will sell for £100 Ster[lin]^g.[8]

Wheatley's poems continued to circulate in manuscript through her network of women friends. On 30 January 1773 Elizabeth Wallcut (1721–1811) wrote to the youngest of her three sons, Thomas (1758–1840), who was attending Dartmouth College, "according to your Desire I have Sent you Dr Sewalls picture and the Verses on his Death Composd by phillis wheetly which with a piece She made on our Colledg ["To the University of Cambridge"] She Sends as a present to you..."[9] Thomas Wallcut was five years younger than Phillis, who corresponded with him initially through his mother, and soon directly. He was one of the earliest (and youngest) admirers of Wheatley's poetry, and she actively promoted his education.[10]

Phillis Wheatley herself continued to distribute her work in manuscript, as well as in print. She wrote "To the Right Honourable WILLIAM, Earl of Dartmouth, His Majesty's Principal Secretary of State for North America, &c." in October 1772 at the suggestion of Thomas Wooldridge (d. 1795), an Englishman who had gone to America to assess the state of the colonies for Dartmouth (1731–1801). Dartmouth had been appointed secretary of state for the colonies and president of the Board of Trade and

---

[7] Massachusetts Historical Society: Andrews-Eliot MS N-1774, #7.
[8] Massachusetts Historical Society: Andrews-Eliot MS N-1774, #16.
[9] Massachusetts Historical Society: Thomas Wallcut Papers.
[10] Thomas Wallcut later became an author, copier of documents, and an antiquarian.

Foreign Plantations in August 1772, during the ministry of Lord North (1732–92), a position Dartmouth held until November 1775. Wooldridge forwarded Wheatley's poem, with its accompanying letter from her, to Dartmouth in November 1772.

"To His Honour the Lieutenant-Governor, on the Death of his Lady. *March* 24, 1773" made its public appearance in Wheatley's *Poems* in 1773, but she probably gave a manuscript copy of it privately to Andrew Oliver (1706–74), lieutenant governor of Massachusetts, soon after the death on 17 March 1773 of his wife, Mary Sanford Oliver. Like Thomas Hubbard, Andrew Oliver was sufficiently impressed by Wheatley's poem on the death of his loved one to later publicly vouch for the authenticity of her poetry.

By the end of 1772 Phillis Wheatley had been ill for months. She had yet to find a publisher. And she still had not heard back from the Countess of Huntingdon directly since sending her the elegy on Whitefield in 1770. Wheatley knew through intermediaries, however, that the Countess had received her letter and poem. The Countess was so intrigued by what she had read that she turned to members of what was commonly called her Huntingdonian Connexion to try to learn more about the young poet's Christian piety and authenticity as an author. Richard Cary (1717–90), who lived in Charlestown, Massachusetts, reported to the Countess on 25 May 1772 that "The Negro Girl of Mrs Wheatley's, by her Virtuous Behaviour and Conversation in Life, gives Reason to believe, she's a Subject of Divine Grace—remarkable for her Piety, of an extraordinary Genius, and in full Communion with one of the Churches, the Family, & Girl, was affected at the kind enquiry Your Ladiship made after her."[11]

On 19 March 1773 Bernard Page, another of the Countess's American correspondents, corroborated Cary's account of Phillis's piety and talent. Shortly after Page had written to the Countess, Susanna Wheatley informed Reverend Samson Occom that the process of finding a publisher and patron in London had already been set in motion. Robert Calef, who frequently conducted transatlantic business for the Wheatleys, sailed for London on 15 November 1772, arriving at the mouth of the River Thames on 17 December.[12] On 29 March Susanna Wheatley sent Occom a copy of a 5 January letter that she had received from captain Calef. Calef had brought a copy of Phillis's book manuscript to England with him. Acting as her literary agent, Calef had enlisted Archibald Bell to publish her book,

---

[11] Huntingdon Papers at the Cheshunt Foundation, Westminster College, Cambridge, UK: A3/5/6.
[12] *Boston Post Boy*, 16 November 1772; *London Chronicle*, 17 December 1772.

if a patron could be found. Susanna told Occom that Bell's mission as a go-between to gain Phillis her patron had been successful.

Phillis no doubt concurred with Susanna and John Wheatley that she should go to London before the publication of her book. Nathaniel Wheatley would accompany her. He had business to conduct for the family, and a marriage to arrange for himself in London. Phillis and Nathaniel Wheatley sailed from Boston with Robert Calef on the *London Packet* on 8 May 1773. Concern about her health, rather than a desire to publicize her forthcoming book, was given as the primary motive for having her go. Phillis's owners were making an extraordinary investment in her celebrity, and taking a considerable risk that her health and the ship would survive an always-dangerous transatlantic voyage. Events would show that she probably had her own even more powerful motive for going to London: the opportunity to gain her freedom.

Everything related to Wheatley's trip to London suggests that a marketing mastermind lay behind its preparation and execution. Colonial newspapers announced her imminent and eventual departure.[13] To ensure that potential colonial readers remained aware of Phillis, new poems by her were published in North America during her absence. The *Boston Post-Boy* published on 10 May "To the Empire of America, Beneath the Western Hemisphere. Farewell to America. To Mrs. S.W.," dated 7 May 1773. Other colonial newspapers republished it during the following weeks.[14] And on 3 June 1773 the *New-York Journal* published a variant of Wheatley's 1772 poem to Dartmouth. On 15 June 1773, two days before Phillis Wheatley arrived in London, the *Morning Post and Daily Advertiser* published there the most recent advertisement of her "Proposals."

For the London market Phillis and Susanna Wheatley anticipated questions about the authenticity of Phillis's poetry. A sophisticated publicity campaign was mounted on both sides of the Atlantic. Phillis Wheatley's own contribution to the production, publication, and distri-

---

[13] The *Boston News-Letter* (6 May), the *Connecticut Journal and New-Haven Post-Boy* (7 May), the *Providence Gazette* (8 May), the *Boston Evening Post* (10 May), the *Boston Gazette* (10 May), the *Boston Post-Boy* (10 May), the *Connecticut Courant* (11 May), the *Boston News-Letter* (13 May), the *Pennsylvania Chronicle* (17 May), the *Pennsylvania Packet* (24 May), and the *New York Gazette and Weekly Post-Boy* (27 May).

[14] The *Boston Evening Post* (10 May), the *Boston News-Letter* (13 May), the *Essex Gazette* (18 May), the *Pennsylvania Packet* (24 May), the *Connecticut Courant* (25 May), the *Massachusetts Spy* (27 May), and the *New Hampshire Gazette* (18 June). The *London Chronicle* (1–3 July) also published Wheatley's "Farewell," with a letter from Boston addressed to the printer of the *London Chronicle* dated 10 May that expand the dedication to "S.W." to read "Susanna W—."

bution of the first book in English by a person of African descent should not be underestimated. She played a very active role in getting her poems into print by gathering the signatures needed to certify her authorship. Solicitations for subscribers to the forthcoming London edition of Phillis Wheatley's book appeared in Boston and London newspapers before she left Boston.

Potential buyers were told that the 1773 book will be "Dedicated by Permission" to the Countess of Huntingdon, and "adorned with an elegant Frontispiece, representing the Author." The booksellers Edward Cox and Edward Berry received subscriptions in Boston. The advertisements in the London *Morning Post and Daily Advertiser* on 21 April and 1 May 1773 include the same information as that found in the Boston newspapers, but are much more elaborate. The London advertisements include the address to the public, the attestation, and the letter from John Wheatley that would appear in the published book. Booksellers from one end of greater London to the other, as well as in Nova Scotia, Canada, solicited subscriptions for the book.

The pre-publication marketing that Phillis participated in during her stay in London continued after she left England on 26 July 1773. *The Morning Post and Daily Advertiser* published further advertisements for her forthcoming book on 6 and 11 August. Archibald Bell registered Wheatley's *Poems* with the Stationers' Company on 10 September to protect his copyright on the first book by an English-speaking author of African descent. The first advertisement of the book itself had appeared in the *London Chronicle* the previous day.

Wheatley, or Bell, or both, revised the volume she had proposed in 1772 to be more appropriate for a London audience. Whereas the 1772 proposal identifies Phillis as "at present a Slave," the 1773 proposal for a primarily London market more appropriately describes her euphemistically as "A Negro Servant to Mr. Wheatley of *Boston*." Titles of poems were changed to be less circumstantial for readers unfamiliar with Boston residents. For example, "To Mrs. *Leonard*, on the Death of her Husband" became "To a Lady on the Death of her Husband." Changes in the titles of the elegies emphasized more strongly than before that the subject of the poems was the theological insignificance of mortality, rather than the social significance of the particular persons who had died. Many of the works in Wheatley's *Poems* written after she published her 1772 "Proposals" deal with philosophical and belletristic subjects intended to appeal to a general audience: "Thoughts on the Works of Providence," "An Hymn to the Morning," "An Hymn to the Evening," "On Recollection," "On Imagination," and

"An Hymn to Humanity."[15] Many of these poems notably contain theistic
but not specifically Christian elements. Unsurprisingly, the earliest reviewers
of Wheatley's *Poems on Various Subjects, Religious and Moral* most often
cite and quote her belletristic works.[16]

Wheatley's references in these more recently written works to her ethnicity and enslaved status are subdued and indirect. For example, the
speaker in "On Recollection" refers to herself as a "vent'rous *Afric*" (l. 2),
without further comment on her origin. Readers of "On Imagination"
were presumably expected to note the contrast between the "silken fetters"
(l. 11) and "soft captivity" (l. 12) imposed by "roving *Fancy*" (l. 9), and
the harsh reality of chattel slavery.[17] Poems whose subjects were likely to
be politically inflammatory to a British readership were dropped from the
1773 *Poems*: "On the Death of Master *Seider*, who was killed by *Ebenezer
Richardson*"; "On the Arrival of the Ships of War, and landing of the
Troops"; and "On the Affray in King-Street, on the Evening of the 5th of
March."

Wheatley returned to Boston before she had the chance to savor the
excitement of the publication and reception of her book. No doubt in part
because of Huntingdon's patronage and protection, nine British periodicals
soon reviewed Wheatley's *Poems*. The reviews are generally favorable,
although usually somewhat patronizing. Many of the reviews include
exemplary poems from the collection. Before reproducing the text of "To
Maecenas," the anonymous writer in the *Critical Review* opines that "[t]he
Negroes of Africa are generally treated as a dull, ignorant, and ignoble race
of men, fit only to be slaves, and incapable of any considerable attainments
in the liberal arts and sciences." Wheatley is a "literary phaenomenon"
because "[t]here are several lines in this piece, which would be no discredit

---

[15] Frank Shuffleton, "Phillis Wheatley, the Aesthetic, and the Form of Life," in *Studies in
Eighteenth-Century Culture* 26, ed. Syndy M. Conger and Julie C. Hayes (Baltimore: Johns
Hopkins University Press, 1998), 73–85. James A. Levernier, "Style as Protest in the Poetry
of Phillis Wheatley," *Style* 27:2 (Summer 1993), 172–93.

[16] On the reviews and Wheatley's visit to London, see William H. Robinson, "Phillis
Wheatley in London," *CLA Journal* 21 (December 1977), 187–201; Mukhtar Ali Isani,
"Wheatley's Departure for London and her 'Farewell to America,'" *South Atlantic Bulletin* 42
(November 1979), 123–9; Mukhtar Ali Isani, "The Contemporaneous Reception of Phillis
Wheatley: Newspaper and Magazine Notices during the Years of Fame, 1765–1774," *The
Journal of Negro History* 85:4 (Autumn 2000), 260–73.

[17] Shields, *Phillis Wheatley's Poetics of Liberation*, argues "that Wheatley developed what
we may term a relaxed Christianity...[that] begins to appear in the middle of 1771" (146).
John C. Shields, *Phillis Wheatley and the Romantic Age* (Knoxville: University of Tennessee
Press, 2010), 49, argues that the theme of the freedom of the imagination appealed to
Wheatley in part because of her own physical enslavement: "While the exterior world of
Boston...would confine her in the shackles of slavery, Wheatley claims ownership of her
own interior, limitless mind."

to an English poet. The whole is indeed extraordinary, considered as the production of a young Negro, who was, but a few years since, an illiterate barbarian."[18] The anonymous critic in the *London Magazine* includes Wheatley's "Hymn to the Morning" to vindicate his assessment that "These poems display no astonishing power of genius; but when we consider them as the productions of a young untutored African...we cannot suppress our admiration of talents so vigorous and lively. We are the more surprised too, as we find her verses interspersed with the poetical names of the ancients, which she has in every instance used with strict propriety."[19]

Political considerations also affected literary judgments. In the *Gentleman's Magazine*, Richard Gough (1735–1809) reprints "On Recollection," lamenting that "Youth, innocence, and piety, united with genius, have not yet been able to restore her to the condition and character with which she was invested by the Great Author of her being. So powerful is custom in rendering the heart insensible to the rights of nature, and the claims of excellence."[20] Although the anonymous commentator in the *Monthly Review* acknowledges that Wheatley "has written many good lines, and now and then one of superior character," his judgment of her works as a whole is harsh: "[t]he poems written by this young negro bear no endemial [endemic] marks of solar fire or spirit" because "[t]hey are merely imitative; and, indeed, most of those people have a turn for imitation, though they have little or none for invention." He is nonetheless "much concerned to find that this ingenious young woman is yet a slave. The people of Boston boast themselves chiefly on their principles of liberty. One such act as the purchase of her freedom, would, in our opinion, have done them more honour than hanging a thousand trees with ribbons and emblems."[21]

While Phillis Wheatley was on her way back to Boston, the *Pennsylvania Chronicle*, a weekly newspaper published in Philadelphia, raised the possibility in its 16–23 August issue that "the purchase of her freedom" may have motivated Phillis to have her *Poems* published in London:

It is to be hoped (though it is not so expressed) that the profit of this publication will in the first place be applied towards purchasing the freedom of the author; and, if, so, it is not doubted but every friend to the rights of humanity will liberally

---

[18] *Critical Review* 36 (September 1773), 232–3.
[19] *London Magazine* 42 (September 1773), 456.
[20] *Gentleman's Magazine* 43 (September 1773), 456.
[21] *Monthly Review* 49 (December 1773), 457–9. The nine reviews are reproduced in Mukhtar Ali Isani, "The British Reception of Wheatley's *Poems on Various Subjects*," *Journal of Negro History* 66:2 (Summer 1981), 144–9.

contribute to such an emancipation both of mind and body, always dreadful, but felt with double poignancy by genius and sensibility.

Although the first edition of Wheatley's *Poems* arrived in Boston by the beginning of December 1773, the Boston Tea Party interrupted its distribution to her American subscribers. The *Boston Gazette* first advertised the book by "Phillis Wheatley, a Negro Girl" on 24 January 1774.[22] The three hundred copies of the second edition arrived by the beginning of May. Subscribers could pick up their copies at the booksellers' shop, and new buyers could purchase a bound copy for three shillings and four pence. By the end of the year Wheatley's book was also on sale in New York, Pennsylvania, Connecticut, and Nova Scotia, Canada.[23] The advertisements no longer identify Phillis Wheatley as "A Negro Servant to John Wheatley," now that she was "on [her] own footing."

Phillis Wheatley continued to produce poetry on demand for people, as she had before publishing her book and gaining her freedom. She also continued to publish poems in response to current events after her return to Boston. Her elegy on the death of the Presbyterian minister John Moorhead, published as a broadside on 15 December 1773, stresses the effect of "the afflicting Providence" felt by those he left behind, rather than the theme of Christian consolation that pervades her earlier elegies. Wheatley took part in a light-hearted and somewhat flirtatious exchange of poems with a member of the royal navy in the first two issues of the *Royal American Magazine*, published in Boston in December 1774 and January 1775 during a period of rapidly deteriorating relations between Britain and its North American colonies.

Prior to the British occupation of Boston, Phillis Wheatley had quite carefully balanced her public expressions of revolutionary and loyalist sentiments. Her agreement to return to Boston from London in 1773 had set her on the path to fully embracing an African American identity. As her "To His Excellency General Washington" demonstrates, in 1775 she pledged

---

[22] The *Boston Gazette* repeated the advertisement on 31 January and 7 February. The *Boston Weekly News-Letter* carried the advertisement on 3, 10, 17 February.

[23] *Rivington's New York Gazeteer*, 14 April 1774; *Pennsylvania Journal and Weekly Advertiser*, 17 August 1774; *Connecticut Gazette; and the Universal Intelligencer*, 17 June; *Nova Scotia Gazette and Weekly Chronicle*, 11 May, 1 June 1774. The printer of the *Connecticut Gazette; and the Universal Intelligencer*, Timothy Green (1737–96), advertised that not only was he selling copies of Wheatley's *Poems*, but that "a few of the above are likewise to be sold by Samson Occom." The week before the *Nova Scotia Gazette and Weekly Chronicle* reprinted Wheatley's "Farewell," as well as the full London advertisement for her *Poems*, it reprinted the extract of Wheatley's letter to Rev. Occom. Cox and Berry re-advertised Wheatley's *Poems* as "This Day is Published . . . for the Benefit of the Author" in the *Boston Post-Boy* on 4, 11, and 18 July 1774.

her allegiance to the revolutionary cause, no doubt hoping that even the
most eminent slave owner in the colonies would ultimately apply the revolutionary ideology of equality and liberty to people of African as well as
European descent. Wheatley's poem and the letter that accompanied it
established a claim to the status of the unofficial poet laureate of the new
nation-in-the-making. But although Wheatley represents herself in her letter and poem to Washington (1732–99) as deeply invested in the revolutionary cause, she seems to hedge her bets on the outcome of the American
Revolution when she describes herself to Obour Tanner (1750?–1835) in
February 1776 as "a mere spectator... of this unnatural civil Contest."

National politics was not the only public subject on which the now-free
Wheatley commented during the 1770s. During the same period she
joined the developing transatlantic opposition to slavery and the slave
trade with the widely distributed publication in March 1774 of part of a
letter that she had recently written to Samson Occom. Occom was helping
her to sell copies of her *Poems*. The *Connecticut Gazette; and the Universal
Intelligencer* was the first of many colonial newspapers that reprinted
Wheatley's most direct condemnation of slavery and the hypocrisy of self-
styled freedom fighters.[24]

Wheatley's *Poems* and separately published works made her widely
known in the English-speaking world and beyond. She quickly gained
continental American attention. Benjamin Rush (1745–1813) refers to her
in a footnote on the second page of his *An Address to the Inhabitants of the
British Settlements in America, on the Slavery of Negroes in America*, which
he published anonymously in Philadelphia in February 1773. Rush, a
prominent Philadelphia physician, uses Wheatley, whom he does not identify by name, to prove that "We have [as] many well-attested anecdotes of
as sublime and disinterested virtue among [Negroes] as ever adorned a
Roman or a Christian character." Not all the attention that Wheatley's
early works received was positive, however. In *Slavery not Forbidden by
Scripture. Or a Defence of the West-India Planters, From the Aspersions
Thrown out against them, by the Author of a Pamphlet, Entitled, "An Address
to the Inhabitants of the British Settlements in America, upon Slave-Keeping."
By a West-Indian* (Philadelphia, 1773), Richard Nisbet anonymously dis-
putes Rush's citation of Wheatley as evidence for the equality of people of
African descent.

---

[24] The *Connecticut Gazette* (11 March 1774), *Boston Evening Post* (21 March), *Essex
Gazette* (22, 29 March), *Boston Post-Boy* (22 March), *Boston News-Letter* (24 March),
Massachusetts Spy (24 March), *Providence Gazette* (26 March), *Essex Journal and Merrimack
Packet* (30 March), *Connecticut Journal* (1 April), *Newport Mercury* (11 April), *Nova Scotia
Gazette and Weekly Chronicle* (3 May).

To Bernard Romans (1741–84), Wheatley was one of a kind, rather than representative of people of African descent:

Do we not see Solomon's words verified in Negroes? *A servant will not answer though he understand.*[25] The very perverse nature of this black race seems to require the harsh treatment they generally receive, but like all things, this is carried into the extreme; far be it from me to approve or recommend the vile usage to which this useful part of the creation is subjected by some of our western nabobs, but against the Phyllis of Boston (who is the *Phoenix* of her race) I could bring at least twenty well known instances of the contrary effect of education on this sable generation.[26]

The celebrity that Wheatley had enjoyed in London during her brief six-week visit in 1773 continued during the 1770s and 1780s. She quickly gained recognition as an author in the growing tradition of women writers. In his 1774 poem, "Wrote after reading some Poems composed by PHILLIS WHEATLLY [*sic*]," the pseudonymous "Alexis" praises "Afric's muse" as emblematic of what people of African descent could achieve if given access to education.[27] In *The Female Advocate*, a poem published in London in 1774, Mary Scott [Taylor] (1752–93) celebrates the literary achievements of her female English contemporaries, including Hannah More (1745–1833), as well as the "Poems by Phillis Wheateley [*sic*], a Negro Servant to Mr. Wheateley [*sic*] of Boston."[28] *The Female Advocate* effectively enrolls Phillis Wheatley in the informal society of British literary women known as the Bluestockings. The lines, diction, and footnotes in *The Female Advocate* devoted to Wheatley place her in the canons of English and philosophical poetry. Wheatley was clearly an alien figure in 1781, however, to Mary Deverell (fl. 1774–97), who seeks to praise her in "On Reading the Poems of Phillis Wheatley." Deverell's rather clumsily constructed eighteen-line poem transforms Wheatley into an Indian maid.

Mary Scott [Taylor]'s association of Wheatley with Hannah More did not go unchallenged. The anonymous critic of *The Female Advocate* in the November 1774 issue of the *Monthly Review* contends, "Surely Miss Scott has impeached her own judgment in thus associating the celebrated Miss

[25] Proverbs 29:19: "A servant will not be corrected by words; for though he understand he will not answer."

[26] Bernard Romans, *A Concise Natural History of East and West Florida.* 2 vols. (New York: Printed for the Author, 1775), 1:105.

[27] *Sentimental Magazine, or, General Assemblage of Science, Taste, and Entertainment* (London), 2 (September 1774), 416.

[28] Scott [Taylor], *The Female Advocate: A Poem Occasioned by Reading Mr. Duncombe's Feminead* (London, 1774), vii, viii.

More with the poor Negro girl, whose talent for poetical imitation we mentioned some time ago." Three satirical essays appeared in the London newspaper the *Public Advertiser* on 11 June, 14 July, and 23 July 1777. Their anonymous author depicts Wheatley as a threatening hypersexual mannish figure in the series of misogynistic attacks on the achievements of contemporaneous literary women.

Wheatley's *Poems* also brought her to the attention of prominent continental Europeans. Both sides in contemporaneous arguments about the intellect, educability, and literary achievements of people of African descent quoted and cited her. In France, Voltaire (1694–1778) wrote to a correspondent in 1774 that Wheatley's very fine English verse disproved the contention by Bernard le Bovier de Fontenelle (1657–1757) that no black poets existed.[29] Although François, Marquis de Barbé-Marbois (1745–1837) was impressed by Wheatley's abilities during his travels in America in 1779, he considered her freakish rather than representative:

> I shall tell you instead about Phyllis, one of the strangest creatures in the country and perhaps in the whole world.
>
> Phyllis is a negress, born in Africa, brought to Boston at the age of ten, and sold to a citizen of that city. She learned English with unusual ease, eagerly read and re-read the Bible, the only book which had been put in her hands, became steeped in the poetic images of which it is full, and at the age of seventeen published a number of poems in which there is imagination, poetry, and zeal, though no correctness nor order nor interest. I read them with some surprise. They are printed, and in the front of the book there are certificates of authenticity which leave no doubt that she is its author.[30]

Phillis Wheatley was a pioneer in the developing transatlantic tradition of authors of sub-Saharan African descent. Although Wheatley never met Reverend Philip Quaque (1741?–1816), an African Anglican priest in present-day Ghana, their mutual correspondent, Congregationalist Reverend Samuel Hopkins (1721–1803), made them known to each other.[31] Hopkins sent Quaque a copy of Wheatley's 1772 "Proposals," and he wrote to her about Quaque's missionary work in Africa. Hopkins also published in

---

[29] Mason, *The Poems of Phillis Wheatley*, 30, quoting Edward Derbyshire Seeber, *Anti-Slavery Opinion in France during the Second Half of the Eighteenth Century* (Baltimore: Johns Hopkins Press, 1937), 57, n. 54.

[30] *Our Revolutionary Forefathers: The Letters of François, Marquis de Barbé-Marbois [1745–1837], During His Residence in the United States as Secretary of the French Legation, 1779–1785*, ed. and trans. Eugene P. Chase (New York: Duffield & Company, 1929), 84–5.

[31] *The Life and Letters of Philip Quaque: The First African Anglican Missionary*, ed. Vincent Carretta and Ty M. Reese (Athens, GA: University of Georgia Press, 2010).

1776 parts of letters to him from both Quaque and Wheatley in an appeal for support of a planned, but never-executed, missionary project in Africa.

Wheatley's piety, especially as expressed in her "On Being Brought from Africa to America," in 1778 earned her the public praise of Jupiter Hammon (1711–c.1800) in Hartford, Connecticut. Wheatley's allegedly fortunate fall into Christianity through enslavement is the theme of Hammon's *AN ADDRESS to Miss PHILLIS WHEATLY* [sic], *Ethiopian Poetess, in Boston, who came from Africa at eight years of age, and soon became acquainted with the Gospel of Jesus Christ.*

To Ignatius Sancho (1729?–1780) in London, however, Wheatley's enslavement exposed the hypocrisy of slave owners who called themselves Christians, and who used Wheatley's talent as an excuse for self-congratulation on the "wanton power" they exercised over "a genius superior" to themselves. Sancho, a free African Briton who had been a slave and servant before becoming a grocer, thought that Wheatley's return to Boston was a tragic move. He wrote on 27 January 1778 to the Quaker Joshua Fisher (1707–1783) of Philadelphia to thank him for having sent Sancho an anti-slavery book by the Quaker abolitionist Anthony Benezet (1713–84), as well as a copy of Wheatley's *Poems*. Sancho's letter establishes him as the first Black Atlantic literary critic. It also offers the first critical comments on Wheatley's work by another African Briton. Unaware that Wheatley had been free since 1773, Sancho expresses his concern about her status in America:

Phyllis's poems do credit to nature—and put art—merely as art—to the blush.— It reflects nothing either to the glory or generosity of her master—if she is still his slave—except he glories in the *low vanity* of having in his wanton power a mind animated by Heaven—a genius superior to himself—the list of splendid—titled—learned names, in confirmation of her being the real authoress.—alas! shews how very poor the acquisition of wealth and knowledge are—without generosity—feeling—and humanity.—These good great folks—all know—and perhaps admired—nay, praised Genius in bondage--and then, like the Priests and the Levites in sacred writ, passed by—not one good Samaritan amongst them.[32]

Wheatley's 1779 "Proposals" for her unpublished second book proves that she continued to write during the last eight years of her life, but very few of her poems and letters from that period have yet been discovered. For example, her 1779 "Proposals" includes a poem usually entitled "On the Capture of General Lee," whose surviving manuscript she dates 30 December 1776, but never published. Only three of Wheatley's poems were first published between 1776 and her death in 1784.

---

[32] Sancho, *Letters of the Late Ignatius Sancho, an African*, ed. Vincent Carretta (Peterborough, Canada: Broadview Press, 2015), 165–6.

On 15 July 1778 Phillis sent a letter signed "Phillis Wheatley" from John
Peters's residence in Queen Street to David Wooster's widow, Mary Clap
Wooster, whom she had never met. The enclosed poem, entitled "On the
Death of General Wooster" in Wheatley's 1779 Proposals, was occasioned
by Wooster's death on 2 May 1777. It is a eulogy for "a martyr in the Cause
of Freedom." Wheatley uses Wooster's imagined dying speech to castigate
the hypocrisy of fighting for the freedom to enslave others. Sending the
poem to Wooster's widow also gave Wheatley the occasion for tending to
business. As soon as the poem ends, Wheatley addresses Mrs. Wooster:
"You will do me a great favour by returning to me by the first oppy [oppor-
tunity] those books that remain unsold and remitting the money for those
that are sold—I can easily dispose of them here for 12 [shillings]/Lm.o
[lawful money] each—I am greatly obliged to you for the care you show me,
and your condescention [i.e., generosity] in taking so much pains for my
Interest." Wheatley's *Poems* was obviously still in demand five years after
having been first published in 1773. The higher price of twelve shillings
lawful money she expected to be able to charge for each copy reflects both
the continued demand for her work and the inflationary effects of the war.

Phillis apologized to Obour Tanner on 10 May 1779 for having "been
Silent" due to "a variety of hindrances," one of which was her preparation
of a second volume for publication, this time to include her correspondence as well as her poems. The description of the proposed book, which
was to be dedicated to Benjamin Franklin, is elaborate and ambitious.
It was to be approximately twice as long as her first book. The description
of the author in the advertisement does not assume that prospective buyers
would be familiar with her. The contents of the proposed book, however,
indicate a writer of transatlantic stature.

The number of poems concerning prominent American military figures
is balanced by those addressed to corresponding British figures. The
national events that are subjects of the poems, as well as the status of her
correspondents, reflect the maturation of Phillis Wheatley Peters as an
author, and her enhanced public profile. The titles and addressees demonstrate her growing interest in more secular rather than specifically Christian
subjects first evident in 1772. Her writings since 1772 also reflect her
increasing emphasis on the equality of people of European descent with
those of African descent, based on natural rights and political theory,
rather than solely on theological doctrine.

The proposed volume was front-page news in the 30 October 1779 issue
of the *Boston Evening Post and General Advertiser*, the newspaper produced by the intended publishers of the book. The lengthy advertisement
takes up more than the whole first column on the front page, under the

newspaper's motto, "Hail LIBERTY Divine, and PEACE, First-born of Heaven." The same newspaper repeated the advertisement on 6 and 27 November and 4, 11, and 18 December.

The absence of any reference to Phillis's maiden name may indicate that her husband played a dominant role in the planning of the proposed book. As a *feme covert*, the former Phillis Wheatley was now legally the property of her husband, as was anything she owned. She no longer had the right to sign contracts independently of him. Given his experience with the law, John Peters was undoubtedly well aware of his legal rights and authority. Hence, he was probably responsible for the decision to use only their surname in the advertisement. He may also have been responsible for pricing the book. It was to be significantly more expensive than Phillis's first book, even after accounting for the difference in the size and scope of the proposed larger volume, as well as the depreciation of continental currency. The proposed book was never published.

Phillis was not completely out of the public eye in Boston during her years of silence between 1780 and 1784. A woodcut portrait based on the frontispiece of her 1773 *Poems* appeared in *Bickerstaff's Boston Almanack…1782* (Boston, 1781). Phillis probably played no role in John Wesley's publication in his Methodist *Arminian Magazine* in London in 1781 and 1784 of variants of eight of her previously published poems. Abolitionist as well as religious concerns probably motivated Wesley's interest in Wheatley and her writings. Unlike Whitefield and the Countess of Huntingdon, John Wesley opposed the institution of slavery.

Shortly after John and Phillis Wheatley Peters returned to Boston from Middleton, Phillis published *An Elegy, Sacred to the Memory of that Great Divine, the Reverend and Learned Dr. Samuel Cooper* in early 1784. She also published in 1784 the pamphlet *LIBERTY AND PEACE, A POEM. By PHILLIS PETERS* to celebrate the Peace of Paris that Congress ratified in January. Not surprisingly given its subject, the poem exudes joy and optimism. The tone is even somewhat self-congratulatory. In her description of "Freedom," Phillis Wheatley Peters self-referentially quotes from her earlier poem to Washington: "*She moves divinely fair,* | *Olive and Laurel bind her golden Hair.*" Unfortunately, her vision that "So Freedom comes array'd with Charms divine, | And in her Train Commerce and Plenty shine" would not include her and her husband.[33] John Peters was arrested for debt soon after he and Phillis returned to Boston.

---

[33] Phillis and John Peters were unaffected by two consequential court rulings involving people of African descent made while they were out of Boston. Both were decided on generous applications of the statement in the preamble of Massachusetts' state constitution that "All men are born free and equal." The first case was won by an enslaved woman named

Phillis remained a subject of public interest. On 20 May 1784 Boston's *Independent Chronicle and Universal Advertiser* published "The Choice," by "the late Mr. Heman Harris" of Wrentham, Massachusetts, which contains the lines

> And to delight the studious mind,
> I'd in the next gradation find
> The Poets in a pleasing throng,
> From the great source of Grecian Song
> That shines in the page
> Down to the PHILLIS of our age.
>
> (ll. 48–53)

The *Independent Chronicle and Universal Advertiser* reprinted next to "The Choice" an emancipationist attack on slavery that a London newspaper had first published two months earlier.

Phillis tried again to reassert her own agency during her husband's absence by advertising in the September 1784 issue of the *Boston Magazine* another proposal for a second volume of her writings. The advertisement includes a hitherto unpublished poem that Phillis had written before her marriage. The difference between her elaborate and very confident-sounding 1779 "Proposals" and her rather desperate-sounding final one, however, is striking.

We can only speculate as to why Phillis Wheatley Peters could not publish her proposed second volume. Her first book had been published in England in 1773 because she was either unable or unwilling to use an American publisher in 1772. Unfortunately, the ongoing war effectively closed the British market to colonial authors in 1779. Her would-be publishers had failed to exploit her continuing celebrity by not referring to her premarital identity as Phillis Wheatley in advertising her proposed book. Her husband may have been responsible for that imprudent decision. Phillis probably did not have much time to promote her proposed book in 1779 before she and her husband left Boston and disappeared from public view for several years. There is no evidence that anyone had approached Benjamin Franklin about having the book dedicated to him. Assuming

---

Elizabeth, nicknamed Bett or Mum Bett (*c*.1742–1829), who gained her freedom in 1781 and promptly appropriated a surname befitting her new legal status: Freeman. In the second case, which began simultaneously with Mum Bett's, Quok Walker finally won his freedom in 1783 in a ruling by Chief Justice William Cushing that undermined the institution of slavery in Massachusetts. Although the state had not outlawed slavery, Cushing's ruling that it was unconstitutional meant that any slave who sued for his or her freedom in court would win.

that he would have been agreeable to such a gesture reflects an impressive amount of confidence. If John Peters was as arrogant as some early sources say, he may have been the source of such confidence. He may also be responsible for the mistake of overpricing the proposed book in a period of economic depression and wartime turmoil.

John Peters was almost certainly in jail for debt when Phillis Peters included a reference to her former identity, Phillis Wheatley, in re-advertising the proposed volume in 1784. When she was on her own she showed some of the same business acumen that she had displayed in the production and distribution of her *Poems* before her marriage to Peters. He was probably still incarcerated when the *Independent Chronicle and Universal Advertiser* notified its Boston readers on 9 December 1784 of the death four days earlier of "Phillis Peters formerly Phillis Wheatley aged 31, known to the literary world by her celebrated miscellaneous poems." Phillis Wheatley Peters's second volume never appeared. Two months after Phillis's death, John Peters sought to recover the "volume of manuscript poems && of Phillis Peters, formerly Phillis Wheatley, deceased" from "[t]he person who borrowed" it.[34] On 2 June 1791, Ebenezer Turrell Andrews (1766-1851) informed his co-publisher and co-bookseller in Boston, Isaiah Thomas (1749-1831), that he had told Peters they would publish the manuscript "if sufficient Subscribers appeared" (American Antiquarian Society: Box 1, Folder 16 of the Isaiah Thomas Papers). The manuscript included two of Phillis Wheatley's poems, [46] and [47] that Thomas had published in the *Royal American Magazine* in 1774-1775. Phillis Wheatley Peters' proposed second volume was never published. The now-missing manuscript is not included among John Peters' effects recorded after his death in 1801.[35]

The death of Phillis Wheatley Peters was quickly noted not only in the northern United States, but in the South as well.[36] Indeed, by far the most

[34] Peters placed the advertisement for the missing manuscript in the *Independent Chronicle and Universal Advertiser*, 10 February 1785.
[35] American Antiquarian Society: Box 1, Folder 16 of the Isaiah Thomas Papers. I thank Ashley Cataldo at the American Antiquarian Society for having brought this letter to my attention. "The Inventory of sundry Effects Belonging to the Estate of John Peters late of Charlestown dec^d tak^n the 6 day of augs^t 1801 by the apprisers," Massachusetts Archives: Middlesex County Probate Court File Papers 17255.
[36] The *Massachusetts Centinel* (Boston), 8 December 1784; the *Connecticut Courant, and Weekly Intelligencer* (Hartford), 9 December 1784; *Thomas's Massachusetts Spy: or, Worcester Gazette* (Worcester), 16 December 1784; the *Norwich Packet or, The Chronicle of Freedom* (Norwich, CT), 16 December 1784; the *Freeman's Journal: or, The North-American Intelligencer* (Philadelphia), 22 December 1784; the *New-York Journal, and State Gazette* (New York, NY), 23 December 1784; the *Connecticut Gazette; and the Universal*

extensive contemporaneous reaction to her death appeared in the *Virginia Journal and Alexandria Advertiser* (Alexandria, Virginia) on 6 January 1785:

A Letter from Boston mentions the death of PHILLIS PETERS, formerly PHILLIS WHEATLY [*sic*], known to the literary world by her celebrated miscellaneous poems.—This Negro Poetess is an instance, amongst numberless others, that the Supreme Being doth not confine his gifts to any particular colour; that the Africans are capable of improvement by education, and being rational creatures, are entitled to every humane attention—and as we derive wealth from their labours, it is highly reasonable that we educate and improve their minds in the great principles of Christianity, and thus compensate them for the severities of slavery.

Wheatley was the first person of sub-Saharan African descent to publish a book, and consequently the first international celebrity of African descent. She also founded the literary tradition of English-speaking authors of African descent. Although Wheatley never met her contemporaries Jupiter Hammon, an enslaved African American poet, Philip Quaque, an African-born Christian missionary to Africa, or Ignatius Sancho, a renowned contemporaneous African British author, they all knew of her and her writings. Sancho calls her a "Genius in Bondage." Eighteenth-century opponents of the transatlantic slave trade, as well as nineteenth-century antebellum American abolitionists, cited Wheatley's poetry as proof of the humanity, equality, and literary talents of people of African descent.

But Wheatley and her work have not always been so highly valued. Arguments about the significance of Wheatley and her writings, from her own lifetime on, reflect the evolving reassessment of African American and African British culture. Some commentators, black as well as white, have questioned the literary quality of her writings, or the political and social significance of her life, in support of their own ideological positions on whether and how people of African descent could or should produce literature. The most notorious was Thomas Jefferson, who denied that she was a poet. During the period from the late nineteenth century to the 1970s, a number of critics expressed neo-Jeffersonian denunciations of Wheatley's literary abilities, as well as of her racial loyalty.[37]

Intelligencer (New London, CT), 24 December 1784; the *Independent Gazeteer* (Philadelphia), 24 December 1784; the *South-Carolina State Gazette and Daily Advertiser* (Charleston, SC), 13 January 1785.
[37] For a somewhat tendentious survey of the criticism, see Shields, *Phillis Wheatley's Poetics of Liberation*, 43–69. See also Vincent Carretta, "Phillis Wheatley Peters," *Oxford Bibliographies Online* http://www.oxfordbibliographies.com/ and Dayton, Cornelia H. "Lost Years Recovered: John Peters and Phillis Wheatley Peters in Middleton." *New England Quarterly* 94:3 (2021).

Phillis Wheatley's place not only in the developing tradition of early transatlantic literature by people of African descent, but also in the universal canon of poetry, is undisputed today. Her role as a founder of African American literature is now finally secure even though the first American edition of her *Poems*, published in Philadelphia, did not appear until 1786. The many ways in which she subtly and indirectly confronts the issues of racism, sexism, and slavery have been increasingly appreciated. The prophecy offered by the pseudonymous "Matilda" in "On Reading the Poems of Phillis Wheatley, the African Poetess" (*New York Magazine*, October 1796) has been realized:

> A PHILLIS rises, and the world no more
> Denies the sacred right to mental pow'r;
> While, Heav'n-inspir'd, she proves *her Country's* claim
> To Freedom, and *her own* to deathless Fame.

FURTHER READING

Balkun, Mary McAleer. "Phillis Wheatley's Construction of Otherness and the Rhetoric of Performed Ideology." *African American Review* 36:1 (Spring 2002): 121–36.

Bassard, Katherine C. "Diaspora Subjectivity and Transatlantic Crossings: Phillis Wheatley's Poetics of Recovery"; "'The Too Advent'rous Strain': Slavery, Conversion, and Poetic Empowerment in Phillis Wheatley's Elegies." In *Spiritual Interrogations: Culture, Gender, and Community in Early American Women's Writing*. Princeton: Princeton University Press, 1999. 28–70.

Bilbro, Jeffrey. "Who Are Lost and How They're Found: Redemption and Theodicy in Wheatley, Newton, and Cowper." *Early American Literature* 47:3 (2012): 561–89.

Brooks, Joanna. "Our Phillis, Ourselves." *American Literature* 82:1 (2010): 1–28.

Burke, Helen. "Problematizing American Dissent: The Subject of Phillis Wheatley." In *Cohesion and Dissent in America*. Ed. Carol Colatrella and Joseph Alkana. Albany: State University of New York Press, 1994. 193–209.

Bynum, Tara. "Phillis Wheatley on Friendship." *Legacy* 31:1 (2014): 42–51.

Carretta, Vincent. *Phillis Wheatley Peters: Biography of a Genius in Bondage*. Athens, GA: University of Georgia Press, 2023.

Carretta, Vincent. "Phillis Wheatley Peters." *Oxford Bibliographies Online* www.oxfordbibliographies.com.

Chiles, Katy L. "'To Make a Poet Black.'" In *Transformable Race: Surprising Metamorphoses in the Literature of Early America*. New York: Oxford University Press, 2014. 49–63.

Cook, William W. and James Tatum. *African American Writers and Classical Tradition*. Chicago: University of Chicago Press, 2010.

Dayton, Cornelia H. "Lost Years Recovered: John Peters and Phillis Wheatley Peters in Middleton." *New England Quarterly* 94:3 (2021): 309–51.

Fichtelberg, Joseph. "Phillis Wheatley's Feminine Sublime." In *Risk Culture: Performance and Danger in Early America*. Ann Arbor: University of Michigan Press, 2010. 94–121.

Foster, Frances Smith. "'Sometimes by Simile, a Victory's Won.'" In *Written by Herself: Literary Production by African American Women, 1746–1892*. Bloomington: Indiana University Press, 1993. 30–43.

Franke, Astrid. "Phillis Wheatley, Melancholy Muse." *The New England Quarterly* 77:2 (2004): 224–51.

Gates, Jr., Henry Louis. *The Trials of Phillis Wheatley: America's First Black Poet and Her Encounters with the Founding Fathers*. New York: Basic Books, 2003.

Grimsted, David. "Anglo-American Racism and Phillis Wheatley's 'Sable Veil,' 'Length'ned Chain,' and 'Knitted Heart.'" In *Women in the Age of the American*

Revolution. Ed. Ronald Hoffman and Peter J. Albert. Charlottesville: University of Virginia Press, 1989. 338–444.

Hodgson, Lucia. "Infant Muse: Phillis Wheatley and the Revolutionary Rhetoric of Childhood." *Early American Literature* 49:3 (2014): 663–82.

Levernier, James A. "Phillis Wheatley and the New England Clergy." *Early American Literature* 26 (1991): 21–38.

Loscocco, Paula. *Phillis Wheatley's Miltonic Poetics*. New York: Palgrave Macmillan, 2014.

McBride, Dwight A. "Appropriating the Word: Phillis Wheatley, Religious Rhetoric, and the Poetics of Liberation."In *Impossible Witnesses: Truth, Abolitionism, and Slave Testimony*. New York: New York University Press, 2001. 103–19.

Mason, Jr., Julian D. ed., *The Poems of Phillis Wheatley: Revised and Enlarged Edition with an Additional Poem* (Chapel Hill: University of North Carolina Press, 1966; rev. ed. 1989).

Nott, Walt. "From 'Uncultivated Barbarian' to 'Poetical Genius': The Public Presence of Phillis Wheatley." *MELUS* 18:3 (1993): 21–32.

O'Neale, Sondra. "A Slave's Subtle War: Phillis Wheatley's Use of Biblical Myth and Symbol." *Early American Literature* 21 (1986). 144–65.

Reising, Russell J. "Trafficking in White: Phillis Wheatley's Semiotics of Racial Representation." *Genre* 22 (1989): 231–61.

Richards, Phillip M. "Phillis Wheatley and Literary Americanization." *American Quarterly* 44 (June 1992): 163–91.

Robinson, William H. *Phillis Wheatley: A Bio-Bibliography*. Boston: G.K. Hall, 1981.

Robinson, William H. *Phillis Wheatley and Her Writings*. New York: Garland, 1984.

Scruggs, Charles. "Phillis Wheatley and the Poetic Legacy of Eighteenth-Century England." *Studies in Eighteenth-Century Culture* 10 (1981): 279–95.

Shields, John C. *Phillis Wheatley's Poetics of Liberation: Backgrounds and Contexts*. Knoxville: University of Tennessee Press, 2008.

Shields, John C. *Phillis Wheatley and the Romantic Age*. Knoxville: University of Tennessee Press, 2010.

Shields, John C. and Eric D. Lamore, eds. *New Essays on Phillis Wheatley*. Knoxville: University of Tennessee Press, 2011.

Shuffelton, Frank. "On Her Own Footing: Phillis Wheatley in Freedom." In *Genius in Bondage: Literature of the Early Black Atlantic*. Ed. Vincent Carretta and Philip Gould. Lexington: University Press of Kentucky, 2001. 175–89.

Slauter, Eric. *The State as a Work of Art: The Cultural Origins of the Constitution*. Chicago: University of Chicago Press, 2011. 169–214.

Slauter, Eric. "Looking for Scipio Moorhead: An 'African Painter' in Revolutionary North America." In *Slave Portraiture in the Atlantic World*. Ed. Agnes Lugo-Ortiz and Angela Rosenthal. Cambridge: Cambridge University Press, 2013. 89–116.

Smith, Cynthia. "'To Maecenas': Phillis Wheatley's Invocation of an Idealized Reader." *Black American Literature Forum* 23:3 (Fall 1989): 579–92.

Stoddard, Roger E., compiler. David R. Whitesell, ed. *A Bibilographical Description of Books and Pamphlets of American Verse Printed from 1610 through 1820.* University Park, PA: Pennsylvania State University Press, 2012. 243–7.

Thorn, Jennnifer. "Seduction, Juvenile Death Literature, and Phillis Wheatley's Child Elegies." In *Atlantic Worlds in the Long Eighteenth Century: Seduction and Sentiment.* Ed. Toni Bowers and Tita Chico. New York: Palgrave Macmillan, 2012. 189–204.

Waldstreicher, David. *The Odyssey of Phillis Wheatley: A Poet's Journeys through American Slavery and Independence.* New York: Farrar, Straus and Giroux, 2023.

Walsh, Megan. "Phillis Wheatley and the Durability of the Author Portrait." In *The Portrait and the Book: Illustration and Literary Culture in Early America.* Iowa City: University of Iowa Press, 2017. 63–102.

Weyler, Karen A. "Mourning New England: Phillis Wheatley and the Broadside Elegy." In *Empowering Words: Outsiders and Authorship in Early America.* Athens, GA: University of Georgia Press, 2013. 25–75.

Wilcox, Kirstin. "The Body into Print: Marketing Phillis Wheatley." *American Literature* 71:1 (March 1999): 1–29.

Zafar, Rafia Zafar. *We Wear the Mask: African Americans Write American Literature, 1760–1870.* New York: Columbia University Press, 1997. 15–39.

EDITORIAL NOTE

This edition includes all of Phillis Wheatley's known surviving writings. Of the fifty-seven poems, as well as their authoritative variants, forty-six were published during her lifetime. Versions of nine of them were published before September 1773. Wheatley published thirty-eight works in *Poems on Various Subjects, Religious and Moral* (London, 1773). Only seven of her poems were published between 1773 and her death in 1784. Eleven poems survive only in manuscript versions. This edition also includes all of Wheatley's extant prose writings: twenty-three letters and four subscription proposals. It includes as well the three known surviving letters written to Wheatley. Excluded are the variant versions of several of Wheatley's poems that during her lifetime either appeared in the *Arminian Magazine* in London, or were transcribed by others: she apparently played no role in either their publication or their revision.

The organization of this edition of Wheatley's writings differs significantly from earlier ones, in which her book, *Poems on Various Subjects, Religious and Moral*, is followed by discrete chronologically arranged categories of individually published poems, manuscript poems, and correspondence.[1] This edition, however, reproduces Wheatley's writings in the chronological order in which they first appeared in manuscript or print to enable the reader to trace Wheatley's development as an author. And to avoid as much as possible disrupting the reader's experience of reading her works, textual and explanatory notes have been placed in a separate section following the primary texts.

Unless indicated otherwise, this edition retains the capitalization, format, italics, punctuation, spelling, and underscoring in Wheatley's manuscript and published texts. Comparing Wheatley's manuscripts with her published writings, however, shows that, like most of her contemporaries, she was inconsistent in her use of underscoring and punctuation. Hence, critical interpretations dependent on accidentals in Wheatley's writings, especially in her printed works, must appreciate that contemporaneous publishing house styles rather than Wheatley herself may have been

---

[1] William H. Robinson, *Phillis Wheatley and Her Writings* (New York: Garland, 1984); John C. Shields, *The Collected Works of Phillis Wheatley* (New York: Oxford University Press, 1988); Julian D. Mason, Jr., ed., *The Poems of Phillis Wheatley: Revised and Enlarged Edition with an Additional Poem* (Chapel Hill: University of North Carolina Press, 1966; rev. ed. 1989); Vincent Carretta, *Phillis Wheatley: Complete Writings* (New York: Penguin, 2001).

responsible for them. For example, printers conventionally italicized proper names. The eighteenth-century *long s* in all texts included in this edition has been replaced with the modern *s*. Distinguishing between Wheatley's holograph upper-case *S* and lower-case *s* is usually very difficult, and often open to dispute. An asterisk * in this edition indicates a footnote in the original text. This edition indicates Wheatley's holograph insertions with carets ^^. My editorial interventions are enclosed within brackets [ ].

The centerpiece of this edition of Phillis Wheatley's writings is of course her magnum opus, *Poems on Various Subjects, Religious and Moral* (London, 1773): 8°: [A]⁴ B–Q⁴; v, [4], 10–124, [4] pp.: [i] title-page, [ii] Entered at Stationer's [or Stationers] Hall., [iii] dedication, [iv]v Preface., [vi] The following is a copy of a letter sent by the author's master to the publisher., John Wheatley. Boston, Nov. 14, 1772., [vii] To the publick [an attestation]., [viii] blank, [9] 10–124 Poems on various subjects., [125–7] Contents. [128] publisher's (A[rchibald]. Bell's) ads.

Roger E. Stoddard and David R. Whitesell examined twenty-six copies of Phillis Wheatley's *Poems on Various Subjects, Religious and Moral* to identify two distinct editions, many variants, and two states of the frontispiece portrait.[2] Edition 2 "is a line-for-line resetting (with minor textual variants) of Edition 1 . . ., except that pp. [iv]–[vi] appear to be in identical setting. The two editions can be easily distinguished by the imprint spacing and the direction of the chainlines" (244). The vertical distance on the title-pages between the words "London" and "Printed" is twice as great in Edition 2 than in Edition 1. Stoddard and Whitesell identify two states of Edition 1 (twenty-three copies). The variants between the two states of Edition 1, and between Edition 1 and Edition 2 (three copies) are in spacing and accidentals (the capitalization, format, italics, punctuation, and spelling). Stoddard and Whitesell note that the copper plate for the inserted engraved frontispiece portrait "was re-worked in order to strengthen the lines for a second impression" during the production of Edition 1: "State A [has] no diagonal crosshatching behind the subject on the right side," while "State B" has. Edition 2 includes State B of the frontispiece (245). The variants in accidentals that Stoddard and Whitesell note between Edition 1 and Edition 2, especially in punctuation, line numbering, and catch words are corrections, albeit inconsequential ones.

    ² Roger E. Stoddard, compiler, and David R. Whitesell, editor, *A Bibliographical Description of Books and Pamphlets of American Verse Printed from 1610 through 1820* (University Park, PA: Published by the Pennsylvania State Press for the Bibliographical Society of America, 2012), 243–7.

Edition 1 of Wheatley's *Poems*, which probably comprised 300 copies, was published in London in September 1773, and arrived at Boston on 28 November 1773. But the books could not be distributed until 24 January 1774 because of the uproar surrounding the Boston Tea Party. Edition 2, published in London, probably in late February or early March 1774, arrived at Boston on 26 April 1774: Wheatley wrote to a friend on 6 May 1774, "I have recᵈ by some of the last Ships 300 more of my Poems."[3] Wheatley could not have been responsible for the differences that Stoddard and Whitesell identify in the two states of Edition 1 because she was at sea on her way back to Boston while her book was in-press in London. Rather than Wheatley herself, Bell's printer, who worked from Wheatley's manuscript, was most likely the person responsible for the variants in the two states of Edition 1. Given the brief period between the distribution in Boston of Edition 1 and the publication in London of Edition 2, Wheatley likely was not responsible for the very minor variant accidentals in the two editions.

My copy-text of Wheatley's *Poems on Various Subjects, Religious and Moral* is the Library of Congress copy of State B of Edition 1, with State A of the frontispiece. The corrections in accidentals made in Edition 2 are noted and incorporated in my edition. A digitized facsimile of the Library of Congress volume is freely accessible at https://memory.loc.gov/ammem/aaohtml/exhibit/aopart2.html.

Digitized facsimiles of the copies of State B of Edition 1 at Emory University, and at the University of Illinois at Urbana-Champaign, neither of which Stoddard and Whitesell examined, are freely available online at https://www.hathitrust.org/. The Emory copy bears Phillis Wheatley's signature.

A digital facsimile of the copy of state A of Edition 1 of Wheatley's *Poems* in the Columbia Department of Rare Books & Special Collections at the University of South Carolina, which Stoddard and Whitesell did not examine, is also freely accessible, as well as searchable, without a fee or subscription, at http://library.sc.edu/spcoll/wheatley/wheatleyp.html.

More than one state of the address "To the PUBLICK" exists. The South Carolina copy probably predates the Library of Congress copy: the variant misspellings "Huchinson," "Cheuney," and "Joon Moorhead"

---

[3] Letter to Obour Tanner, 6 May 1774 [42, below]. The 25 April to 2 May 1774 issue of the *Boston Post-Boy* reports that "Capt. White arrived here last Monday, and on Tuesday [26 April] Capt. [Robert] Calef, from London." Calef conducted trade between Boston and London for Phillis Wheatley's owners. He brought the 300 copies of Edition 2 of her *Poems* from London to Boston aboard the *London Packet*, the same vessel on which he had taken Phillis from Boston to and from London in 1773.

under "To the PUBLICK" in the South Carolina copy are subsequently corrected, respectively, to "Hutchinson," "Chauncy," and "John Moorhead" in Editions 1 and 2. The "E. Pemberton" in the South Carolina copy is subsequently changed in Editions 1 and 2 to "Ed. Pemberton," a misprint of the abbreviation for Ebenezer.

Digitized facsimiles of Wheatley's manuscript correspondence and poems are increasingly available online. For example, the digitized manuscripts at the Massachusetts Historical Society can be seen at https:// www.masshist.org/. Because an acquisition stamp mars the title page of the Library of Congress copy, the frontispiece and title page of Wheatley's *Poems* included in this edition are reproduced from the Massachusetts Historical Society copy of Edition 1 (Wat. Library C.VI.6).

A NOTE ON MONEY

Before 1971, when the British monetary system was decimalized, British money was counted in pounds sterling (£), shillings (s.), pence, or pennies (d.), and farthings. One pound sterling = 20 shillings; 5 shillings = 1 crown; 1 shilling = 12 pennies; 1 farthing = 1/4 pence. One guinea = 21 shillings. The coin was so named because the gold from which it was made came from the Gold Coast of Africa and because the coin was first struck to celebrate the founding in 1663 of the slave-trading monopoly the Royal Adventurers into Africa.

Each colony issued its own local paper currency, and a colonial pound was worth less than a pound sterling, with the conversion rates for the currencies of the various colonies fluctuating throughout the eighteenth century. The price of Wheatley's 1773 volume was advertised in pounds sterling. In 1774, 135 Massachusetts pounds equalled 100 pounds sterling in value. After the onset of hostilities the value of a Massachusetts pound depreciated rapidly. Between January 1777 and December 1779, when Wheatley sought subscribers for her proposed second volume of works, the value of a Massachusetts pound depreciated nearly thirtyfold. But even at that rate of depreciation, adjusted for inflation, the price in Massachusetts pounds asked by John Peters for Phillis's proposed second volume was still approximately three times the value in pounds sterling asked for her 1772 volume.

THE WRITINGS OF PHILLIS WHEATLEY PETERS

Phillis Wheatley's writings in chronological order

Phillis Wheatley's poems not published in Poems on Various Subjects *in chronological order*

[8] Ms. "America" [1768], p. 12.

[10] Ms. "To the Honble Commodore Hood on his Pardoning a Deserter" [February 1769], p. 14.

[12] Ms. "On Friendship" [15 July 1769], p. 20.

[13] Ms. "On the Death of M^r. Snider Murder'd by Richardson" [late February or early March 1770], p. 20.

[36] Ms. "Ocean" [September 1773], p. 107.

[35] *An Elegy to Miss Mary Moorhead, on the Death of her Father, the Rev. Mr. John Moorhead* [Boston, 15 December 1773], p. 114.

[46] [To a Gentleman of the Navy] [dated 30 October 1774; published in the *Royal American Magazine*, Boston, December 1774], p. 126.

[47] "Philis's [*sic*] Reply to the Answer in our last by the Gentleman in the Navy" [dated 5 December 1774; published in the *Royal American Magazine*, Boston, January 1775], p. 128.

[48] "To his Excellency General Washington" [dated 26 October 1775; published in the *Pennsylvania Magazine*, Philadelphia, April 1776], p. 129.

[51] Ms. "On the Capture of General Lee" [30 December 1776], p. 129.

[53] Ms. "On the Death of General Wooster" [15 July 1778], p. 135.

[56] *An Elegy, Sacred to the Memory of that Great Divine, the Reverend and Learned Dr. Samuel Cooper* [Boston, January 1784], p. 139.

[57] *Liberty and Peace, a Poem* [Boston, 1784], p. 141.

[59] "To Mr. and Mrs.—, on the Death of their Infant Son" [probably written between May 1773 and 26 November 1778; published in the *Boston Magazine*, September 1784], p. 143.

Variants of Phillis Wheatley's published poems in chronological order

[6] Ms. "To the University of Cambridge, wrote in 1767," p. 10.

[9] Ms. "To The King's Most Excellent Majesty on His Repealing the American Stamp Act" [1768], p. 14.

[11] Ms. "On the Decease of the Revd Doct^r Sewall" [presumably soon after 27 June 1769], p. 15.

[11a] Ms. "On the Decease of the rev'd Dr Sewell" [presumably soon after 27 June 1769], p. 17.

[11b] Ms. "On the Death of the Rev'd D^r. Sewall. 1769" [presumably soon after 27 June 1769], p. 18.

Phillis Wheatley's correspondence in chronological order

Proposals for volumes of Phillis Wheatley's writings in chronological order

The Writings of Phillis Wheatley Peters

[1]

Untitled handwritten transcriptions in Reverend Jeremy Belknap's 1773 diary, Massachusetts Historical Society.

> Mrs Thacher's Son is gone ^Unto^ ^Salvation^ her Daughter too
> 　　　　　　　　　　　　　　　　　　　　so I conclude
> 　　They are both gone to be renewed

Belknap's second transcription, immediately following the first, presents the text as a four-line poem, framed in the manuscript by an opening bracket:

> Mrs Thacher's Son is gone
> Unto Salvation
> Her Daughter too, so I conclude
> They are both gone to be renewed

[2]

"Atheism—"

Where now shall I begin this Spacious Feild
To tell what curses unbeleif doth yield
Thou that dost daily feel his hand and rod
And dare deny the essence of a god
If there's no god from whence did all things spring　　　5
He made the greatest and minutest thing
If there's no heaven whither wilt thou go
Make thy Elysium in the shades below
With great astonishment my soul is struck
O rashness great hast thou thy sense forsook　　　10
Hast thou forgot the preterperfect days
They are recorded in the Book of praise
If twas not written by the hand of God
Why was it sealed with Immanuel's blood
Tho 'tis a second point thou dost deny　　　15
Unmeasur'd vengeance Scarlet sins do cry
Turn now I pray thee from the dangerous road
Rise from the dust and seek the mighty God
By whose great mercy we do move and live
Whose Loving kindness doth our sins forgive　　　20

Tis Beelzebub our adversary great
Withholds from us the kingdom and the seat
Bliss weeping waits us in her arms to fly
To the vast regions of Felicity
Perhaps thy Ignorance will ask us where   25
Go to the corner stone it will declare
Thy heart in unbeleif will harder grow
Altho thou hidest it for pleasure now
Thou tak'st unusual means, the path forbear
Unkind to Others to thyself severe   30
Methinks I see the consequence thou art blind
Thy unbeleif disturbs the peaceful mind
The endless Scene too far for me to tread
Too great to Accomplish from so weak a head
If men such wise inventions then should know   35
In the high Firmament who made the bow
That covenant was made for to ensure
Made to establish lasting to endure
Who made the heavens and earth a lasting spring
Of Admiration. to whom dost thou bring   40
Thy thanks, and tribute, Adoration pay,
To heathen Gods, can wise Apollo say
Tis I that saves thee from the deepest hell
Minerva teach thee all thy days to tell
Doth Pluto tell thee thou shalt see the shade   45
Of fell perdition for thy learning made
Doth Cupid in thy breast that warmth inspire
To Love thy brother which is Gods desire
Look thou above and see who made the sky
Nothing more Lucid to an Atheist's eye   50
Look thou beneath, behold each purling stream
It surely can not a Delusion Seem
Mark rising Pheobus when he spreads his ray
And his commission for to guide the day
At night keep watch, and see a Cynthia bright   55
And her commission for to guide the night
See how the stars when the[y] do sing his praise
Witness his essence in celestial Lays

[1767]

[2a]

"Atheism—Boston July 1769"

Where now shall I begin this Spacious Feild
To tell what curses unbeleif doth yeild
Thou that dost daily feel his hand and rod—
And dare deny the essence of a God
If there's no heaven whither wilt thou go?   5
Make thy elysium in the shades below
If there's no God from whence Did all things spring
He made the greatest and minutest thing
With great astonishment my Soul is struck
O rashness great; hast thou thy sense forsook   10
Hast thou forgot the preterperfect days
They are recorded in the book of praise
If twas not written by the hand of God
Why was it sealed with Immanuels blood
Tho' tis a second point thou dost deny.   15
Unmeasur'd vengence scarlet sins do cry
Now turn I pray thee from the dangerous road
Rise from the dust and seek the mighty God
By whose great mercy we do move and live
Whose loving kindness doth our sins forgive   20
'Tis beelzebub our adversary great
With holds from us the kingdom and the seat
Bliss weeping waits us in her arms to fly
To the vast regions of Felicity—
Perhaps thy Ignorance will ask us where   25
Go to the corner stone, it will declare
Thy heart in unbelief will harder grow
Altho' thou hidest it for pleasure now
Methinks I see the consequence thou'rt blind
Thy unbeleif disturbs the peaceful mind   30
The endless Scene too far for me to tread
Too great, to accomplish from so weak a head
If men such wise inventions then should know
In the high Firmament who made the bow
That covenant was made for to ensure   35
Made to establish lasting to endure
Who made the heavens and earth, a lasting spring

Of admiration; to whom dost thou bring
Thy thanks, and tribute, adoration pay
To heathen Gods? can wise apollo say   40
Tis I that saves from the lowest hell
Minerva teach thee all thy days to tell.
Doth Pluto tell thee thou shalt see the shade
Of fell perdition for thy learning made
Doth Cupid in thy breast that warmth inspire   45
To love thy brother, which is gods desire
Look thou above and see who made the sky—
Nothing more lucid to an atheists eye
Look thou beneath and see each purling stream
It surely cannot a delusion seem   50
Mark rising Pheobus when he spreads his ray
And his Commission for to guide the day
At night keep watch and see a Cynthia bright
And her commission for to guide the night—
See how the stars when they do sing his praise   55
Witness his essence in celestial Lays

[3]

"An Address to the Atheist, by P. Wheatley at the Age of 14 Years—1767—"

Muse! where shall I begin the spacious feild
To tell what curses unbeleif doth yeild?
Thou who dost daily feel his hand, and rod
Darest thou deny the Essence of a God!—
If there's no heav'n, ah! whither wilt thou go   5
Make thy Ilysium in the shades below?
If there's no God from whom did all things Spring
He made the greatest and minutest Thing
Angelic ranks no less his Power display
Than the least mite scarce visible to Day   10
With vast astonishment my soul is struck
Have Reason'g powers thy darken'd breast forsook?
The Laws deep Graven by the hand of God,
Seal'd with Immanuel's all-redeeming blood:
This second point thy folly dares deny   15
On thy devoted head for vengeance cry—

Turn then I pray thee from the dangerous road
Rise from the dust and seek the mighty God.
His is bright truth without a dark disguise
And his are wisdom's all beholding Eyes: 20
With labour'd snares our Adversary great
Withholds from us the Kingdom and the seat.
Bliss weeping waits thee, in her Arms to fly
To her own regions of felicity—
Perhaps thy ignorance will ask us where?   25
Go to the <u>Corner stone</u> he will declare.
Thy heart in unbelief will harden'd grow
Tho' much indulg'd in vicious pleasure now—
Thou tak'st unusual means; the path forbear
Unkind to others to thy self Severe—   30
Methinks I see the consequence thou'rt blind
Thy unbelief disturbs the peaceful Mind.
The endless scene too far for me to tread
Too great to utter from so weak a head.
That man his maker's love divine might know   35
In heavens high firmament he placed his Bow
To shew his covenant for ever sure
To endless Age unchanging to endure—
He made the Heavens and earth that lasting Spring
Of admiration! To whom dost thou bring   40
Thy grateful tribute? Adoration pay
To heathen Gods? Can wise <u>Apollo</u> say
Tis I that saves thee from the deepest hell;
<u>Minerva</u> teach thee all thy days to tell?
Doth <u>Pluto</u> tell thee thou Shalt see the shade   45
Of fell perdition for transgression made?
Doth <u>Cupid</u> in thy breast that warmth inspire
To love thy Brother, which is God's desire?
Atheist! behold the wide extended skies
And wisdom infinite shall strike thine eyes   50
Mark rising Sol when far he spreads his Ray
And his Commission read—To rule the Day
At night behold that silver Regent bright
And her command to lead the train of Night
Lo! how the Stars all vocal in his praise   55
Witness his Essence in celestial lays!

[1767]

[4]
"Deism"

Must Ethiopians be imploy'd for you
Greatly rejoice if any good I do
I ask O unbeleiver satan's child
Has not thy saviour been to meek & mild
The auspicious rays that round his head do shine   5
Do still declare him to be christ divine
Doth not the Omnipotent call him son?
And is well pleas'd with his beloved One
How canst thou thus divide the trinity
What can'st thou take up for to make the three   10
Tis satans snares a Fluttering in the wind
Whereby he hath ensnar'd thy Foolish mind
God the eternal Orders this to be
Sees thy vain arg'ments to divide the three
Canst thou not see the consequence in store   15
Begin the Omnipotent to adore
Arise the pinions of Persuasions here
Seek the Eternal while he is so near
At the last day where wilt thou hide thy face
The day approaching is no time for grace   20
Then wilt thou cry thyself undone and lost
Proclaiming Father, Son, and Holy Ghost
Who trod the wine press of Jehovahs wrath
Who taught us prayer and gave us grace and faith
Who but the great and the supreme who bless'd   25
Ever and ever in Immortal rest
The meanest prodigal that comes to God
Is not cast off, but brought by Jesus Blood
When to the faithless Jews he oft did cry
One call'd him Teacher some made him a lye   30
He came to you in mean apparell clad
He came to save you from your sins and had
Far more Compassion than I can express
Pains his companions, and his Friends Distress
Immanuel God with us these pains did bear   35
Must the Eternal our Petitions hear?

Ah! cruel distiny his life he Laid
Father Forgive them thus the saviour said
They nail'd King Jesus to the cross for us
For our Transgressions he did bear the curse.   40

May I O Eternal salute aurora to begin thy Praise, shall mortal dust do that
which Immortals scarcely can comprehend, then O omnipotent I will
humbly ask, after imploring thy pardon for this presumption, when shall
we approach thy majestys presence crown'd with celestial Dignities When
shall we see the resting place of the great Supreme When shall we behold
thee. O redeemer in all the resplendent Graces of a suffering God,
 Ye 6 wise men Sent from the Orient clime
Now led by seraphs to the bless'd abode

[1767]

[5]
"An Address to the Deist—1767—"

Must Ethiopians be employ'd for you?
Much I rejoice if any good I do.
I ask O unbeleiver, Satan's child
Hath not thy Saviour been too much revil'd
Th' auspicious rays that round his temples shine   5
Do still declare him to be Christ divine
Doth not the great <u>Eternal</u> call him Son
Is he not pleas'd with his beloved One—?
How canst thou thus divide the Trinity—
The blest the Holy the eternal three   10
Tis Satan's Snares are fluttering in the wind
Whereby he doth insnare thy foolish mind
God, the Eternal Orders this to be
Sees thy vain arg'ments to divide the three
Cans't thou not see the Consequence in store?   15
Begin th' Almighty monarch to adore
Attend to Reason whispering in thine ear
Seek the Eternal while he is so near.
Full in thy view I point each path I know
Lest to the vale of black dispair I go.   20

At the last day where wilt thou hide thy face
That <u>Day</u> approaching is no time for Grace.
Too late percieve thyself undone and lost
To late own Father, Son, and Holy Ghost.
Who trod the wine-press of Jehovah's wrath?   25
Who taught us prayer, and promis'd grace and faith—?
Who but the Son, who reigns supremely blest
Ever, and ever, in immortal rest.? [*sic*]
The vilest prodigal who comes to God
Is not cast out but bro't by Jesus' blood.   30
When to the faithless Jews he oft did cry
Some own'd this teacher Some made him a lye
He came to you in mean apparel clad
He came to Save us from our Sins, and had
Compassion more than language can express.   35
Pains his companions, and his friends distress
Immanuel on the cross those pains did bear—
Will the eternal our petitions hear?
Ah! wondrous Distiny his life he laid.
"Father forgive them," thus the Saviour pray'd   40
Nail'd was King Jesus on the cross for us.
For our transgressions he sustain'd the Curse.

[1767]

[6]
"To the University of Cambridge, wrote in 1767—"

While an intrinsic ardor bids me write
The muse doth promise to assist my pen.
'Twas but e'en now I left my native shore
The sable Land of error's darkest night
There, sacred Nine! for you no place was found,   5
Parent of mercy, 'twas thy Powerfull hand
Brought me in Safety from the dark abode.
   To you, Bright youths! he points the heights of Heav'n
To you, the knowledge of the depths profound.
Above, contemplate the ethereal Space   10
And glorious Systems of revolving worlds.

Still more, ye sons of science! you've reciev'd
The pleasing sound by messengers from heav'n,
The saviour's blood, for your Redemption flows.
S[ee] Him, with hands stretch'd out upon the Cross!   15
Divine compassion in his bosom glows.
He hears revilers with oblique regard.
What Condescention in the Son of God!
When the whole human race, by sin had fal'n;
He deign'd to Die, that they might rise again,   20
To live with him beyond the starry sky
Life without death, and Glory without End.—
    Improve your privileges while they stay:
Caress, redeem each moment, which with haste
Bears on its rapid wing Eternal bliss.   25
Let hateful vice so baneful to the soul,
Be still avoided with becoming care;
Suppress the sable monster in its growth,
Ye blooming plants of human race, divine
An Ethiop tells you, tis your greatest foe   30
Its present sweetness turns to endless pain
And brings eternal ruin on the soul.

[7]
"On Messrs. Hussey and Coffin."

TO THE PRINTER [*Newport Mercury*, December 21, 1767].

Please to insert the following Lines, composed by a Negro Girl (belonging
to one Mr. Wheatley of Boston) on the following Occasion, viz. Messrs
Hussey and Coffin, as undermentioned, belonging to Nantucket, being
bound from thence to Boston, narrowly escaped being cast away on Cape-
Cod, in one of the late Storms; upon their Arrival, being at Mr. Wheatley's,
and, while at Dinner, told of their narrow Escape, this Negro Girl at the
same Time 'tending Table, heard the Relation, from which she composed
the following Verses.

On Messrs. Hussey and Coffin.
Did Fear and Danger so perplex your Mind,
As made you fearful of the Whistling Wind?
Was it not Boreas knit his angry Brow

Against you? or did Consideration bow?
To lend you Aid, did not his Winds combine?   5
To stop your passage with a churlish Line,
Did haughty Eolus with Contempt look down
With Aspect windy, and a study'd Frown?
Regard them not;—the Great Supreme, the Wise,
Intends for something hidden from our Eyes.   10
Suppose the groundless Gulph had snatch'd away
Hussey and Coffin to the raging Sea;
Where wou'd they go? where wou'd be their Abode?
With the supreme and independent God,
Or made their Beds down in the Shades below,   15
Where neither Pleasure nor Content can flow.
To Heaven their Souls with eager Raptures soar,
Enjoy the Bliss of him they wou'd adore.
Had the soft gliding Streams of Grace been near,
Some favourite Hope their fainting hearts to cheer,   20
Doubtless the Fear of Danger far had fled:
No more repeated Victory crown their Heads.

Had I the Tongue of a Seraphim, how would I exalt thy Praise; thy Name as Incense to the Heavens should fly, and the Remembrance of thy Goodness to the shoreless Ocean of Beatitude!—Then should the Earth glow with seraphick Ardour.

Blest Soul, which sees the Day while Light doth shine,
To guide his Steps to trace the Mark divine.

Phillis Wheatley

[8]
"America"

New England first a wilderness was found
Till for a continent 'twas destin'd round
From feild to feild the savage monsters run
E'r yet Brittania had her work begun
Thy Power, O Liberty, makes strong the weak   5
And (wond'rous instinct) Ethiopians speak

Sometimes by Simile, a victory's won
A certain lady had an only son
He grew up daily virtuous as he grew
Fearing his Strength which she undoubted knew   10
She laid some taxes on her darling son
And would have laid another act there on
Amend your manners I'll the task remove
Was said with seeming Sympathy and Love
By many scourges she his goodness try'd   15
Untill at length the Best of Infants cry'd
He wept, Brittania turn'd a sens^eless ear
At last awaken'd by maternal fear
Why weeps americus why weeps my Child
Thus spake Brittania, thus benign and mild   20
My dear mama said he, shall I repeat—
Then Prostrate fell, at her maternal feet
What ails the rebel, great Brittania Cry'd
Indeed said he, you have no cause to Chide
You see each day my fluent tears my food.   25
Without regard, what no more English blood?
Has length of time drove from our English viens
The kindred he to Great Brittania deigns?
Tis thus with thee O Brittain keeping down
New English force, thou fear'st his Tyranny and thou didst frown   30
He weeps afresh to feel this Iron chain
Turn, O Brittania claim thy child again
Riecho Love drive by thy powerful charms
Indolence Slumbering in forgetful arms
See Agenoria diligent imploy's   35
Her sons, and thus with rapture she replys
Arise my sons with one consent arise
Lest distant continents with vult'ring eyes
Should charge America with Negligence
They praise Industry but no pride commence   40
To raise their own Profusion, O Brittain See
By this, New England will increase like thee

[1768]

[9]
"To the King's Most Excellent Majesty on his Repealing the American Stamp Act"

Your Subjects hope
The crown upon your head may flourish long
And in great wars your royal arms be strong
May your Sceptre many nations sway
Resent it on them that dislike Obey   5
But how shall we exalt the British king
Who ruleth france Possessing every thing
The sweet remembrance of whose favours past
The meanest peasants bless the great the last
May George belov'd of all the nations round   10
Live and by earths and heavens blessings crownd
May heaven protect and Guard him from on high
And at his presence every evil fly
Thus every clime with equal gladness See
When kings do Smile it sets their Subjects free   15
When wars came on the proudest rebel fled
God thunder'd fury on their guilty head

Phillis
[1768]

[10]
"To the Hon.ble Commodore Hood on his pardoning a deserter"

It was thy noble soul and high desert
That caus'd these breathings of my grateful heart
You sav'd a soul from Pluto's dreary shore
You sav'd his body and he asks no more
This generous act Immortal wreaths shall bring   5
To thee for meritorious was the spring
From whence from whence, [sic] this candid ardor flow'd
To grace thy name, and Glorify thy God
The Eatherial spirits in the realms above

Rejoice to see thee exercise thy Love   10
Hail: Commodore may heaven delighted pour
Its blessings plentious in a silent shower
The voice of pardon did resound on high
While heaven consented, and he must not die
On thee, fair victor be ^the^ Blessing shed   15
And rest for ever on thy matchless Head

Phillis
[1769]

[11]
"On the Decease of the Rev'd Doct^r Sewall"

E'er yet the morning heav'd its Orient head
Behold him praising with the happy dead—
Hail happy Saint, on the Immortal Shore
We hear thy warnings and advice no more
Then let each one behold with wishful eyes   5
The saint ascending to his native skies
From hence the prophet wing'd his rapturous way
To mansions pure to fair Celestial day—
Then begging for the Spirit of the Gods
And panting eager for the bless'd Abodes   10
Let every one with the same vigour Soar
To bliss and happiness Unseen before
Then be Christs Image on our minds impressd
And plant a Saviour in each glowing breast
Thrice happy thou Arriv'd to Joy at last   15
What compensation for the evil past
Thou Lord incomprehensible, unknown—
By sense; we bow at thy exalted throne—
While thus we beg thy excellence to feel
Thy sacred spirit to our hearts reveal   20
To make each One of us that grace partake
Which thus we ask for the redeemers Sake—
["]Sewall is dead[,"] Swift-piniond fame thus cryd
["]Is Sewall dead[?"] my trembling heart replyd
Behold to us a benefit deny^d   25

But when Our Jesus had ascended high
With captive bands he led captivity
And gifts receiv'd for such as knew not God
Lord send a Pastor for thy Churches Good
["]O ruin'd world[,"] my mournful tho'ts reply^d   30
["]And ruin'd continent[,"] the mountains cry^d
How Oft for us the Holy prophet pray^d
But now behold him in his clay cold bed
Ye Powers above my weeping verse to close
I'll on his tomb an epitaph compose—   35

Here lies a man bought with Christs precious blood
Once a Poor sinner now a saint with God
Behold ye rich and poor and fools and wise
Nor let this monitor your hearts surprize
I'll tell you all what this great saint has done   40
That makes him Brighter than the Glorious Sun
Listen ye Happy from the seats above
I speak Sincerely and with truth and Love
He sought the paths of virtue and of truth
Twas this, that made him happy in his youth   45
In Blooming years he found that grace divine
That gives admittance to the sacred shrine—
Mourn him ye Indigent whom he has fed
Seek yet more earnest for the Living bread
E'n Christ your bread descend from above   50
Implore his pity and his grace and Love.
Mourn him ye youth whom he has Often told
Gods bounteous mercy from the times of Old
I too, have cause this heavy loss to mourn:
Because my monitor will not return   55
Now this faint semblance of his complete:
He is thro' Jesus made divinely great
And set a Glorious Pattern to repeat
But when shall we to this blessd State arrive?
When the Same graces in Our hearts do thrive   60

Phillis Wheatley
[1769]

[11a]
"On the Decease of the rev'd Dr. Sewell—"

E'r yet the morning heav'd its Orient head
Behold him praising with the happy dead,
Hail happy saint, on the Immortal shore
We hear thy warnings and advice no more
Then let each one, behold with wishful eyes 5
The saint ascending to his native skies
From hence the Prophet wing'd his rapturous way
To mansions pure, to fair celestial day—
Then begging for the Spirit of his God
And panting eager for the blest abode 10
Let every one with the same vigour soar
To bliss and happiness unseen before
Then be christs image on our minds impress'd
And plant a saviour in each glowing breast
Thrice happy thou, arriv'd to Joy at last 15
What compensation for the evil past—
Thou Lord incomprehensible unknown
By sense;—we bow at thy exalted throne
While thus we beg thy excellence to feel
Thy Sacred Spirit in our hearts reveal 20
To make each one of us thy grace partake
Which thus we ask for the Redeemers Sake
["]Sewell is dead["]; swift-pinion'd fame thus cry'd
["]Is Sewell dead[?"], my trembling heart reply'd
Behold, to us, a benefit deny'd— 25
But when our Jesus had ascended high
With captive bands he led captivity
And gifts receiv'd, for such as knew not God
Lord, send a Pastor for thy Church'es good;
["]O ruin'd world,["] my mournful tho'ts reply'd 30
["]And ruin'd continent[,"] the ecco cry'd
How oft for us the holy Prophet pray'd
But now behold him in his clay cold bed
By duty urg'd my weeping verse to close
I'll on his Tomb, an Epitaph compose. 35
Here lies a man bought with Christ's precious blood
Once a poor Sinner, now a saint with God

Behold ye rich and poor and fools and wise
Nor let this monitor your hearts Surprize
I'll tell you all, what this great saint has done   40
That makes him brighter than the glorious sun
Listen ye happy, from the seats above.
I speak sincerely and with truth and Love
He sought the paths of virtue and of truth
'Twas this that made him happy in his Youth   45
In blooming years he found that grace divine
That gives admittance to the Sacred Shrine
Mourn him ye indigent, whom he has fed
Seek yet more earnest for the living bread
Even Christ, your bread that cometh from above   50
Implore his pity and his grace and Love
Mourn him ye youth whom he hath often told
Gods bounteous mercy from the times of old
I too have cause this heavy loss to mourn
For this my monitor will not return   55
Now this faint semblance of his life complete
He is thro' Jesus made divinely great
And Set a Glorious pattern to repeat—
But when shall we to this bless'd state Arrive
When the same graces in our hearts do thrive   60

Phillis Wheatley
[1769]

[11b]

"On the Death of the Rev'd D.ʳ Sewall. 1769—"

E'er yet the morning heav'd its Orient head
Behold him praising with the happy dead.
Hail! happy Saint, on the immortal shore
We hear thy warnings and advice no more:
Then let each one behold with wishful eyes   5
The saint ascending to his native skies,
From hence the Prophet wing'd his rapturous way
To mansions pure, to fair celestial day.
    Then begging for the spirit of his God

And panting eager for the bless'd abode,   10
Let every one, with the same vigour soar
To bliss, and happiness, unseen before
Then be Christ's image on our minds impress'd
And plant a saviour in each glowing Breast.
Thrice happy thou, arriv'd to Joy at last;   15
What compensation for the evil past!
   Thou Lord, incomprehensible, unknown,
To sense, we bow, at thy exalted Throne!
While thus we beg thy excellence to feel,
Thy sacred spirit, in our hearts reveal   20
And make each one of us, that grace partake
Which thus we ask for the Redeemer's sake
   "Sewall is dead." swift pinion'd fame thus cry'd ⎫
"Is Sewall dead?" my trembling heart reply'd ⎬
O what a blessing in thy flight deny'd! ⎭   25
But when our Jesus had ascended high,
With Captive bands he led Captivity;
And gifts reciev'd for such as knew not God
Lord! Send a Pastor, for thy Churche's [good]
O ruin'd world! bereft of thee, we cry'd,   30
(The rocks responsive to the voice, reply'd.)
How oft for us this holy Prophet pray'd:
But ah! behold him in his Clay-cold bed
By duty urg'd, my weeping verse to close,
I'll on his Tomb, an Epitaph compose.   35
   Lo! here, a man bought with Christ's precious blood
Once a poor sinner, now a Saint with God.—
Behold ye rich and poor, and fools and wise;
Nor Let this monitor your hearts surprize!
I'll tell you all, what this great Saint has done   40
Which makes him ~~greater~~ ^Brighter^ than the Glorious Sun.—
Listen ye happy from your seats above
I speak sincerely and with truth and Love.
He sought the Paths of virtue and of Truth
Twas this which made him happy in his Youth.   45
In Blooming years he found that grace divine
Which gives admittance to the sacred Shrine.
Mourn him, ye Indigent, Whom he has fed,
Seek yet more earnest for the living Bread:
E'en Christ your Bread, who cometh from above   50

Implore his pity and his grace and Love.
Mourn him ye Youth, whom he hath often told
God's bounteous Mercy from the times of Old.
I too, have cause this mighty loss to mourn
For this my monitor will not return.   55
    Now this faint semblance of his life complete
He is, thro' Jesus, made divinely great
And left a glorious pattern to repeat
    But when Shall we, to this bless'd state arrive?
When the same graces in our hearts do thrive.   60

[12]
"On Friendship"

Let amicitia in her ample reign
Extend her notes to a Celestial strain
Benevolent far more divinely Bright
Amor like me doth triumph at the sight
~~To let~~ When my thoughts in gratitude imploy   5
Mental Imaginations give me Joy
Now let my thoughts in Contemplation steer
The Footsteps of the Superlative fair

Written by Phillis Wheatley
Boston July 15 1769

[13]
"On the Death of Mr Snider Murder'd by Richardson"

In heavens eternal court it was decreed
How the first martyr for the cause should bleed
To clear the country of the hated brood
He whet his courage for the common good
Long hid before, a vile infernal here   5
Prevents Achilles in his mid career
Where'er this fury darts his Pois'nous breath
All are endanger'd to the shafts of death.
The generous Sires beheld the fatal wound

Saw their young champion gasping on the ground   10
They rais'd him up. but to each present ear
What martial glories did his tongue declare
The wretch appal'd no longer can despise
But from the Striking victim turns his eyes—
When this young martial genius did appear   15
The Tory cheifs no longer could forbear.
Ripe for destruction, see the wretches doom
He waits the curses of the age to come
In vain he flies, by Justice Swiftly chaced
With unexpected infamy disgraced   20
Be Richardson for ever banish'd here
The grand Usurpers bravely vaunted Heir.
We bring the body from the watry bower
To lodge it where it shall remove no more
Snider behold with what Majestic Love   25
The Illustrious retinue begins to move
With Secret rage fair freedoms foes beneath
See in thy corse ev'n Majesty in Death

Phillis
[Late February or early March 1770]

[14]

AN ELEGIAC | POEM, | On the DEATH of that celebrated Divine,
and eminent Servant of *JESUS CHRIST, the late Reverend, and pious* |
*GEORGE WHITEFIELD, | Chaplain to the Right Honourable the Countess
of Huntingdon, &c &c. | Who made his Exit from this transitory State, to
dwell in the celestial Realms of Bliss, on LORD'S-DAY, 30th of September,
1770, when he was seiz'd with a Fit of the Asthma, at NEWBURY-PORT,
near BOSTON, in NEW-ENGLAND. In which is a Condolatory Address to
His truly noble Benefactress the worthy and pious Lady HUNTINGDON,—
and the Orphan-Children in GEORGIA; who, with many Thousands, are
left, by the Death of this great Man, to lament the Loss of a Father, Friend, and
Benefactor.//*

*By PHILLIS, a Servant Girl of 17 Years of Age, belonging to
Mr. J. WHEATLEY, of Boston:—And has been but 9 Years in this Country
from Africa.*

Hail happy Saint on thy immortal throne!
To thee complaints of grievance are unknown;
We hear no more the music of thy tongue,
Thy wonted auditories cease to throng.
Thy lessons in unequal'd accents flow'd!   5
While emulation in each bosom glow'd;
Thou didst, in strains of eloquence refin'd,
Inflame the soul, and captivate the mind.
Unhappy we, the setting Sun deplore!
Which once was splendid, but it shines no more;   10
He leaves this earth for Heaven's unmeasur'd height:
And worlds unknown, receive him from our sight;
There WHITEFIELD wings, with rapid course his way,
And sails to Zion, through vast seas of day.

When his AMERICANS were burden'd sore,   15
When streets were crimson'd with their guiltless gore!
Unrival'd friendship in his breast now strove:
The fruit thereof was charity and love
Towards *America*—couldst thou do more
Than leave thy native home, the *British* shore,   20
To cross the great Atlantic's wat'ry road,
To see *America's* distress'd abode?
Thy prayers, great Saint, and thy incessant cries,
Have pierc'd the bosom of thy native skies!
Thou moon hast seen, and ye bright stars of light   25
Have witness been of his requests by night!
He pray'd that grace in every heart might dwell:
He long'd to see *America* excell;
He charg'd its youth to let the grace divine
Arise, and in their future actions shine;   30
He offer'd THAT he did himself receive,
A greater gift not GOD himself can give:
He urg'd the need of HIM to every one;
It was no less than GOD's co-equal SON!
Take HIM ye wretched for your only good;   35
Take HIM ye starving souls to be your food.
Ye thirsty, come to his life giving stream:
Ye Preachers, take him for your joyful theme:
Take HIM, "my dear AMERICANS," he said,
Be your complaints in his kind bosom laid: 40

Take HIM ye *Africans*, he longs for you;
Impartial SAVIOUR, is his title due;
If you will chuse to walk in grace's road,
You shall be sons, and kings, and priests to GOD.

 Great COUNTESS! we *Americans* revere   45
Thy name, and thus condole thy grief sincere:
We mourn with thee, that TOMB obscurely plac'd,
In which thy Chaplain undisturb'd doth rest.
New-England sure, doth feel the ORPHAN's smart;
Reveals the true sensations of his heart: 50
Since this fair Sun, withdraws his golden rays,
No more to brighten these distressful days!
His lonely *Tabernacle*, sees no more
A WHITEFIELD landing on the *British* shore:
Then let us view him in yon azure skies: 55
Let every mind with this lov'd object rise.
No more can he exert his lab'ring breath,
Seiz'd by the cruel messenger of death.
What can his dear AMERICA return?
But drop a tear upon his happy urn,   60
Thou tomb, shalt safe retain thy sacred trust,
Till life divine re-animate his dust.

Sold by EZEKIEL RUSSELL, in Queen-Street, and JOHN BOYLES, in Marlboro-Street

[October 1770]

[15]

To the R.ᵗ Hon'ble the Countess of Huntingdon

Most noble Lady,

 The Occasion of my addressing your Ladiship will, I hope, Apologize for this my boldness in doing it; it is to enclose a few lines on the decease of your worthy Chaplain, the Rev'd Mʳ. Whitefield, in the loss of whom I sincerely sympathize with your Ladiship; but your great loss which is his Greater gain, will, I hope, meet with infinite reparation, in the presence of God, the Divine Benefactor whose image you bear by filial imitation.

The Tongues of the Learned, are insufficient, much less the pen of an untutor'd African, to paint in lively characters, the excellencies of this Citizen of Zion! I beg an Interest in your Ladiship's Prayers and Am,

With great humility
your Ladiship's most Obedient
Humble Servant
Phillis Wheatley

Boston Oct. 25, 1770

[16]
To Mrs. LEONARD, *on the Death of her* HUSBAND.

GRIM Monarch! see depriv'd of vital breath,
A young Physician in the dust of death!
Dost thou go on incessant to destroy:
The grief to double, and impair the joy?
Enough thou never yet wast known to say,   5
Tho' millions die thy mandate to obey.
Nor youth, nor science nor the charms of love,
Nor aught on earth thy rocky heart can move.
The friend, the spouse, from his dark realm to save,
In vain we ask the tyrant of the grave.   10

    Fair mourner, there see thy own LEONARD spread,
Lies undistinguish'd from the vulgar dead;
Clos'd are his eyes, eternal slumbers keep,
His senses bound in never-waking sleep,
Till time shall cease; till many a shining world,   15
Shall fall from Heav'n, in dire confusion hurl'd:
Till dying Nature in wild torture lies;
Till her last groans shall rend the brazen skies!
And not till then, his active Soul shall claim,
Its body, now, of more than mortal frame.   20
But ah! methinks the rolling tears apace,
Pursue each other down the alter'd face.
Ah! cease ye sighs, nor rend the mourner's heart:

Cease thy complaints, no more thy griefs impart.
From the cold shell of his great soul arise!   25
And look above, thou native of the skies!
There fix thy view, where fleeter than the wind
Thy LEONARD flies, and leaves the earth behind.

   Thyself prepare to pass the gloomy night,
To join forever in the fields of light;   30
To thy embrace, his joyful spirit moves,
To thee the partner of his earthly loves;
He welcomes thee to pleasures more refin'd
And better suited to the deathless mind.

Phillis Wheatley.
[June 1771]

[17]
"On the Death of Dʳ. Samuel Marshall"

Thro' thickest glooms, Look back, immortal Shade;
On that confusion which thy flight hath made.
Or from Olympus height, look down, and see,
A Town involv'd in grief, bereft of thee.
His Lucy sees him mix among the Dead,   5
And rends the gracefull tresses from her head.
Frantic with woe, with griefs unknown, oppress'd,
Sigh follows Sigh, and heaves the downy breast;
Too quickly fled, ah! whither art thou gone?
Ah! lost forever to thy wife and son!   10
The hapless child, thy only hope, and heir,
Clings round the neck, and weeps his Sorrows there
The loss of thee, on Tyler's Soul returns.
And Boston too, for her Physician mourns.
When Sickness call'd for Marshall's kindly hand,   15
Lo! how with pitty would his heart expand!
The Sire, the friend in him we oft have found;
With gen'rous friendship, did his Soul abound.
Could Esculapius then no Longer stay,
To bring his lingring Infant in to Day?   20

The Babe unborn, in dark confiens is toss'd
And Seems in anguish for its Father Lost.
Gone is Apollo! from his house of earth!
And leaves the memorial of his worth.
From yonder worlds unseen he Comes no more,   25
The common parent, whom we thus deplore:
Yet in our hopes, immortal Joys attend,
The Sire, the Spouse, the universal freind.

[17a]
On the Death of Doctor SAMUEL MARSHALL.

Thro' thickest glooms, look back, immortal Shade!
On that confusion which thy flight has made.
Or from Olympus' height look down, and see
A Town involv'd in grief for thee:
His *Lucy* sees him mix among the dead.   5
And rends the graceful tresses from her head:
Frantic with woe, with griefs unknown, oppres'd,
Sigh follows sigh, and heaves the downy breast.

Too quickly fled, ah! whither art thou gone!
Ah! lost for ever to thy Wife and Son!   10
The hapless child, thy only hope and heir,
Clings round her neck, and weeps his sorrows there.
The loss of thee on *Tyler's* soul returns,
And *Boston* too, for her Physician mourns.
When sickness call'd for *Marshall's* kindly hand,   15
Lo! how with pity would his heart expand!
The sire, the friend, in him we oft have found,
With gen'rous friendship did his soul abound.

Could Esculapius then no longer stay?
To bring his ling'ring infant into day!   20
The babe unborn, in dark confines is toss'd
And seems in anguish for it's father lost.

Gone, is Apollo! from his house of earth,
And leaves the sweet memorials of his worth.
From yonder world unseen, he comes no more,   25

The common parent, whom we thus deplore:
Yet, in our hopes, immortal joys attend
The Sire, the Spouse, the universal Friend.

[18]

"Proposals for Printing by Subscription"

A Collection of POEMS, wrote at several times, and upon various occasions, by PHILLIS, a Negro Girl, from the strength of her own Genius, it being but a few Years since she came to this Town an uncultivated Barbarian from *Africa*. The Poems having been seen and read by the best Judges, who think them well worthy of the Publick View; and upon critical examination, they find that the declared Author was capable of writing them. The Order in which they were penned, together with the Occasion, are as follows;

On the Death of the Rev. Dr. *Sewell*, when sick, 1765—;
On Virtue, [17]66—;
On two Friends, who were cast away, d[itt]o. —;
To the University of Cambridge, 1767—;
An Address to the Atheist, do.—;
An Address to the Deist, do.—;
On America, 1768—;
On the King, do.—;
On Friendship, do.—;
Thoughts on being brought from Africa to America, do.—;
On the Nuptials of Mr. *Spence* to Miss *Hooper*, do.—;
On the Hon. Commodore Hood, on his pardoning a Deserter, 1769—;
On the Death of Reverend Dr. *Sewell*, do.—;
On the Death of Master *Seider*, who was killed by *Ebenezer Richardson*,
    1770.—;
On the Death of the Rev. *George Whitefield*, do.—;
On the Death of a young Miss, aged 5 years, do.—;
On the Arrival of the Ships of War, and landing of the Troops.
    [undated]—;
On the Affray in King-Street, on the Evening of the 5th of March.
    [undated]—;
On the death of a young Gentleman. [undated]—;
To *Samuel Quincy*, Esq; a Panegyrick. [undated]—;

To a Lady on her coming to America for her Health. [undated]—;
To Mrs. *Leonard*, on the Death of her Husband. [undated]—;
To Mrs. Boylston and Children on the Death of her Son and their
    Brother. [undated]—;
To a Gentleman and Lady on the Death of their Son, aged 9 Months.
    [undated]—;
To a Lady on her remarkable Deliverance in a Hurricane. [undated]—;
To *James Sullivan*, Esq; and Lady on the Death of her Brother and
    Sister, and a child *Avis*, aged 12 Months. [undated]—;
Goliah [*sic* for Goliath] of Gath. [undated]—;
On the Death of Dr. *Samuel* Marshall. [undated]—;

It is supposed they will make one small Octavo Volume, and will contain
about 200 Pages.

They will be printed on Demy Paper, and beautiful Types.

The Price to Subscribers, handsomely bound and lettered, will be Four
Shillings.—Stitched in blue, Three Shillings.

It is hoped Encouragement will be given to this Publication, as a reward
to a very uncommon Genius, at present a Slave.

This Work will be put to the Press as soon as three Hundred Copies are
subscribed for, and shall be published with all Speed.

Subscriptions are taken in by E. Russell, in Marlborough Street.

[19]
"Recollection."

To the AUTHOR *of the* LONDON MAGAZINE [March 1772].

Boston, in New-England, Jan. 1, 1772.

SIR,

As your Magazine is a proper repository for any thing valuable or curious, I hope you will excuse the communicating the following by one of
your subscribers.

There is in this town a young *Negro woman*, who left *her* country at ten
years of age, and has been in *this* eight years. She is a compleat sempstress,
an accomplished mistress of her pen, and discovers a most surprising
genius. Some of her productions have seen the light, among which is a
poem on the death of the Rev. Mr. George Whitefield.—The following

was occasioned by her being in company with some young ladies of family, when one of them said she did not remember, among all the poetical pieces she had seen, ever to have met with a poem upon RECOLLECTION. The *African* (so let me call her, for so in fact she is) took the hint, went home to her master's, and soon sent what follows.

"Madam,

Agreeable to your proposing *Recollection* as a subject proper for me to write upon, I enclose these few thoughts upon it; and, as you was the first person who mentioned it, I thought none more proper to dedicate it to; and, if it meets with your approbation, the poem is honoured, and the authoress satisfied. I am, Madam,

Your very humble servant, PHILLIS."

RECOLLECTION.

To Miss A— M—, humbly inscribed by the Authoress.

MNEME, begin; inspire, ye sacred Nine!
Your vent'rous *Afric* in the deep design.
Do ye rekindle the coelestial fire,
Ye god-like powers! the glowing thoughts inspire,
Immortal Pow'r! I trace thy sacred spring,   5
Assist my strains, while I *thy* glories sing.
By *thee*, past acts of many thousand years,
Rang'd in due order, to the mind appears;
The *long-forgot* thy gentle hand conveys,
Returns, and soft upon the fancy plays.   10
Calm, in the visions of the night he pours
Th' exhaustless treasures of his secret stores.
Swift from above he wings his downy flight
Thro' *Phoebe's* realm, fair regent of the night.
Thence to the raptur'd poet gives his aid,   15
Dwells in his heart, or hovers round his head;
To give instruction to the lab'ring mind,
Diffusing light coelestial and refin'd.
Still he pursues, unweary'd in the race,
And wraps his senses in the pleasing maze.   20
The Heav'nly Phantom *points* the actions done
In the past worlds, and tribes beneath the sun.

He, from his throne in ev'ry human breast,
Has *vice* condemn'd, and ev'ry *virtue* bless'd.
Sweet are the sounds in which thy words we hear,   25
Coelestial musick to the ravish'd ear.
We hear thy voice, resounding o'er the plains,
Excelling Maro's sweet Menellian strains.
But awful *Thou*! to that perfidious race,
Who scorn thy warnings, nor the good embrace;   30
By *Thee* unveil'd, the horrid crime appears,
Thy mighty hand redoubled fury bears;
The time mis-spent augments their hell of woes,
While through each breast the dire contagion flows.
Now turn and leave the rude ungraceful scene,   35
And paint fair Virtue in immortal green.
For ever flourish in the glowing veins,
For ever flourish in poetick strains.
Be *Thy* employ to guide my early days,
And *Thine* the tribute of my youthful lays.   40

Now **eighteen years* their destin'd course have run,
In due succession, round the central sun;
How did each folly unregarded pass!
But sure 'tis graven on eternal brass!
To *recollect*, inglorious I return;   45
'Tis mine past follies and past crimes to mourn.
The *virtue*, ah! unequal to the *vice*,
Will scarce afford small reason to rejoice.

Such, RECOLLECTION! is thy pow'r, high-thron'd
In ev'ry breast of mortals, ever own'd.   50
The wretch, who dar'd the vengeance of the skies,
At last awakes with horror and surprise.
By *Thee* alarm'd, he sees impending fate,
He howls in anguish, and repents too late.
But oft *thy* kindness moves with timely fear   55
The furious rebel in his mad career.
Thrice bless'd the man, who in *thy* sacred shrine
Improves the REFUGE from the wrath divine.

*Her age.

[20]

To John Thornton in London

Boston April 21st,, [*sic*] 1772

Hon'd Sir,

I rec'd your instructive fav^r. of Feb. 29, for which, return you ten thousand thanks. I did not flatter myself with the tho'ts of your honouring me with an Answer to my letter, I thank you for recommending the Bible to be my cheif Study, I find and Acknowledge it the best of Books, it contains an endless treasure of wisdom, and knowledge. O that my eyes were more open'd to see the real worth, and true excellence of the word of truth, my flinty heart Soften'd with the grateful dews of divine grace and the stubborn will, and affections, bent on God alone their proper object, and the vitiated palate may be corrected to relish heav'nly things. It has pleas'd God to lay me on a bed of Sickness, and I knew not but my deathbed, but he has been graciously pleas'd to restore me in a great measure. I beg your prayers, that I may be made thankful for his paternal corrections, and that I may make proper use of them to the glory of his grace. I am still very weak & the Physicians seem to think there is danger of a consumpsion. And O that when my flesh and my heart fail me God would be my strength and portion for ever, that I might put my whole trust and Confidence in him, who has promis'd never to forsake those who Seek him with the whole heart. You could not, I am sure have express [*sic*] greater tenderness and affection for me, than by being a welwisher to my Soul, the friends of Souls bear ^some^ resemblance to the father of spirits and are made partakers of his divine Nature.

I am affraid I have entruded on your patient [patience], but if I had not tho't it ungrateful ^to omit writing in answer to your favour^ should not have troubl'd you, but I can't expect you to answer this,

I am Sir with greatest respect,
your very hum. sert.
Phillis Wheatley

[21]

To Arbour Tanner in New Port [Rhode Island]

Boston, May 19.th 1772

Dear Sister

I rec'd your favour of February 6.th for which I give you my sincere thanks. I greatly rejoice with you in that realizing view, and I hope experience, of the saving change which you so emphatically describe. Happy were it for us if we could arrive to that evangelical Repentance, and the true holiness of heart which you mention. Inexpressibly happy should we be could we have a due sense of Beauties and excellence of the Crucified Saviour. In his Crucifixion may be seen marvellous displays of Grace and Love, sufficient to draw and invite us to the rich and endless treasures of his mercy, let us rejoice in and adore the wonders of God's infinite Love in bringing us from a land Semblant of darkness itself, and where the divine light of revelation (being obscur'^d) is as darkness. Here, the knowledge of the true God and eternal life are made manifest; But there, profound ignorance overshadows the Land, Your observation is true, namely, that there was nothing in us to recommend us to God. Many of our fellow creatures are pass'd by, when the bowels of divine love expanded towards us. May this goodness & long suffering of God lead us to unfeign'd repentance.

It gives me very great pleasure to hear of so many of my Nation, seeking with eagerness the way to true felicity. O may we all meet at length in that happy mansion. I hope the correspondence between us will continue, (my being much indispos'd this winter past was the reason of my not answering yours before now) which correspondence I hope may have the happy effect of improving our mutual friendship. Till we meet in the regions of consummate blessedness, let us endeavor by the assistance of divine grace, to live the life, and we Shall die the death of the Righteous. May this be our happy case and of those who are travelling to the region of Felicity, is the earnest request of your affectionate

Friend & hum. Ser.^t Phillis Wheatley

[22]

"To the Rev. M^r. Pitkin, on the Death of his Lady."

Where Contemplation finds her sacred Spring;
Where heav'nly Music makes the Centre ring;
Where Virtue reigns unsull[i]ed, and divine;
Where Wisdom thron'd, and all the Graces shine;
There sits thy Spouse, amid the glitt'ring Throng;   5
There central Beauty feasts the ravish'd Tongue;
With recent Powers, with recent glories crown'd,
The Choirs angelic shout her welcome round.
The virtuous Dead, demand a greateful Tear—
But cease thy Grief a-while, thy Tears forbear,   10
Not thine alone, the Sorrow I relate,
Thy blooming Off-spring feel the mighty Weight;
Thus, from the Bosom of the tender Vine,
The Branches torn, fall, wither, sinke supine.
Now flies the Soul, thro' Aether unconfin'd,   15
Thrice happy State of the immortal Mind!
Still in thy Breast tumultuous Passions rise,
And urge the lucent Torrent from thine Eyes.
Amidst the Seats of Heaven, a Place is free
Among those bright angelic Ranks for thee.   20
For thee, they wait—and with expectant Eye,
Thy Spouse leans forward from th' ethereal Sky
Thus in my Hearing, "Come away," She cries,
"Partake the sacred Raptures of the Skies!
"Our Bliss divine, to Mortals is unknown,   25
"And endless Scenes of Happiness our own;
"May the dear Off-spring of our earthly Love,
"Receive Admittance to the Joys above!
"Attune the Harp to more than mortal Lays,
"And pay with us, the Tribute of their Praise   30
"To him, who died, dread Justice to appease
"Which reconcil'd, holds Mercy in Embrace;
"Creation too, her Maker's Death bemoan'd,
"Retir'd the Sun, and deep the Centre groan'd.
"He in his Death slew ours, and as he rose   35
"He crush'd the Empire of our hated Foes.
"How vain their Hopes to put the God to flight,

"And render Vengeance to the Sons of Light![”]
Thus having spoke she turn'd away her Eyes
Which beam'd celestial Radiance o'er the Skies.   40
Let Grief no longer damp the sacred Fire,
But rise sublime, to equal Bliss aspire;
Thy Sighs no more be wafted by the wind,
Complain no more, but be to Heav'n resign'd.
'Twas thine to shew those treasures all divine,   45
To sooth our woes, the task was also thine.
Now sorrow is recumbent on thy Heart,
Permit the Muse that healing to impart,
Nor can the World, a pittying tear refuse,
They weep, and with them, every heavenly Muse.   50

Phillis Wheatley
Boston, June 16th, 1772

The above Phillis Wheatley, is a Negro Girl, about 18 Years old, who has
been in this Country 11 Years.

[22a]
To the Rev. Mr. Pitkin, *on the DEATH of his LADY.*

WHERE Contemplation finds her sacred Spring;
    Where heav'nly Music makes the Centre ring;
    Where Virtue reigns unsull[i]ed, and divine;
    Where Wisdom thron'd, and all the Graces shine;
There sits thy Spouse, amid the glitt'ring Throng;   5
There central Beauty feasts the ravish'd Tongue;
With recent Powers, with recent glories crown'd,
The Choirs angelic shout her Welcome round.

    The virtuous Dead, demand a grateful Tear—
But cease thy Grief a-while, thy Tears forbear,   10
Not thine alone, the Sorrow I relate,
Thy blooming Off-spring feel the mighty Weight;
Thus, from the Bosom of the tender Vine,
The Branches torn, fall, wither, sink supine.

    Now flies the Soul, thro' Aether unconfin'd.   15
Thrice happy State of the immortal Mind!

Still in thy Breast tumultuous Passions rise,
And urge the lucent Torrent from thine Eyes.
Amidst the Seats of Heaven, a Place is free
Among those bright angelic Ranks for thee.   20
For thee, they wait—and with expectant Eye,
Thy Spouse leans forward from th' ethereal Sky,
Thus in my Hearing, "Come away," she cries,
"Partake the sacred Raptures of the Skies!
"Our Bliss divine, to Mortals is unknown,   25
"And endless Scenes of Happiness our own;
"May the dear Off-spring of our earthly Love,
"Receive Admittance to the Joys above!
"Attune the Harp to more than mortal Lays,
"And pay with us, the Tribute of their Praise   30
"To Him, who died, dread Justice to appease,
"Which reconcil'd, holds Mercy in Embrace;
"Creation too, her MAKER'S Death bemoan'd,
"Retir'd the Sun, and deep the Centre groan'd.
"He in his Death slew ours, and as he rose,   35
"He crush'd the Empire of our hated Foes.
"How vain their Hopes to put the GOD to flight,
"And render Vengeance to the Sons of Light!"

    Thus having spoke she turn'd away her Eyes,
Which beam'd celestial Radiance o'er the Skies.   40
Let Grief no longer damp the sacred Fire,
But rise sublime, to equal Bliss aspire;
Thy Sighs no more be wafted by the Wind,
Complain no more, but be to Heav'n resign'd.
'Twas thine to shew those Treasures all divine,   45
To sooth our Woes, the Task was also thine.
Now Sorrow is recumbent on thy Heart,
Permit the Muse that healing to impart,
Nor can the World, a pitying tear refuse,
They weep, and with them, ev'ry heavenly Muse.   50

Phillis Wheatley.
Boston, June 16th, 1772.

The above *Phillis Wheatley*, is a Negro Girl, about 18 Years old, who
has been in this Country 11 Years.

[23]

To Arbour Tanner In New Port Rhode Island
To the care of M^r. Pease's Servant

Boston, July 19th 1772

My dear friend

I rec'd your kind Epistle a few days ago; much disappointed to hear that you had not rec'd my answer to your first letter.* I have been in a very poor state of health all the past winter and spring, and now reside in the country for the benefit of its more wholesome air. I came to town this morning to spend the Sabbath with my master and mistress: Let me be interested in y^r. Prayers that God would please to bless to me the means us'd for my recovery, if agreable to his holy Will. While my outward Man languishes under weakness and pa[in], may the inward be refresh'd and Strengthend more abundantly by him who declar'd from heaven that his strength was made perfect in weakness! may he correct our vitiated taste, that the meditation of him may be delightful to us. No longer to be so excessively charm'd with fleeting vanities: But pressing forward to the fix'd mark f[or] the prize. How happy that man who is prepar'd for that Nig[ht] Wherein no man can work! Let us be mindful of our high calling, continually on our guard, lest our treacherous hearts Should give the adversary an advantage over us. O! who can think without horror of the Snares of the Devil. Let us, by freque[nt] meditation on the eternal Judgment, prepare for it. May the Lord bless to us these thoughts, and teach us by his Spirit to live to him alone, and when we leave this world may We be his: That this may be our happy case, is the sincere desire

of, your affectionate friend, & humble Servt.
Phillis Wheatley

*I sent the letter to M^r. Whitwell's who said he wou'd forward it.

[24]
"A Poem on the death of Charles Eliot aged 12 m°. To M^r. S Eliot."

Thro' airy realms, he wings his instant flight,
To purer regions of celestial light.

Unmov'd he sees unnumber'd systems roll.
Beneath his feet, the universal whole
In Just succession run their destin'd round   5
And circling wonders spread the dread profound.
Th' ethereal now, and now the starry skies;
With glowing splendors, strike his wond'ring eyes.
    The heav'nly legions, view, with Joy unknown,
Press his soft hand, and seat him on the throne,   10
And smiling, thus. ["]To this divine abode,
The seat of saints, of angels and of God:
Thrice welcome thou.["]—The raptur'd babe replies,
"Thanks to my God, who snatch'd me to the skies!
"E're Vice triumphant had possess'd my heart;   15
"E're yet the tempter claim'd my better part:
"E're yet on sins' most deadly actions bent:
"E're yet I knew temptation's dread intent:
"E're yet the rod for horrid crimes I knew,
"Not rais'd with vanity, or press'd with woe;   20
"But soon arriv'd to heav'n's bright port assign'd.
"New glories rush on my expanding mind!
"A noble ardor now, my bosom fires,
"To utter what the heav'nly muse inspires!"
    Joyful he spoke—exulting cherubs round,   25
Clap loud their pinions, and the plains resound.
Say, parents! why this unavailing moan?
Why heave your bosoms with the rising groan?
To Charles the happy subject of my song,
A happier world, and nobler strains belong.   30
Say, would you tear him from the realms above?
Or make less happy, frantic in your Love.
Doth his beatitude increase your pain,
Or could you welcome to this earth again
The son of bliss.—no, with superior air,   )   35
Methink he answers with a smile severe,   }
"Thrones and dominions cannot tempt me there!")
    But still you cry. "O Charles! thy manly mind,
"Enwrap our souls, and all thy actions bind,
"Our only hope, more dear than vital breath,   40
"Twelve moons revolv'd, and sunk in shades of death.
"Engaging Infant! Nightly visions give
"Thee to our arms, and we with Joy receive,

"We fain would clasp, the phantom to our breast,
"The phantom flies, and leaves the soul unblest!"   45
    Prepare to meet your dearest Infant friend,
Where Joys are pure, and Glory without end.

Boston Septr 1.st 1772. Phil^s Wheatley

[24a]
A Poem on the Death of <u>Charles Eliot</u>, aged 12 Months

Thro' airy realms, he wings his instant flight,
To purer regions of celestial light;
Unmov'd he sees unnumber'd systems roll.
Beneath his feet, the universal whole
In just succession run their destin'd round,   5
And circling wonders spread the dread profound;
Th' etherial now, and now the starry skies,
With glowing splendors, strike his wond'ring eyes.
    The heav'nly legions, view, with joy unknown,
Press his soft hand, and seat him on the throne,   10
And smiling, thus: "To this divine abode,
"The seat of Saints, of Angels, and of GOD:
"Thrice welcome thou."—The raptur'd babe replies,
"Thanks to my God, who snatch'd me to the skies,
"Ere vice triumphant had possess'd my heart;   15
"Ere yet the tempter claim'd my better part;
"Ere yet on sin's most deadly actions bent;
"Ere yet I knew temptation's dread intent;
"Ere yet the rod for horrid crimes I knew,
"Not rais'd with vanity, or press'd with wo;   20
"But soon arriv'd to heav'n's bright port assign'd.
"New glories rush on my expanding mind;
"A noble ardor now, my bosom fires,
"To utter what the heav'nly muse inspires!"
    Joyful he spoke—exulting cherubs round   25
Clap loud their pinions, and the plains resound.
Say, parents! why this unavailing moan?
Why heave your bosoms with the rising groan?
To CHARLES, the happy subject of my song,

A happier world, and nobler strains belong.   30
Say, would you tear him from the realms above?
Or make less happy, frantic in your love?
Doth his beatitude increase your pain,
Or could you welcome to this earth again
The son of bliss?—No, with superior air,   35
Methinks he answers with a smile severe,
"Thrones and dominions cannot tempt me there!"
     But still you cry, "O Charles! thy manly mind,
"Enwrap our souls, and all thy actions bind;
"Our only hope, more dear than vital breath,   40
"Twelve moons revolv'd, and sunk in shades of death!
"Engaging infant! Nightly visions give
"Thee to our arms, and we with joy recieve:
"We fain would clasp the phantom to our breast,
"The phantom flies, and leaves the soul unblest!"   45
     Prepare to meet your dearest infant friend
Where joys are pure, and glory's without end.

                    Boston, Septr. 1st. 1772. Phillis Wheatley.

[24b]
A Poem on the death of Charles Eliot aged 12 months

Thro' Airy realms, he wings his instant flight
To purer regions of celestial Light,
Unmov'd he Sees unnumber'd Systems roll,
Beneath his feet, the Universal whole
In Just Succession run their destin'd round   5
And circling wonders Spread the dread Profound,
Th'etherial now, and now the Starry Skies;
With glowing Splendors, Strike his wondring eyes.
     The heav'nly legions, view with Joy unknown,
Press his soft hand, & Seat him on the throne,   10
And Smiling, thus. ["]To this divine abode,
"The Seat of Saints, of Angels and of God:
"Thrice welcome thou.["]—The raptur'd babe replies,
"Thanks to my God, who Snatch'd me to the Skies!
"E'er Vice triumphant had Posses'd my heart;   15

"E'er yet the tempter claim'd my better part:
"E'er yet on sins most deadly Actions bent;
"E'er yet I knew temptation's dread intent:
"E'er yet the rod for horrid crimes I knew,
"Not raisd with vanity or press'd with woe;   20
"But soon Arriv'd to heav'ns bright Port assign'd
"New glories rush on my expanding Mind.
"A noble ardor now, my bosom fires
"To utter what the heavnly muse inspires!"
  Joyful he Spoke.—exulting cherubs round.   25
Clap loud their pinions, and the plains resound.
Say, parents why this unavailing moan?
Why heave your bosoms with the rising groan?
To Charles the happy Subject of my Song
A happier world, and nobler Strains belong   30
Say, would you tear him from the realms above?
Or make less happy, frantic in your Love.
Doth his beatitude increase your Pain,
Or could you welcome to this earth again
The Son of bliss—No with Superior Air   35
Methink he answers with a Smile Severe,
"Thrones and Dominions cannot tempt me there!["]
  But Still you cry. "O Charles! thy manly mind
"Enwrap our Souls, and all thy actions bind,
"Our only hope, more dear than vital breath,   40
"Twelve moons revolv'd, and Sunk in shades of death
"Engaging Infant! Nightly visions give
"Thee to our Arms, and we with Joy receive,
"We fain would clasp, the Phantom to our breast
"The Phantom flies, and leaves the Soul unblest."   45
Prepare to meet your dearest Infant friend,
Where Joys are pure, and Glory without end.

Boston Septr 1st 1772 Phil^s: Wheatley

[25]

To the Right Hon'ble The Earl of Dartmouth &c. &c. &c. p[e]^r. favour of M^r. Wooldridge.

My Lord,

The Joyful occasion which has given me this Confidence in addressing your Lordship in the enclos'd Piece, will, I hope, Sufficiently apologize for this freedom from an African, who with the (now) happy America, exults with equal transport, in the view of one of its greatest advocates Presiding, with the Special tenderness of a Fatherly heart, over the American department.

Nor can they, my Lord, be insensible of the Friendship so much exemplified in your endeavors in their behalf, during the late unhappy disturbances. I sincerely wish your Lordship all Possible Success, in your undertakings for the Interest of North America.

That the united Blessings of Heaven and Earth, may attend you here, and the endless Felicity of the invisible State, in the presence of the Divine Benefactor, may be your portion here after, is the hearty desire

of, My Lord,

Your Lordship's Most Ob^t. & devoted Hum^l Servt.

Boston, N[ew]. E[ngland]. Oct. 10. 1772}   Phillis Wheatley

To the Right Hon^l. William Earl of Dartmouth, His Majesty's Secretary of State for North America &.c &.c &.c

Hail! happy day! when smiling like the Morn,
Fair Freedom rose, New England to adorn;
The northern clime, beneath her genial ray,
Beholds, exulting, thy Paternal sway,
For big with hope, her race no longer mourns,   5
Each soul expands, each ardent bosom burns,
While in thy hand, with pleasure, we behold
The silken reins, and Freedom's charms unfold!
Long lost to Realms beneath the northern skies,
She shines supreme, while hated Faction dies,   10
Soon as he saw the triumph long desir'd
Sick at the view, he languish'd and expir'd.
Thus from the splendors of the rising Sun.
The sickning Owl explores the dark unknown.

No more of grievance unredress'd complain;   15
Or injur'd Rights, or groan beneath the chain,
Which Wanton Tyranny with lawless hand,
Made to enslave, O Liberty! thy Land.
My soul rekindles at thy glorious name
Thy beams essential to the vital Flame.   20
    The Patrio'ts' breast, what Heav'nly virtue warms! [*sic*]
And adds new lustre to his mental charms;
While in thy speech, the Graces all combine;
Apollos too, with Sons of Thunder join,
Then shall the Race of injur'd Freedom bless   25
The Sire, the Friend, and messenger of Peace.
    While you, my Lord, read o'er th' advent'rous Song
And wonder whence such daring boldness sprung:
Hence, flow my wishes for the common good
By feeling hearts alone, best understood.   30
    From Native clime, when Seeming cruel fate
Me snatch'd from Afric's fancy'd happy Seat
Impetuous.—Ah! what bitter pangs molest
What Sorrows labour'd in the Parent breast!
That more than Stone, ne'er soft compassion mov'd   35
Who from its Father seiz'd his much belov'd.
Such once my case.—Thus I deplore the day
When Britons weep beneath Tyrannic sway.
To thee, our thanks for favours past are due,
To thee, we still Solicite for the new;   40
Since in thy pow'r as in thy Will before,
To sooth the griefs which thou didst then deplore.
    May heav'nly grace, the Sacred Sanction give
To all thy works, and thou for ever live,
Not only on the wing of fleeting Fame,   45
(Immortal Honours grace the Patriots' name!)
Thee to conduct to Heav'ns refulgent fane;
May fiery coursers sweep th' ethereal plain!
Thou, like the Prophet, find the bright abode
Where dwells thy Sire, the *Everlasting God*.   50

[26]

To the Hon'ble Thomas Hubbard, *Esq; On the Death of Mrs.* Thankfull Leonard.

WHILE thus you mourn beneath the Cypress shade
That hand of Death, a kind conductor made
To her whose flight commands your tears to flow
And wracks your bosom with a scene of wo:
Let Recollection bear a tender part   5
To sooth and calm the tortures of your heart:
To still the tempest of tumultous grief;
To give the heav'nly Nectar of relief;
Ah! cease, no more her unknown bliss bemoan!
Suspend the sigh, and check the rising groan.   10
Her virtues shone with rays divinely bright,
But ah! soon clouded with the shades of night.
How free from tow'ring pride, that gentle mind!
Which ne'er the hapless indigent declin'd,
Expanding free, it sought the means to prove   15
Unfailing Charity, unbounded Love!

   She unreluctant flies, to see no more
Her much lov'd Parents on Earth's dusky shore,
'Till dark mortality shall be withdrawn,
And your bless'd eyes salute the op'ning morn.*   20
Impatient heav'n's resplendent goal to gain
She with swift progress scours the azure plain,
Where grief subsides, where passion is no more
And life's tumultous billows cease to roar,
She leaves her earthly mansions for the skies   25
Where new creations feast her won'dring eyes.
To heav'n's high mandate chearfully resign'd
She mounts, she flies, and leaves the rolling Globe behind.
She who late sigh'd for LEONARD to return
Has ceas'd to languish, and forgot to mourn.   30
Since to the same divine dominions come
She joins her Spouse, and smiles upon the Tomb:
And thus addresses;—(let Idea rove)—
["]Lo! this the Kingdom of celestial Love!
Could our fond Parents view our endless Joy,   35

Soon would the fountain of their sorrows dry;
Then would delightful retrospect inspire,
Their kindling bosoms with the sacred fire!
Amidst unutter'd pleasures, whilst I play,
In the fair sunshine of celestial day: 40
As far as grief affects a deathless Soul,
So far doth grief my better mind controul:
To see on Earth, my aged Parents mourn,
And secret, wish for THANKFULL to return!
Let not such thought their latest hours employ   45
But as advancing fast, prepare for equal Joy.["]

* Meaning the Resurrection.

Boston, January 2. 1773. *Phillis Wheatley.*

[27]
PROPOSALS

For Printing in *London* by SUBSCRIPTION,
A Volume of POEMS,
Dedicated by Permission to the Right Hon. the
Countess of Huntingdon.
Written by PHILLIS,
A Negro Servant to Mr. Wheatley of *Boston*
in New-England.
Terms of Subscription.

I. The Book to be neatly printed in 12 mo. on a new Type and a fine Paper, adorned with an elegant Frontispiece, representing the Author.

II. That the Price to Subscribers shall be Two Shillings Sewed or Two Shillings and Six-pence neatly bound.

II[I]. That every Subscriber deposit One Shilling at the Time of subscribing; and the Remainder to be paid on the Delivery of the Book.

Subscriptions are received by Cox & Berry, in *Boston.*

[28]

To the Empire of America, Beneath the Western Hemisphere. Farewell to America.

To Mrs. S.W.

ADIEU NEW ENGLAND'S smiling Meads,
    Adieu the flow'ry Plain:
I leave thy op'ning Charms, O Spring!
    To try the Azure Reign.—

In vain for me the Flowrets rise,   5
    And show their guady [*sic*] Pride,
While here beneath the Northern Skies
    I mourn for Health deny'd.

Thee, charming Maid, while I pursue,
    In thy luxuriant Reign,   10
And sigh, and languish thee to view,
    Thy Pleasures to regain:—

SUSANNA mourns, nor can I bear
    To see the Christal Show'r
Fast falling,—the indulgent Tear,   15
    In sad Departure's Hour!

Not unregarding lo! I see
    Thy Soul with Grief oppress'd:
Ah! curb the rising Groan for me,
    Nor Sighs disturb thy Breast.   20

In vain the feather'd Songsters sing,
    In vain the Garden blooms,
And on the Bosom of the Spring
    Breathes out her sweet Perfumes;—

While for Britannia's distant Shore   25
    We sweep the liquid Plain,
'Till Aura to the Arms restore,
    Of this belov'd Domain.

Lo, Health appears, Celestial Dame!
 Complacent and serene,   30
With Hebe's Mantle o'er her Frame,
 With Soul-delighting Mein.

Deep in a Vale, where London lies,
 With misty Vapours crown'd;
Which cloud Aurora's thousand Dyes,   35
 And veil her Charms around.

Why, P[h]oebus, moves thy Car so slow,
 So slow thy rising Ray;—
Nor give the mantl'd Town to View
 Thee, glorious King of Day!   40

But late from Orient Skies behold,
 He shines benignly bright,
He decks his native Plains with Gold,
 With chearing Rays of Light.

For thee, Britannia, I resign   45
 New England's smiling Face,
To view again her Charms divine,
 One short reluctant Space.

But thou, Temptation, hence away,
 With all thy hated Train   50
Of Ills,—nor tempt my Mind astray
 From Virtue's sacred Strain.

Most happy! who with Sword and Shield
 Is screen'd from dire Alarms,
And fell Temptation on the Field   55
 Of fatal Pow'r disarms.

But cease thy Lays: my Lute forbear;
 Nor frown, my gentle Muse,
To see the secret, falling Tear,
 Nor pitying look refuse.   60

[28a]

BOSTON, MAY 10, 1773 Saturday last Capt. Calef sailed for London, in [with] whom went Passengers Mr. Nathaniel Wheatley, Merchant; also, Phillis, the extraordinary Negro Poet, Servant to Mr. John Wheatley.

FAREWELL TO AMERICA.

To Mrs. S— W—. *By* Phillis Wheatley.

ADIEU New England's smiling Meads;
　　Adieu the flow'ry Plain,
I leave thy opening Charms, O Spring!
　　To try the Azure Reign.

In vain for me the Flow'rets rise　　　　　　　　5
　　And show their gawdy Pride,
While here beneath the Northern Skies
　　I mourn for Health deny'd.

Thee, charming Maid! while I pursue
　　In thy luxuriant Reign;　　　　　　　　　　10
And sigh and languish, thee to view,
　　Thy Pleasures to regain.

Susanna mourns, nor can I bear
　　To see the Christal Show'r
Fast falling—the indulgent Tear　　　　　　　　15
　　In sad Departure's Hour.

Not unregarding lo! I see
　　Thy Soul with Grief oppress'd;
Ah! curb the rising Groan for me,
　　Nor Sighs disturb thy Breast.　　　　　　　　20

In vain the feather'd Songsters sing,
　　In vain the Garden Blooms,
And on the Bosom of the Spring,
　　Breaths out her sweet Perfumes.

While for Britannia's distant Shore,   25
    We sweep the liquid Plain,
Till Aura to the Arms restore
    Of this belov'd Domain.

Lo! Health appears! Celestial Dame,
    Complacent and serene,   30
With Hebe's Mantle o'er her Frame,
    With Soul-delighting Mein.

Deep in a Vale where London lies,
    With misty Vapours crown'd,
Which cloud Aurora's thousand Dyes,   35
    And Veil her Charms around.

Why Phoebus! moves thy Car so slow,
    So slow thy rising Ray;
Nor gives the mantled Town to View
    Thee glorious King of Day!   40

But late from Orient Skies, behold!
    He Shines benignly bright,
He decks his native Plains with Gold,
    With chearing Rays of Light.

For thee Britannia! I resign   45
    New-England's smiling Face,
To view again her Charms divine,
    One short reluctant Space.

But thou Temptation! hence, away,
    With all thy hated Train   50
Of Ills—nor tempt my Mind astray
    From Virtue's sacred Strain.

Most happy! who with Sword and Shield
    Is screen'd from dire Alarms,
And fell Temptation, on the Field,   55
    Of fatal Power disarms.

But cease thy Lays, my Lute forbear
    Nor frown my gentle Muse,
To see the secret falling Tear,
    Nor pitying look refuse.   60

It was mentioned in our last that Phillis[,] the Negro Poet, had taken her Passage for England, in consequence of an Invitation from the Countess of Huntingdon, which was a mistake.

[29]

Poems on Various Subjects, Religious and Moral.

[29a] [Frontispiece]

Phillis Wheatley, Negro Servant to M^r. John Wheatley, of Boston.
Published according to Act of Parliament, Septr. 1, 1773 by Arch^d. Bell,/Bookseller N°. 8 near the Saracens Head Aldgate.

[29b]

[Title-page]

POEMS
ON
VARIOUS SUBJECTS,
RELIGIOUS and MORAL.

BY

PHILLIS WHEATLEY,

NEGRO SERVANT to Mr. JOHN WHEATLEY,

of BOSTON, in NEW ENGLAND.

LONDON:
Printed for A. BELL, Bookseller, Aldgate; and sold by
Messrs. COX and BERRY, King-Street, *BOSTON.*
MDCCLXXIII.

[Title-page verso]

Entered at Stationers Hall

[29c]

DEDICATION.

To the Right Honourable the

COUNTESS OF HUNTINGDON,

THE FOLLOWING

POEMS

Are most respectfully

Inscribed,

By her much obliged,

Very humble,

And devoted Servant,

Phillis Wheatley.

Boston, June 12,
1773.

[29d]

PREFACE.

THE following Poems were written originally for the Amusement of the Author, as they were the Products of her leisure Moments. She had no Intention ever to have published them; nor would they now have made their Appearance, but at the Importunity of many of her best, and most generous Friends; to whom she considers herself, as under the greatest Obligations.

As her Attempts in Poetry are now sent into the World, it is hoped the Critic will not severely censure their Defects; and we presume they will have too much Merit to be cast aside with Contempt, as worthless and trifling Effusions.

As to the Disadvantages she has laboured under, with Regard to Learning, nothing needs to be offered, as her Master's Letter in the following Page will sufficiently shew the Difficulties in this Respect she had to encounter.

With all their Imperfections, the Poems are now humbly submitted to the Perusal of the Public.

[29e]

The following is a Copy of a LETTER sent by the Author's Master to the Publisher.

PHILLIS was brought from *Africa* to *America*, in the Year 1761, between Seven and Eight Years of age. Without any Assistance from School Education, and by only what she was taught in the Family, she, in sixteen Months Time from her arrival, attained the English Language, to which she was an utter Stranger before, to such a Degree, as to read any, the most difficult Parts of the Sacred Writings, to the great Astonishment of all who heard her.

As to her WRITING, her own curiosity led her to it; and this she learnt in so short a Time, that in the Year 1765, she wrote a Letter to the Rev. Mr. OCCOM, the *Indian* Minister, while in *England*.

She has a great Inclination to learn the Latin Tongue, and has made some Progress in it. This Relation is given by her Master who bought her, and with whom she now lives.

JOHN WHEATLEY.
Boston, Nov. 14, 1772.

[29f]

To the PUBLICK.

AS it has been repeatedly suggested to the Publisher, by Persons, who have seen the Manuscript, that Numbers would be ready to suspect they were not really the Writings of PHILLIS, he has procured the following Attestation, from the most respectable Characters in *Boston*, that none might have the least Ground for disputing their *Original*.

WE whose Names are under-written, do assure the World, that the POEMS specified in the following Page,* were (as we verily believe) written by PHILLIS, a young Negro Girl, who was but a few Years since, brought an uncultivated Barbarian from *Africa*, and has ever since been, and now is, under the Disadvantage of serving as a Slave in a Family in this Town. She has been examined by some of the best Judges, and is thought qualified to write them.

His Excellency THOMAS HUTCHINSON, *Governor*,
The Hon. ANDREW OLIVER, *Lieutenant-Governor*.

The Hon. Thomas Hubbard,	*The Rev.* Charles Chauncy, *D.D.*
The Hon. John Erving,	*The Rev.* Mather Byles, *D.D.*
The Hon. James Pitts,	*The Rev.* Ed. Pemberton, *D.D.*
The Hon. Harrison Gray,	*The Rev.* Andrew Elliot, *D.D.*
The Hon. James Bowdoin,	*The Rev.* Samuel Cooper, *D.D.*
John Hancock, *Esq*;	*The Rev.* Samuel Mather, *D.D.*
Joseph Green, *Esq*;	*The Rev.* Mr. John Moorhead, *D.D.*
Richard Carey, *Esq*;	Mr. John Wheatley, *her Master.*

N.B. The original Attestation, signed by the above Gentlemen, may be seen by applying to *Archibald Bell* Bookseller, No. 8, *Aldgate-Street.*

*The Words *"following Page"* allude to the Contents of the Manuscript Copy, which are wrote at the Back of the above Attestation.

POEMS
ON
VARIOUS SUBJECTS.

[29g]

To MAECENAS.

MAECENAS, you, beneath the myrtle shade,
Read o'er what poets sung, and shepherds play'd.
What felt those poets but you feel the same?
Does not your soul possess the sacred flame?

Their noble strains your equal genius shares   5
In softer language, and diviner airs.

 While *Homer* paints lo! circumfus'd in air,
Celestial Gods in mortal forms appear;
Swift as they move hear each recess rebound,
Heav'n quakes, earth trembles, and the shores resound.   10
Great Sire of verse, before my mortal eyes,
The lightnings blaze across the vaulted skies,
And, as the thunder shakes the heav'nly plains,
A deep-felt horror thrills through all my veins.
When gentler strains demand thy graceful song,   15
The length'ning line moves languishing along.
When great *Patroclus* courts *Achilles*' aid,
The grateful tribute of my tears is paid;
Prone on the shore he feels the pangs of love,
And stern *Pelides* tend'rest passions move.   20

 Great *Maro*'s strain in heav'nly numbers flows,
The *Nine* inspire, and all the bosom glows.
O could I rival thine and *Virgil*'s page,
Or claim the *Muses* with the *Mantuan* Sage;
Soon the same beauties should my mind adorn,   25
And the same ardors in my soul should burn:
Then should my song in bolder notes arise,
And all my numbers pleasingly surprise;
But here I sit, and mourn a grov'ling mind
That fain would mount, and ride upon the wind.   30

 Not you, my friend, these plaintive strains become,
Not you, whose bosom is the *Muses* home;
When they from tow'ring *Helicon* retire,
They fan in you the bright immortal fire,
But I less happy, cannot raise the song,   35
The fault'ring music dies upon my tongue.

 The happier *Terence** all the choir inspir'd,
His soul replenish'd, and his bosom fir'd;
But say, ye *Muses*, why this partial grace,
To one alone of *Afric*'s sable race;   40
From age to age transmitting thus his name
With the first glory in the rolls of fame?

Thy virtues, great *Maecenas*! shall be sung
In praise of him, from whom those virtues sprung:
While blooming wreaths around thy temples spread,   45
I'll snatch a laurel from thine honour'd head,
While you indulgent smile upon the deed.

   As long as *Thames* in streams majestic flows,
Or *Naiads* in their oozy beds repose,
While *Phoebus* reigns above the starry train,   50
While bright *Aurora* purples o'er the main,
So long, great Sir, the muse thy praise shall sing,
So long thy praise shall make *Parnassus* ring:
Then grant, *Maecenas*, thy paternal rays,
Hear me propitious, and defend my lays.   55

*He was *African* by birth.

[29h]

On VIRTUE.

   O Thou bright jewel in my aim I strive
To comprehend thee. Thine own words declare
Wisdom is higher than a fool can reach.
I cease to wonder, and no more attempt
Thine height t'explore, or fathom thy profound.   5
But, O my soul, sink not into despair,
Virtue is near thee, and with gentle hand
Would now embrace thee, hovers o'er thine head.
Fain would the heav'n-born soul with her converse,
Then seek, then court her for her promis'd bliss.   10

   Auspicious queen, thine heav'nly pinions spread,
And lead celestial *Chastity* along;
Lo! now her sacred retinue descends,
Array'd in glory from the orbs above.
Attend me, *Virtue*, thro' my youthful years!   15
O leave me not to the false joys of time!
But guide my steps to endless life and bliss.
Greatness, or *Goodness*, say what I shall call thee,

To give an higher appellation still,
Teach me a better strain, a nobler lay,   20
O Thou, enthron'd with Cherubs in the realms of day!

[29i]

To the University of CAMBRIDGE, in NEW-ENGLAND.

WHILE an intrinsic ardor prompts to write,
The muses promise to assist my pen;
'Twas not long since I left my native shore
The land of errors, and *Egyptian* gloom:
Father of mercy, 'twas thy gracious hand   5
Brought me in safety from those dark abodes.

Students, to you 'tis giv'n to scan the heights
Above, to traverse the ethereal space,
And mark the systems of revolving worlds.
Still more, ye sons of science ye receive   10
The blissful news by messengers from heav'n,
How *Jesus*' blood for your redemption flows.
See him with hands out-stretcht upon the cross;
Immense compassion in his bosom glows;
He hears revilers, nor resents their scorn: 15
What matchless mercy in the Son of God!
When the whole human race by sin had fall'n,
He deign'd to die that they might rise again,
And share with him in the sublimest skies,
Life without death, and glory without end.   20

Improve your privileges while they stay,
Ye pupils, and each hour redeem, that bears
Or good or bad report of you to heav'n.
Let sin, that baneful evil to the soul,
By you be shunn'd, nor once remit your guard;   25
Suppress the deadly serpent in its egg.
Ye blooming plants of human race divine,
An *Ethiop* tells you 'tis your greatest foe;

Its transient sweetness turns to endless pain,
And in immense perdition sinks the soul.   30

[29j]
To the KING's Most Excellent Majesty. 1768.

YOUR subjects hope, dread Sire—
The crown upon your brows may flourish long,
And that your arm may in your God be strong!
O may your sceptre num'rous nations sway,
And all with love and readiness obey!   5

But how shall we the *British* king reward!
Rule thou in peace, our father, and our lord!
Midst the remembrance of thy favours past,
The meanest peasants most admire the last.*
May *George*, belov'd by all the nations round,   10
Live with heav'ns choicest constant blessings crown'd!
Great God, direct, and guard him from on high,
And from his head let ev'ry evil fly!
And may each clime with equal gladness see
A monarch's smile can set his subjects free!   15

*The Repeal of the Stamp Act.

[29k]
On being brought from AFRICA to AMERICA.

'TWAS mercy brought me from my *Pagan* land,
Taught my benighted soul to understand
That there's a God, that there's a *Saviour* too:
Once I redemption neither sought nor knew.
Some view our sable race with scornful eye,   5
"Their colour is a diabolic die."
Remember, *Christians*, *Negros*, black as *Cain*,
May be refin'd, and join th' angelic train.

[291]

On the Death of the Rev. Dr. SEWELL. 1769.

ERE yet the morn its lovely blushes spread,
See *Sewell* number'd with the happy dead.
Hail, holy man, arriv'd th' immortal shore,
Though we shall hear thy warning voice no more.
Come, let us all behold with wishful eyes   5
The saint ascending to his native skies;
From hence the prophet wing'd his rapt'rous way
To the blest mansions in eternal day.
Then begging for the Spirit of our God,
And panting eager for the same abode,   10
Come, let us all with the same vigour rise,
And take a prospect of the blissful skies;
While on our minds *Christ's* image is imprest,
And the dear Saviour glows in ev'ry breast.
Thrice happy saint! to find thy heav'n at last,   15
What compensation for the evils past!

Great God, incomprehensible, unknown
By sense, we bow at thine exalted throne.
O, while we beg thine excellence to feel,
Thy sacred Spirit to our hearts reveal,   20
And give us of that mercy to partake,
Which thou hast promis'd for the *Saviour's* sake!

"*Sewell* is dead." Swift-pinion'd *Fame* thus cry'd.
"Is *Sewell* dead," my trembling tongue reply'd,
O what a blessing in his flight deny'd!   25
How oft for us the holy prophet pray'd!
How oft to us the Word of Life convey'd!
By duty urg'd my mournful verse to close,
I for his tomb this epitaph compose.

"Lo, here a Man, redeem'd by *Jesus'* blood,   30
"A sinner once, but now a saint with God;
"Behold ye rich, ye poor, ye fools, ye wise,
"Nor let his monument your heart surprize;
"'Twill tell you what this holy man has done,
"Which gives him brighter lustre than the sun.   35

"Listen, ye happy, from your seats above.
"I speak sincerely, while I speak and love,
"He sought the paths of piety and truth,
"By these made happy from his early youth!
"In blooming years that grace divine he felt, 40
"Which rescues sinners from the chains of guilt.
"Mourn him, ye indigent, whom he has fed,
"And henceforth seek, like him, for living bread;
"Ev'n *Christ*, the bread descending from above,
"And ask an int'rest in his saving love. 45
"Mourn him, ye youth, to whom he oft has told
"God's gracious wonders from the times of old.
"I, too have cause this mighty loss to mourn,
"For he my monitor will not return.
"O when shall we to his blest state arrive? 50
"When the same graces in our bosoms thrive."

[29m]

On the Death of the Rev.
Mr. GEORGE WHITEFIELD. 1770.

HAIL, happy saint, on thine immortal throne,
Possest of glory, life, and bliss unknown;
We hear no more the music of thy tongue,
Thy wonted auditories cease to throng.
Thy sermons in unequall'd accents flow'd, 5
And ev'ry bosom with devotion glow'd;
Thou didst in strains of eloquence refin'd
Inflame the heart, and captivate the mind.
Unhappy we the setting sun deplore,
So glorious once, but ah! it shines no more. 10

Behold the prophet in his tow'ring flight!
He leaves the earth for heav'n's unmeasur'd height,
And worlds unknown receive him from our sight.
There *Whitefield* wings with rapid course his way,
And sails to *Zion* through vast seas of day. 15
Thy pray'rs, great saint, and thine incessant cries

Have pierc'd the bosom of thy native skies.
Thou moon hast seen, and all the stars of light,
How he has wrestled with his God by night.
He pray'd that grace in ev'ry heart might dwell, 20
He long'd to see *America* excel;
He charg'd its youth that ev'ry grace divine
Should with full lustre in their conduct shine;
That Saviour, which his soul did first receive,
The greatest gift that ev'n a God can give, 25
He freely offer'd to the num'rous throng,
That on his lips with list'ning pleasure hung.

"Take him, ye wretched, for your only good,
"Take him ye starving sinners, for your food;
"Ye thirsty, come to this life-giving stream, 30
"Ye preachers, take him for your joyful theme;
"Take him my dear *Americans*, he said,
"Be your complaints on his kind bosom laid:
"Take him, ye *Africans*, he longs for you,
"*Impartial Saviour* is his title due: 35
"Wash'd in the fountain of redeeming blood,
"You shall be sons, and kings, and priests to God."

Great *Countess*,* we *Americans* revere
Thy name, and mingle in thy grief sincere;
New England deeply feels, the *Orphans* mourn, 40
Their more than father will no more return.

But, though arrested by the hand of death,
Whitefield no more exerts his lab'ring breath,
Yet let us view him in th' eternal skies,
Let ev'ry heart to this bright vision rise; 45
While the tomb safe retains its sacred trust,
Till life divine re-animates his dust.

*The Countess of *Huntingdon*, to whom Mr. *Whitefield* was Chaplain.

[29n]

On the Death of a young Lady of Five Years of Age.

FROM dark abodes to fair etherial light
Th' enraptur'd innocent has wing'd her flight;
On the kind bosom of eternal love
She finds unknown beatitude above.
This know, ye parents, nor her loss deplore,   5
She feels the iron hand of pain no more;
The dispensations of unerring grace,
Should turn your sorrows into grateful praise;
Let then no tears for her henceforward flow,
No more distress'd in our dark vale below.   10

Her morning sun, which rose divinely bright,
Was quickly mantled with the gloom of night;
But hear in heav'n's blest bow'rs your *Nancy* fair,
And learn to imitate her language there.
"Thou, Lord, whom I behold with glory crown'd,   15
"By what sweet name, and in what tuneful sound
"Wilt thou be prais'd? Seraphic pow'rs are faint
"Infinite love and majesty to paint.
"To thee let all their grateful voices raise,
"And saints and angels join their songs of praise."   20

Perfect in bliss she from her heav'nly home
Looks down, and smiling beckons you to come;
Why then, fond parents, why these fruitless groans?
Restrain your tears, and cease your plaintive moans.
Freed from a world of sin, and snares, and pain,   25
Why would you wish your daughter back again?
No—bow resign'd. Let hope your grief control,
And check the rising tumult of the soul.
Calm in the prosperous, and adverse day,
Adore the God who gives and takes away;   30
Eye him in all, his holy name revere,
Upright your actions, and your hearts sincere,
Till having sail'd through life's tempestuous sea,
And from its rocks, and boist'rous billows free,
Yourselves, safe landed on the blissful shore,   35
Shall join your happy babe to part no more.

[290]

On the Death of a young Gentleman.

WHO taught thee conflict with the pow'rs of night,
To vanquish Satan in the fields of fight?
Who strung thy feeble arms with might unknown,
How great thy conquest, and how bright thy crown!
War with each princedom, throne, and pow'r is o'er,   5
The scene is ended to return no more.
O could my muse thy seat on high behold,
How deckt with laurel, how enrich'd with gold!
O could she hear what praise thine harp employs,
How sweet thine anthems, how divine thy joys!   10
What heav'nly grandeur should exalt her strain!
What holy raptures in her numbers reign!
To sooth the troubles of the mind to peace,
To still the tumult of life's tossing seas,
To ease the anguish of the parents heart,   15
What shall my sympathizing verse impart?
Where is the balm to heal so deep a wound?
Where shall a sov'reign remedy be found?
Look, gracious Spirit, from thine heav'nly bow'r,
And thy full joys into their bosoms pour;   20
The raging tempest of their grief control,
And spread the dawn of glory through the soul,
To eye the path the saint departed trod,
And trace him to the bosom of his God.

[29p]

To a Lady on the Death of her Husband.

GRIM monarch! see, depriv'd of vital breath,
A young physician in the dust of death:
Dost thou go on incessant to destroy,
Our griefs to double, and lay waste our joy?
Enough thou never yet wast known to say,   5
Though millions die, the vassals of thy sway:
Nor youth, nor science, nor the ties of love,

Nor aught on earth thy flinty heart can move.
The friend, the spouse from his dire dart to save,
In vain we ask the sovereign of the grave.   10
Fair mourner, there see thy lov'd *Leonard* laid,
And o'er him spread the deep impervious shade;
Clos'd are his eyes, and heavy fetters keep
His senses bound in never-waking sleep,
Till time shall cease, till many a starry world   15
Shall fall from heav'n, in dire confusion hurl'd,
Till nature in her final wreck shall lie,
And her last groan shall rend the azure sky:
Not, not till then his active soul shall claim
His body, a divine immortal frame.   20

    But see the softly-stealing tears apace
Pursue each other down the mourner's face;
But cease thy tears, bid ev'ry sigh depart,
And cast the load of anguish from thine heart:
From the cold shell of his great soul arise,   25
And look beyond, thou native of the skies;
There fix thy view, where fleeter than the wind
Thy *Leonard* mounts, and leaves the earth behind.
Thyself prepare to pass the vale of night
To join for ever on the hills of light: 30
To thine embrace his joyful spirit moves
To thee, the partner of his earthly loves;
He welcomes thee to pleasures more refin'd,
And better suited to th' immortal mind.

[29q]
GOLIATH of GATH.

1 Sam. Chap. xvii.

YE martial pow'rs, and all ye tuneful nine,
Inspire my song, and aid my high design.
The dreadful scenes and toils of war I write,
The ardent warriors, and the fields of fight:
You best remember, and you best can sing   5
The acts of heroes to the vocal string:

Resume the lays with which your sacred lyre,
Did then the poet and the sage inspire.

Now front to front the armies were display'd,
Here *Israel* rang'd, and there the foes array'd;   10
The hosts on two opposing mountains stood,
Thick as the foliage of the waving wood;
Between them an extensive valley lay,
O'er which the gleaming armour pour'd the day,
When from the camp of the *Philistine* foes,   15
Dreadful to view, a mighty warrior rose;
In the dire deeds of bleeding battle skill'd,   ·
The monster stalks the terror of the field.
From *Gath* he sprung, *Goliath* was his name,
Of fierce deportment, and gigantic frame: 20
A brazen helmet on his head was plac'd,
A coat of mail his form terrific grac'd,
The greaves his legs, the targe his shoulders prest:
Dreadful in arms high-tow'ring o'er the rest
A spear he proudly wav'd, whose iron head,   25
Strange to relate, six hundred shekels weigh'd;
He strode along, and shook the ample field,
While *Phoebus* blaz'd refulgent on his shield:
Through *Jacob's* race a chilling horror ran,
When thus the huge, enormous chief began: 30

"Say, what the cause that in this proud array
"You set your battle in the face of day?
"One hero find in all your vaunting train,
"Then see who loses, and who wins the plain;
"For he who wins, in triumph may demand   35
"Perpetual service from the vanquish'd land:
"Your armies I defy, your force despise,
"By far inferior in *Philistia's* eyes:
"Produce a man, and let us try the fight,
"Decide the contest, and the victor's right."   40

Thus challeng'd he: all *Israel* stood amaz'd,
And ev'ry chief in consternation gaz'd;
But *Jesse's* son in youthful bloom appears,
And warlike courage far beyond his years:
He left the folds, he left the flow'ry meads,   45

And soft recesses of the sylvan shades.
Now *Israel's* monarch, and his troops arise, ⎫
With peals of shouts ascending to the skies; ⎬
In *Elah's* vale the scene of combat lies. ⎭

When the fair morning blush'd with orient red,   50
What *David's* sire enjoin'd the son obey'd,
And swift of foot towards the trench he came,
Where glow'd each bosom with the martial flame.
He leaves his carriage to another's care,
And runs to greet his brethren of the war.   55
While yet they spake the giant-chief arose,
Repeats the challenge, and insults his foes:
Struck with the sound, and trembling at the view,
Affrighted *Israel* from its post withdrew.
"Observe ye this tremendous foe, they cry'd,   60
"Who in proud vaunts our armies hath defy'd:
"Whoever lays him prostrate on the plain,
"Freedom in *Israel* for his house shall gain;
"And on him wealth unknown the king will pour,
"And give his royal daughter for his dow'r."   65

Then *Jesse's* youngest hope: "My brethren say,
"What shall be done for him who takes away
"Reproach from *Jacob*, who destroys the chief,
"And puts a period to his country's grief.
"He vaunts the honours of his arms abroad,   70
"And scorns the armies of the living God."

Thus spoke the youth, th' attentive people ey'd
The wond'rous hero, and again reply'd:
"Such the rewards our monarch will bestow,
"On him who conquers, and destroys his foe."   75

Eliab heard, and kindled into ire
To hear his shepherd-brother thus inquire,
And thus begun? [*sic*] "What errand brought thee? say
"Who keeps thy flock? or does it go astray?
"I know the base ambition of thine heart,   80
"But back in safety from the field depart."

Eliab thus to *Jesse's* youngest heir,
Express'd his wrath in accents most severe.

When to his brother mildly he reply'd,
"What have I done? or what the cause to chide?" 85

 The words were told before the king, who sent
For the young hero to his royal tent:
Before the monarch dauntless he began,
"For this *Philistine* fail no heart of man:
"I'll take the vale, and with the giant fight: 90
"I dread not all his boasts, nor all his might."
When thus the king: "Dar'st thou a stripling go,
"And venture combat with so great a foe?
"Who all his days has been inur'd to fight,
"And made its deeds his study and delight: 95
"Battles and bloodshed brought the monster forth,
"And clouds and whirlwinds usher'd in his birth."
When *David* thus: "I kept the fleecy care,
"And out there rush'd a lion and a bear;
"A tender lamb the hungry lion took, 100
"And with no other weapon than my crook
"Bold I pursu'd, and chas'd him o'er the field,
"The prey deliver'd, and the felon kill'd:
"As thus the lion and the bear I slew,
"So shall *Goliath* fall, and all his crew: 105
"The God, who sav'd me from these beasts of prey,
"By me this monster in the dust shall lay."
So *David* spoke. The wond'ring king reply'd;
"Go thou with heav'n and victory on thy side:
"This coat of mail, this sword gird on," he said, 110
And plac'd a mighty helmet on his head:
The coat, the sword, the helm he laid aside,
Nor chose to venture with those arms untry'd,
Then took his staff, and to the neighb'ring brook
Instant he ran, and thence five pebbles took. 115
Mean time descended to *Philistia's* son
A radiant cherub, and he thus begun:
"Goliath, well thou know'st thou hast defy'd
"Yon Hebrew armies, and their God deny'd:
"Rebellious wretch! audacious worm! forbear, 120
"Nor tempt the vengeance of their God too far:
"Them, who with his omnipotence contend,
"No eye shall pity, and no arm defend:
"Proud as thou art, in short liv'd glory great,

"I come to tell thee thine approaching fate.   125
"Regard my words. The judge of all the gods,
"Beneath whose steps the tow'ring mountain nods,
"Will give thine armies to the savage brood,
"That cut the liquid air, or range the wood.
"Thee too a well-aim'd pebble shall destroy,   130
"And thou shalt perish by a beardless boy:
"Such is the mandate from the realms above, ⎞
"And should I try the vengeance to remove, ⎬
"Myself a rebel to my king would prove. ⎠
"*Goliath* say, shall grace to him be shown,   135
"Who dares heav'ns monarch, and insults his throne?"

    "Your words are lost on me," the giant cries, ⎞
While fear and wrath contended in his eyes, ⎬
When thus the messenger from heav'n replies: ⎠
"Provoke no more *Jehovah's* awful hand   140
"To hurl its vengeance on thy guilty land:
"He grasps the thunder, and, he wings the storm,
"Servants their sov'reign's orders to perform."

    The angel spoke, and turn'd his eyes away,
Adding new radiance to the rising day.   145

    Now *David* comes: the fatal stones demand
His left, the staff engag'd his better hand:
The giant mov'd, and from his tow'ring height
Survey'd the stripling, and disdain'd the sight,
And thus began: "Am I a dog with thee?   150
"Bring'st thou no armour, but a staff to me?
"The gods on thee their vollied curses pour,
"And beasts and birds of prey thy flesh devour."

    David undaunted thus, "Thy spear and shield
"Shall no protection to thy body yield: 155
"*Jehovah's* name—no other arms I bear,
"I ask no other in this glorious war.
"To-day the Lord of Hosts to me will give
"Vict'ry, to-day thy doom thou shalt receive;
"The fate you threaten shall your own become,   160
"And beasts shall be your animated tomb,
"That all the earth's inhabitants may know
"That there's a God, who governs all below:

"This great assembly too shall witness stand,
"That needs nor sword, nor spear, th' Almighty's hand: 165
"The battle his, the conquest he bestows,
"And to our pow'r consigns our hated foes."

　　Thus *David* spoke; *Goliath* heard and came
To meet the hero in the field of fame.
Ah! fatal meeting to thy troops and thee,   170
But thou wast deaf to the divine decree;
Young *David* meets thee, meets thee not in vain;
'Tis thine to perish on th' ensanguin'd plain.

　　And now the youth the forceful pebble flung,
Philistia trembled as it whizz'd along: 175
In his dread forehead, where the helmet ends,
Just o'er the brows the well-aim'd stone descends,
It pierc'd the skull, and shatter'd all the brain,
Prone on his face he tumbled to the plain:
Goliath's fall no smaller terror yields   180
Than riving thunders in aerial fields:
The soul still ling'red in its lov'd abode,
Till conq'ring *David* o'er the giant strode:
Goliath's sword then laid its master dead,
And from the body hew'd the ghastly head;   185
The blood in gushing torrents drench'd the plains,
The soul found passage through the spouting veins.

　　And now aloud th' illustrious victor said,
"Where are your boastings now your champion's dead?"
Scarce had he spoke, when the *Philistines* fled: 190
But fled in vain; the conqu'ror swift pursu'd:
What scenes of slaughter! and what seas of blood!
There *Saul* thy thousands grasp'd th' impurpled sand
In pangs of death the conquest of thine hand;
And *David* there were thy ten thousands laid: 195
Thus *Israel's* damsels musically play'd.

　　Near *Gath* and *Ekron* many an hero lay,
Breath'd out their souls, and curs'd the light of day:
Their fury, quench'd by death, no longer burns,
And *David* with *Goliath's* head returns,   200
To *Salem* brought, but in his tent he plac'd

The load of armour which the giant grac'd.
His monarch saw him coming from the war,
And thus demanded of the son of *Ner*.
"Say, who is this amazing youth?" he cry'd,   205
When thus the leader of the host reply'd;
"As lives thy soul I know not whence he sprung,
"So great in prowess though in years so young:"
"Inquire whose son is he," the sov'reign said,
"Before whose conq'ring arm *Philistia* fled."   210
Before the king behold the stripling stand,
Goliath's head depending from his hand:
To him the king: "Say of what martial line
"Art thou, young hero, and what sire was thine?"
He humbly thus; "the son of *Jesse* I: 215
"I came the glories of the field to try.
"Small is my tribe, but valiant in the fight;
"Small is my city, but thy royal right."
"Then take the promis'd gifts," the monarch cry'd,
Conferring riches and the royal bride: 220
"Knit to my soul for ever thou remain
"With me, nor quit my regal roof again."

[29r]
Thoughts on the WORKS of PROVIDENCE.

ARISE, my soul, on wings enraptur'd, rise
To praise the monarch of the earth and skies,
Whose goodness and beneficence appear
As round its centre moves the rolling year,
Or when the morning glows with rosy charms,   5
Or the sun slumbers in the ocean's arms:
Of light divine be a rich portion lent
To guide my soul, and favour my intent.
Celestial muse, my arduous flight sustain,
And raise my mind to a seraphic strain!   10

Ador'd for ever be the God unseen,
Which round the sun revolves this vast machine,
Though to his eye its mass a point appears:

Ador'd the God that whirls surrounding spheres,
Which first ordain'd that mighty *Sol* should reign   15
The peerless monarch of th' ethereal train:
Of miles twice forty millions is his height,
And yet his radiance dazzles mortal sight
So far beneath—from him th' extended earth
Vigour derives, and ev'ry flow'ry birth: 20
Vast through her orb she moves with easy grace
Around her *Phoebus* in unbounded space;
True to her course th' impetuous storm derides,
Triumphant o'er the winds, and surging tides.

Almighty, in these wond'rous works of thine,   25
What *Pow'r*, what *Wisdom*, and what *Goodness* shine?
And are thy wonders, Lord, by men explor'd,
And yet creating glory unador'd!

Creation smiles in various beauty gay,
While day to night, and night succeeds to day: 30
That *Wisdom*, which attends *Jehovah's* ways,
Shines most conspicuous in the solar rays:
Without them, destitute of heat and light,
This world would be the reign of endless night:
In their excess how would our race complain,   35
Abhorring life! how hate its length'ned chain!
From air adust what num'rous ills would rise?
What dire contagion taint the burning skies?
What pestilential vapours, fraught with death,
Would rise, and overspread the lands beneath?   40

Hail, smiling morn, that from the orient main
Ascending dost adorn the heav'nly plain!
So rich, so various are thy beauteous dies,
That spread through all the circuit of the skies,
That, full of thee, my soul in rapture soars,   45
And thy great God, the cause of all adores.
O'er beings infinite his love extends,
His *Wisdom* rules them, and his *Pow'r* defends.
When tasks diurnal tire the human frame,
The spirits faint, and dim the vital flame,   50
Then too that ever active bounty shines,

Which not infinity of space confines.
The sable veil, that *Night* in silence draws,
Conceals effects, but shews th' *Almighty Cause*;
Night seals in sleep the wide creation fair,   55
And all is peaceful but the brow of care.
Again, gay *Phoebus*, as the day before,
Wakes ev'ry eye, but what shall wake no more;
Again the face of nature is renew'd,
Which still appears harmonious, fair, and good.   60
May grateful strains salute the smiling morn,
Before its beams the eastern hills adorn!

    Shall day to day, and night to night conspire
To show the goodness of the Almighty Sire?
This mental voice shall man regardless hear,   65
And never, never raise the filial pray'r?
To-day, O hearken, nor your folly mourn
For time mispent, that never will return.

    But see the sons of vegetation rise,
And spread their leafy banners to the skies.   70
All-wise Almighty providence we trace
In trees, and plants, and all the flow'ry race;
As clear as in the nobler frame of man,
All lovely copies of the Maker's plan.
The pow'r the same that forms a ray of light,   75
That call'd creation from eternal night.
"Let there be light," he said: from his profound
Old *Chaos* heard, and trembled at the sound:
Swift as the word, inspir'd by pow'r divine,
Behold the light around its maker shine,   80
The first fair product of th' omnific God,
And now through all his works diffus'd abroad.

    As reason's pow'rs by day our God disclose,
So we may trace him in the night's repose:
Say what is sleep? and dreams how passing strange!   85
When action ceases, and ideas range
Licentious and unbounded o'er the plains,
Where *Fancy*'s queen in giddy triumph reigns.
Hear in soft strains the dreaming lover sigh

To a kind fair, or rave in jealousy;   90
On pleasure now, and now on vengeance bent,
The lab'ring passions struggle for a vent.
What pow'r, O man! thy *reason* then restores,
So long suspended in nocturnal hours?
What secret hand returns the mental train,   95
And gives improv'd thine active pow'rs again?
From thee, O man, what gratitude should rise! ⎫
And, when from balmy sleep thou op'st thine eyes, ⎬
Let thy first thoughts be praises to the skies. ⎭
How merciful our God who thus imparts   100
O'erflowing tides of joy to human hearts,
When wants and woes might be our righteous lot,
Our God forgetting, by our God forgot!

 Among the mental pow'rs a question rose,
"What most the image of th' Eternal shows?"   105
When thus to *Reason* (so let *Fancy* rove)
Her great companion spoke immortal *Love.*

 "Say, mighty pow'r, how long shall strife prevail,
"And with its murmurs load the whisp'ring gale?
"Refer the cause to *Recollection's* shrine,   110
"Who loud proclaims my origin divine,
"The cause whence heav'n and earth began to be,
"And is not man immortaliz'd by me?
"*Reason* let this most causeless strife subside."
Thus *Love* pronounc'd, and *Reason* thus reply'd.   115

 "Thy birth, celestial queen! 'tis mine to own,
"In thee resplendent is the Godhead shown;
"Thy words persuade, my soul enraptur'd feels
"Resistless beauty which thy smile reveals."
Ardent she spoke, and, kindling at her charms,   120
She clasp'd the blooming goddess in her arms.

 Infinite *Love* wher'er we turn our eyes
Appears: this ev'ry creature's wants supplies;
This most is heard in *Nature's* constant voice,
This makes the morn, and this the eve rejoice;   125
This bids the fost'ring rains and dews descend
To nourish all, to serve one gen'ral end,

The good of man: yet man ungrateful pays
But little homage, and but little praise.
To him, whose works array'd with mercy shine,   130
What songs should rise, how constant, how divine!

[29s]

To a Lady on the Death of Three Relations.

WE trace the pow'r of Death from tomb to tomb,
And his are all the ages yet to come.
'Tis his to call the planets from on high,
To blacken *Phoebus*, and dissolve the sky;
His too, when all in his dark realms are hurl'd,   5
From its firm base to shake the solid world;
His fatal sceptre rules the spacious whole,
And trembling nature rocks from pole to pole.

Awful he moves, and wide his wings are spread:
Behold thy brother number'd with the dead!   10
From bondage freed, the exulting spirit flies
Beyond *Olympus*, and these starry skies.
Lost in our woe for thee, blest shade, we mourn
In vain; to earth thou never must return.
Thy sisters too, fair mourner, feel the dart   15
Of Death, and with fresh torture rend thine heart.
Weep not for them, who wish thine happy mind
To rise with them, and leave the world behind.

As a young plant by hurricanes up torn,
So near its parent lies the newly born—   20
But 'midst the bright ethereal train behold
It shines superior on a throne of gold:
Then, mourner, cease; let hope thy tears restrain,
Smile on the tomb, and sooth the raging pain.
On yon blest regions fix thy longing view,   25
Mindless of sublunary scenes below;
Ascend the sacred mount, in thought arise,
And seek substantial and immortal joys;
Where hope receives, where faith to vision springs,
And raptur'd seraphs tune th' immortal strings   30

To strains extatic. Thou the chorus join,
And to thy father tune the praise divine.

[29t]

To a Clergyman on the Death of his Lady.

WHERE contemplation finds her sacred spring,
Where heav'nly music makes the arches ring,
Where virtue reigns unsully'd and divine,
Where wisdom thron'd, and all the graces shine,
There sits thy spouse amidst the radiant throng,   5
While praise eternal warbles from her tongue;
There choirs angelic shout her welcome round,
With perfect bliss, and peerless glory crown'd.

While thy dear mate, to flesh no more confin'd,
Exults a blest, an heav'n-ascended mind,   10
Say in thy breast shall floods of sorrow rise?
Say shall its torrents overwhelm thine eyes?
Amid the seats of heav'n a place is free,
And angels ope their bright ranks for thee;
For thee they wait, and with expectant eye   15
Thy spouse leans downward from th' empyreal sky:
"O come away, her longing spirit cries,
"And share with me the raptures of the skies.
"Our bliss divine to mortals is unknown;
"Immortal life and glory are our own.   20
"There too may the dear pledges of our love
"Arrive, and taste with us the joys above;
"Attune the harp to more than mortal lays,
"And join with us the tribute of their praise
"To him, who dy'd stern justice to atone,   25
"And make eternal glory all our own.
"He in his death slew ours, and, as he rose,
"He crush'd the dire dominion of our foes;
"Vain were their hopes to put the God to flight,
"Chain us to hell, and bar the gates of light."   30

She spoke, and turn'd from mortal scenes her eyes,
Which beam'd celestial radiance o'er the skies.

Then thou, dear man, no more with grief retire, ⎫
Let grief no longer damp devotion's fire,   ⎬
But rise sublime, to equal bliss aspire.   ⎭   35
Thy sighs no more be wafted by the wind,
No more complain, but be to heav'n resign'd.
'Twas thine t' unfold the oracles divine,
To sooth our woes the task was also thine;
Now sorrow is incumbent on thy heart,   40
Permit the muse a cordial to impart;
Who can to thee their tend'rest aid refuse?
To dry thy tears how longs the heav'nly muse!

[29u]

An HYMN to the MORNING.

ATTEND my lays, ye ever honour'd nine,
Assist my labours, and my strains refine;
In smoothest numbers pour the notes along,
For bright *Aurora* now demands my song.

Aurora hail, and all the thousand dies,   5
Which deck thy progress through the vaulted skies:
The morn awakes, and wide extends her rays,
On ev'ry leaf the gentle zephyr plays;
Harmonious lays the feather'd race resume,
Dart the bright eye, and shake the painted plume.   10

Ye shady groves, your verdant gloom display
To shield your poet from the burning day:
Calliope awake the sacred lyre,
While thy fair sisters fan the pleasing fire:
The bow'rs, the gales, the variegated skies   15
In all their pleasures in my bosom rise.

See in the east th' illustrious king of day!
His rising radiance drives the shades away—
But Oh! I feel his fervid beams too strong,
And scarce begun, concludes th' abortive song.   20

[29v]

An HYMN to the EVENING.

SOON as the sun forsook the eastern main
The pealing thunder shook the heav'nly plain;
Majestic grandeur! From the zephyr's wing,
Exhales the incense of the blooming spring.
Soft purl the streams, the birds renew their notes,   5
And through the air their mingled music floats.

   Through all the heav'ns what beauteous dies are spread!
But the west glories in the deepest red:
So may our breasts with ev'ry virtue glow,
The living temples of our God below!   10

   Fill'd with the praise of him who gives the light,
And draws the sable curtains of the night,
Let placid slumbers sooth each weary mind,
At morn to wake more heav'nly, more refin'd;
So shall the labours of the day begin   15
More pure, more guarded from the snares of sin.

   Night's leaden sceptre seals my drowsy eyes,
Then cease, my song, till fair *Aurora* rise.

[29w]

Isaiah lxiii. 1–8.

   SAY, heav'nly muse, what king, or mighty God,
That moves sublime from *Idumea's* road?
In *Bozrah's* dies, with martial glories join'd,
His purple vesture waves upon the wind.
Why thus enrob'd delights he to appear   5
In the dread image of the *Pow'r* of war?

   Compress'd in wrath the swelling wine-press groan'd,
It bled, and pour'd the gushing purple round.

   "Mine was the act," th' Almighty Saviour said,
And shook the dazzling glories of his head,   10

"When all forsook I trod the press alone,
"And conquer'd by omnipotence my own;
"For man's release sustain'd the pond'rous load,
"For man the wrath of an immortal God:
"To execute th' Eternal's dread command   15
"My soul I sacrific'd with willing hand;
"Sinless I stood before the avenging frown,
"Atoning thus for vices not my own."

    His eye the ample field of battle round
Survey'd, but no created succours found;   20
His own omnipotence sustain'd the fight,
His vengeance sunk the haughty foes in night;
Beneath his feet the prostrate troops were spread,
And round him lay the dying, and the dead.

    Great God, what light'ning flashes from thine eyes?   25
What pow'r withstands if thou indignant rise?

    Against thy *Zion* though her foes may rage,
And all their cunning, all their strength engage,
Yet she serenely on thy bosom lies,
Smiles at their arts, and all their force defies.   30

[29x]

On RECOLLECTION.

    MNEME begin. Inspire, ye sacred nine,
Your vent'rous *Afric* in her great design.
Mneme, immortal pow'r, I trace thy spring:
Assist my strains, while I thy glories sing:
The acts of long departed years, by thee   5
Recover'd, in due order rang'd we see:
Thy pow'r the long-forgotten calls from night,
That sweetly plays before the *fancy's* sight.

    Mneme in our nocturnal visions pours
The ample treasure of her secret stores;   10
Swift from above she wings her silent flight
Through *Phoebe's* realms, fair regent of the night;

And, in her pomp of images display'd,
To the high-raptur'd poet gives her aid,
Through the unbounded regions of the mind,   15
Diffusing light celestial and refin'd.
The heav'nly *phantom* paints the actions done
By ev'ry tribe beneath the rolling sun.

   Mneme, enthron'd within the human breast,
Has vice condemn'd, and ev'ry virtue blest.   20
How sweet the sound when we her plaudit hear?
Sweeter than music to the ravish'd ear,
Sweeter than *Maro's* entertaining strains
Resounding through the groves, and hills, and plains.
But how is *Mneme* dreaded by the race,   25
Who scorn her warnings and despise her grace?
By her unveil'd each horrid crime appears,
Her awful hand a cup of wormwood bears.
Days, years mispent, O what a hell of woe!
Hers the worst tortures that our souls can know.   30

   Now eighteen years their destin'd course have run,
In fast succession round the central sun.
How did the follies of that period pass
Unnotic'd, but behold them writ in brass!
In Recollection see them fresh return,   35
And sure 'tis mine to be asham'd, and mourn.

   O *Virtue*, smiling in immortal green,
Do thou exert thy pow'r, and change the scene;
Be thine employ to guide my future days,
And mine to pay the tribute of my praise.   40

   Of *Recollection* such the pow'r enthron'd
In ev'ry breast, and thus her pow'r is own'd.
The wretch, who dar'd the vengeance of the skies,
At last awakes in horror and surprize,
By her alarm'd, he sees impending fate,   45
He howls in anguish, and repents too late.
But O! what peace, what joys are hers t'impart
To ev'ry holy, ev'ry upright heart!
Thrice blest the man, who, in her sacred shrine,
Feels himself shelter'd from the wrath divine!   50

[29y]

On IMAGINATION.

THY various works, imperial queen, we see,
How bright their forms! how deck'd with pomp by thee!
Thy wond'rous acts in beauteous order stand,
And all attest how potent is thine hand.

From *Helicon's* refulgent heights attend,   5
Ye sacred choir, and my attempts befriend:
To tell her glories with a faithful tongue,
Ye blooming graces, triumph in my song.

Now here, now there, the roving *Fancy* flies,
Till some lov'd object strikes her wand'ring eyes,   10
Whose silken fetters all the senses bind,
And soft captivity involves the mind.

Imagination! who can sing thy force?
Or who describe the swiftness of thy course?
Soaring through air to find the bright abode,   15
Th' empyreal palace of the thund'ring God,
We on thy pinions can surpass the wind,
And leave the rolling universe behind:
From star to star the mental optics rove,
Measure the skies, and range the realms above.   20
There in one view we grasp the mighty whole,
Or with new worlds amaze th' unbounded soul.

Though *Winter* frowns to *Fancy's* raptur'd eyes
The fields may flourish, and gay scenes arise;
The frozen deeps may break their iron bands,   25
And bid their waters murmur o'er the sands.
Fair *Flora* may resume her fragrant reign,
And with her flow'ry riches deck the plain;
Sylvanus may diffuse his honours round,
And all the forest may with leaves be crown'd: 30
Show'rs may descend, and dews their gems disclose,
And nectar sparkle on the blooming rose.

Such is thy pow'r, nor are thine orders vain,
O thou the leader of the mental train:
In full perfection all thy works are wrought,   35
And thine the sceptre o'er the realms of thought.
Before thy throne the subject-passions bow,
Of subject-passions sov'reign ruler Thou,
At thy command joy rushes on the heart,
And through the glowing veins the spirits dart.   40

    Fancy might now her silken pinions try
To rise from earth, and sweep th' expanse on high;
From *Tithon's* bed now might *Aurora* rise, }
Her cheeks all glowing with celestial dies,
While a pure stream of light o'erflows the skies.}   45
The monarch of the day I might behold,
And all the mountains tipt with radiant gold,
But I reluctant leave the pleasing views,
Which *Fancy* dresses to delight the *Muse*;
Winter austere forbids me to aspire,   50
And northern tempests damp the rising fire;
They chill the tides of *Fancy's* flowing sea,
Cease then, my song, cease the unequal lay.

[29z]

A Funeral POEM on the Death of C.E.
an Infant of Twelve Months.

    THROUGH airy roads he wings his instant flight
To purer regions of celestial light;
Enlarg'd he sees unnumber'd systems roll,
Beneath him sees the universal whole,
Planets on planets run their destin'd round,   5
And circling wonders fill the vast profound.
Th' ethereal now, and now th' empyreal skies
With growing splendors strike his wond'ring eyes:
The angels view him with delight unknown,
Press his soft hand, and seat him on his throne;   10
Then smiling thus. "To this divine abode,
"The seat of saints, of seraphs, and of God,
"Thrice welcome thou." The raptur'd babe replies,

"Thanks to my God, who snatch'd me to the skies,
"E'er vice triumphant had possess'd my heart,   15
"E'er yet the tempter had beguil'd my heart,
"E'er yet on sin's base actions I was bent,
"E'er yet I knew temptation's dire intent;
"E'er yet the lash for horrid crimes I felt,
"E'er vanity had led my way to guilt,   20
"But, soon arriv'd at my celestial goal,
"Full glories rush on my expanding soul."
Joyful he spoke: exulting cherubs round
Clapt their glad wings, the heav'nly vaults resound.

Say, parents, why this unavailing moan?   25
Why heave your pensive bosoms with the groan?
To *Charles*, the happy subject of my song,
A brighter world, and nobler strains belong.
Say would you tear him from the realms above
By thoughtless wishes, and prepost'rous love?   30
Doth his felicity increase your pain?
Or could you welcome to this world again
The heir of bliss? with a superior air
Methinks he answers with a smile severe,
"Thrones and dominions cannot tempt me there."   35
But still you cry, "Can we the sigh forbear,
"And still and still must we not pour the tear?
"Our only hope, more dear than vital breath,
"Twelve moons revolv'd, becomes the prey of death;
"Delightful infant, nightly visions give   40
"Thee to our arms, and we with joy receive,
"We fain would clasp the *Phantom* to our breast,
"The *Phantom* flies, and leaves the soul unblest."

To yon bright regions let your faith ascend, ⎫
Prepare to join your dearest infant friend   ⎬   45
In pleasures without measure, without end.   ⎭

[29aa]

To Captain H—D, of the 65th Regiment.

SAY, muse divine, can hostile scenes delight
The warrior's bosom in the fields of fight?

Lo! here the christian, and the hero join
With mutual grace to form the man divine.
In H—d see with pleasure and surprize,   5
Where *valour* kindles, and where *virtue* lies:
Go, hero brave, still grace the post of fame,
And add new glories to thine honour'd name,
Still to the field, and still to virtue true:
Britannia glories in no son like you.   10

[29bb]

To the Right Honourable WILLIAM,
Earl of DARTMOUTH, His Majesty's Principal
Secretary of State for North-America, &c.

HAIL, happy day, when, smiling like the morn,
Fair *Freedom* rose *New-England* to adorn:
The northern clime beneath her genial ray,
Dartmouth, congratulates thy blissful sway:
Elate with hope her race no longer mourns,   5
Each soul expands, each grateful bosom burns,
While in thine hand with pleasure we behold
The silken reins, and *Freedom's* charms unfold.
Long lost to realms beneath the northern skies
She shines supreme, while hated *faction* dies: 10
Soon as appear'd the *Goddess* long desir'd,
Sick at the view, she lanquish'd and expir'd;
Thus from the splendors of the morning light
The owl in sadness seeks the caves of night.

No more, *America*, in mournful strain   ⎫   15
Of wrongs, and grievance unredress'd complain, ⎬
No longer shalt thou dread the iron chain,   ⎭
Which wanton *Tyranny* with lawless hand
Had made, and with it meant t'enslave the land.

Should you, my lord, while you peruse my song,   20
Wonder from whence my love of *Freedom* sprung,
Whence flow these wishes for the common good,
By feeling hearts alone best understood,

I, young in life, by seeming cruel fate
Was snatch'd from *Afric's* fancy'd happy seat: 25
What pangs excruciating must molest,
What sorrows labour in my parent's breast?
Steel'd was that soul and by no misery mov'd
That from a father seiz'd his babe belov'd:
Such, such my case. And can I then but pray   30
Others may never feel tyrannic sway?

For favours past, great Sir, our thanks are due,
And thee we ask thy favours to renew,
Since in thy pow'r, as in thy will before,
To sooth the griefs, which thou did'st once deplore.   35
May heav'nly grace the sacred sanction give
To all thy works, and thou for ever live
Not only on the wings of fleeting *Fame*,
Though praise immortal crowns the patriot's name,
But to conduct to heav'ns refulgent fane,   40
May fiery coursers sweep th' ethereal plain,
And bear thee upwards to that blest abode,
Where, like the prophet, thou shalt find thy God.

[29cc]

ODE to NEPTUNE.

On Mrs. W—'s Voyage to England.

I.

WHILE raging tempests shake the shore,
While *AE'lus'* thunders round us roar,
And sweep impetuous o'er the plain
Be still, O tyrant of the main;
Nor let thy brow contracted frowns betray,   5
While my *Susannah* skims the wat'ry way.

II.

The *Pow'r* propitious hears the lay,
The blue-ey'd daughters of the sea
With sweeter cadence glide along,

And *Thames* responsive joins the song.   10
Pleas'd with their notes *Sol* sheds benign his ray,
And double radiance decks the face of day.

III.

To court thee to *Britannia's* arms
    Serene the climes and mild the sky,
Her region boasts unnumber'd charms,   15
    Thy welcome smiles in ev'ry eye.
Thy promise, *Neptune* keep, record my pray'r,
Nor give my wishes to the empty air.

                    Boston, October 10, 1772.

[29dd]

To a LADY on her coming to North-America with her Son, for the Recovery of her Health.

INdulgent muse! my grov'ling mind inspire,
And fill my bosom with celestial fire.

See from *Jamaica's* fervid shore she moves,
Like the fair mother of the blooming loves,
When from above the *Goddess* with her hand   5
Fans the soft breeze, and lights upon the land;
Thus she on *Neptune's* wat'ry realm reclin'd
Appear'd, and thus invites the ling'ring wind.

    "Arise, ye winds, *America* explore,
"Waft me, ye gales, from this malignant shore;   10
"The *Northern* milder climes I long to greet,
"There hope that health will my arrival meet."
Soon as she spoke in my ideal view
The winds assented, and the vessel flew.

    Madam, your spouse bereft of wife and son,   15
In the grove's dark recesses pours his moan;
Each branch, wide-spreading to the ambient sky,
Forgets its verdure, and submits to die.

From thence I turn, and leave the sultry plain,
And swift pursue thy passage o'er the main: 20
The ship arrives before the fav'ring wind,
And makes the *Philadelphian* port assign'd,
Thence I attend you to *Bostonia's* arms,
Where gen'rous friendship ev'ry bosom warms:
Thrice welcome here! may health revive again,   25
Bloom on thy cheek, and bound in ev'ry vein!

Then back return to gladden ev'ry heart,
And give your spouse his soul's far dearer part,
Receiv'd again with what a sweet surprize,
The tear in transport starting from his eyes!   30
While his attendant son with blooming grace
Springs to his father's ever dear embrace.
With shouts of joy *Jamaica's* rocks resound,
With shouts of joy the country rings around.

[29ee]

To a LADY on her remarkable Preservation in an Hurricane in *North-Carolina*.

THOUGH thou did'st hear the tempest from afar,
And felt'st the horrors of the wat'ry war,
To me unknown, yet on this peaceful shore
Methinks I hear the storm tumultuous roar,
And how stern *Boreas* with impetuous hand   5
Compell'd the *Nereids* to usurp the land.
Reluctant rose the daughters of the main,
And slow ascending glided o'er the plain,
Till *AEolus* in his rapid chariot drove
In gloomy grandeur from the vault above: 10
Furious he comes. His winged sons obey
Their frantic sire, and madden all the sea.
The billows rave, the wind's fierce tyrant roars,
And with his thund'ring terrors shakes the shores:
Broken by waves the vessel's frame is rent,   15
And strows with planks the wat'ry element.

But thee, *Maria*, a kind *Nereid's* shield
Preserv'd from sinking, and thy form upheld:
And sure some heav'nly oracle design'd
At that dread crisis to instruct thy mind   20
Things of eternal consequence to weigh,
And to thine heart just feelings to convey
Of things above, and of the future doom,
And what the births of the dread world to come.

From tossing seas I welcome thee to land.   25
"Resign her, *Nereid*," 'twas thy God's command.
Thy spouse late buried, as thy fears conceiv'd,
Again returns, thy fears are all reliev'd:
Thy daughter blooming with superior grace
Again thou see'st, again thine arms embrace;   30
O come, and joyful show thy spouse his heir,
And what the blessings of maternal care!

[29ff]

To a LADY and her Children, on the Death of her Son and their Brother.

O'Erwhelming sorrow now demands my song:
From death the overwhelming sorrow sprung.
What flowing tears? What hearts with grief opprest?
What sighs on sighs heave the fond parent's breast?
The brother weeps, the hapless sisters join   5
Th' increasing woe, and swell the crystal brine;
The poor, who once his gen'rous bounty fed,
Droop, and bewail their benefactor dead.
In death the friend, the kind companion lies,
And in one death what various comfort dies!   10

Th' unhappy mother sees the sanguine rill
Forget to flow, and nature's wheels stand still,
But see from earth his spirit far remov'd,
And know no grief recals your best-belov'd:
He, upon pinions swifter than the wind,   15
Has left mortality's sad scenes behind

For joys to this terrestrial state unknown,
And glories richer than the monarch's crown.
Of virtue's steady course the prize behold!
What blissful wonders to his mind unfold!   20
But of celestial joys I sing in vain:
Attempt not, muse, the too advent'rous strain.

    No more in briny show'rs, ye friends around,
Or bathe his clay, or waste them on the ground:
Still do you weep, still wish for his return?   25
How cruel thus to wish, and thus to mourn?
No more for him the streams of sorrow pour,
But haste to join him on the heav'nly shore,
On harps of gold to tune immortal lays,
And to your God immortal anthems raise.   30

[29gg]
To a GENTLEMAN and LADY on the Death
of the Lady's Brother and Sister, and a Child
of the Name *Avis*, aged one Year.

    ON *Death's* domain intent I fix my eyes,
Where human nature in vast ruin lies:
With pensive mind I search the drear abode,
Where the great conqu'ror has his spoils bestow'd;
[W]here there the offspring of six thousand years   5
In endless numbers to my view appears:
Whole kingdoms in his gloomy den are thrust,
And nations mix with their primeval dust:
Insatiate still he gluts the ample tomb;
His is the present, his the age to come.   10
See here a brother, here a sister spread,
And a sweet daughter mingled with the dead.

    But, *Madam*, let your grief be laid aside,
And let the fountain of your tears be dry'd,
In vain they flow to wet the dusty plain,   15
Your sighs are wafted to the skies in vain,
Your pains they witness, but they can no more,
While *Death* reigns tyrant o'er this mortal shore.

The glowing stars and silver queen of light
At last must perish in the gloom of night: 20
Resign thy friends to that Almighty hand,
Which gave them life, and bow to his command;
Thine *Avis* give without a murm'ring heart,
Though half thy soul be fated to depart.
To shining guards consign thine infant care   25
To waft triumphant through the seas of air:
Her soul enlarg'd to heav'nly pleasure springs,
She feeds on truth and uncreated things.
Methinks I hear her in the realms above,
And leaning forward with a filial love,   30
Invite you there to share immortal bliss
Unknown, untasted in a state like this.
With tow'ring hopes, and growing grace arise,
And seek beatitude beyond the skies.

[29hh]
On the Death of Dr. SAMUEL MARSHALL. 1771.

THROUGH thickest glooms look back, immortal shade,
On that confusion which thy death has made;
Or from *Olympus'* height look down, and see
A *Town* involv'd in grief bereft of thee.
Thy *Lucy* sees thee mingle with the dead,   5
And rends the graceful tresses from her head,
Wild in her woe, with grief unknown opprest
Sigh follows sigh deep heaving from her breast.

Too quickly fled, ah! whither art thou gone?
Ah! lost for ever to thy wife and son!   10
The hapless child, thine only hope and heir,
Clings round his mother's neck, and weeps his sorrows there.
The loss of thee on *Tyler's* soul returns,
And *Boston* for her dear physician mourns.

When sickness call'd for *Marshall's* healing hand,   15
With what compassion did his soul expand?
In him we found the father and the friend:
In life how lov'd! how honour'd in his end!

And must not then our *AEsculapius* stay
To bring his ling'ring infant into day?   20
The babe unborn in the dark womb is tost,
And seems in anguish for its father lost.

Gone is *Apollo* from his house of earth,
But leaves the sweet memorials of his worth:
The common parent, whom we all deplore,   25
From yonder world unseen must come no more,
Yet 'midst our woes immortal hopes attend
The spouse, the sire, the universal friend.

[29ii]
To a GENTLEMAN on his Voyage to
Great-Britain for the Recovery of his Health.

WHILE others chant of gay *Elysian* scenes,
Of balmy zephyrs, and of flow'ry plains,
My song more happy speaks a greater name,
Feels higher motives and a nobler flame.
For thee, O R—, the muse attunes her strings,   5
And mounts sublime above inferior things.

I sing not now of green embow'ring woods,
I sing not now the daughters of the floods,
I sing not of the storms o'er ocean driv'n,
And how they howl'd along the waste of heav'n,   10
But I to R— would paint the *British* shore,
And vast *Atlantic*, not untry'd before:
Thy life impair'd commands thee to arise,
Leave these bleak regions and inclement skies,
Where chilling winds return the winter past,   15
And nature shudders at the furious blast.

O thou stupendous, earth-enclosing main
Exert thy wonders to the world again!
If ere thy pow'r prolong'd the fleeting breath,
Turn'd back the shafts, and mock'd the gates of death,   20
If ere thine air dispens'd an healing pow'r,
Or snatch'd the victim from the fatal hour,

This equal case demands thine equal care,
And equal wonders may this patient share.
But unavailing, frantic is the dream   25
To hope thine aid without the aid of him
Who gave thee birth, and taught thee where to flow,
And in thy waves his various blessings show.

  May R— return to view his native shore
Replete with vigour not his own before,   30
Then shall we see with pleasure and surprize,
And own thy work, great Ruler of the skies!

[29jj]

To the Rev. Dr. THOMAS AMORY on reading his Sermons on DAILY DEVOTION, in which that Duty is recommended and assisted.

  TO cultivate in ev'ry noble mind
Habitual grace, and sentiments refin'd,
Thus while you strive to mend the human heart,
Thus while the heav'nly precepts you impart,
O may each bosom catch the sacred fire,   5
And youthful minds to *Virtue's* throne aspire!

  When God's eternal ways you set in sight,
And *Virtue* shines in all her native light,
In vain would *Vice* her works in night conceal,
For *Wisdom's* eye pervades the sable veil.   10

  Artists may paint the sun's effulgent rays,
But *Amory's* pen the brighter God displays:
While his great works in *Amory's* pages shine,
And while he proves his essence all divine,
The Atheist sure no more can boast aloud   15
Of chance, or nature, and exclude the God;
As if the clay without the potter's aid
Should rise in various forms, and shapes self-made,
Or worlds above with orb o'er orb profound
Self-mov'd could run the everlasting round.   20

It cannot be—unerring *Wisdom* guides
With eye propitious, and o'er all presides.

    Still prosper, *Amory*! still may'st thou receive
The warmest blessings which a muse can give,
And when this transitory state is o'er,   25
When kingdoms fall, and fleeting *Fame's* no more,
May *Amory* triumph in immortal fame,
A noble title, and superior name!

[29kk]
On the Death of J.C. an Infant.

NO more the flow'ry scenes of pleasure rise,
Nor charming prospects greet the mental eyes,
No more with joy we view that lovely face
Smiling, disportive, flush'd with ev'ry grace.

    The tear of sorrow flows from ev'ry eye,   5
Groans answer groans, and sighs to sighs reply;
What sudden pangs shot thro' each aching heart,
When, *Death*, thy messenger dispatch'd his dart?
Thy dread attendants, all-destroying *Pow'r*,
Hurried the infant to his mortal hour.   10
Could'st thou unpitying close those radiant eyes?
Or fail'd his artless beauties to surprize?
Could not his innocence thy stroke controul,
Thy purpose shake, and soften all thy soul?

    The blooming babe, with shades of *Death* o'erspread,   15
No more shall smile, no more shall raise its head,
But, like a branch that from the tree is torn,
Falls prostrate, wither'd, languid, and forlorn.
"Where flies my *James*?" 'tis thus I seem to hear
The parent ask, "Some angel tell me where   20
"He wings his passage thro' the yielding air?"
Methinks a cherub bending from the skies
Observes the question, and serene replies,
"In heav'ns high palaces your babe appears:

"Prepare to meet him, and dismiss your tears." 25
Shall not th'intelligence your grief restrain,
And turn the mournful to the chearful strain?
Cease your complaints, suspend each rising sigh,
Cease to accuse the Ruler of the sky.
Parents, no more indulge the falling tear: 30
Let *Faith* to heav'n's refulgent domes repair,
There see your infant, like a seraph glow:
What charms celestial in his numbers flow
Melodious, while the soul-enchanting strain
Dwells on his tongue, and fills th'ethereal plain? 35
Enough—for ever cease your murm'ring breath;
Not as a foe, but friend converse with *Death*,
Since to the port of happiness unknown
He brought that treasure which you call your own.
The gift of heav'n intrusted to your hand 40
Chearful resign at the divine command:
Not at your bar must sov'reign *Wisdom* stand.

[29ll]

An HYMN to HUMANITY.

To   S.P.G.   Esq;

I.

LO! for this dark terrestrial ball
Forsakes his azure-paved hall
   A prince of heav'nly birth!
Divine *Humanity* behold.
What wonders rise, what charms unfold 5
   At his descent to earth!

II.

The bosoms of the great and good
With wonder and delight he view'd,
   And fix'd his empire there:
Him, close compressing to his breast, 10
The sire of gods and men address'd,
   "My son, my heav'nly fair!

III.

"Descend to earth, there place thy throne;
"To succour man's afflicted son
  "Each human heart inspire: 15
"To act in bounties unconfin'd
"Enlarge the close contracted mind,
  "And fill it with thy fire."

IV.

Quick as the word, with swift career
He wings his course from star to star,   20
  And leaves the bright abode.
The *Virtue* did his charms impart;
Their G——! then thy raptur'd heart
  Perceiv'd the rushing God:

V.

For when thy pitying eye did see   25
The languid muse in low degree,
  Then, then at thy desire
Descended the celestial nine;
O'er me methought they deign'd to shine,
  And deign'd to string my lyre.   30

VI.

Can *Afric's* muse forgetful prove?
Or can such friendship fail to move
  A tender human heart?
Immortal *Friendship* laurel-crown'd
The smiling *Graces* all surround   35
  With ev'ry heav'nly *Art*.

[29mm]

To the Honourable T.H. Esq;
on the Death of his Daughter.

WHILE deep you mourn beneath the cypress-shade
The hand of Death, and your dear daughter laid
In dust, whose absence gives your tears to flow,

And racks your bosom with incessant woe,
Let *Recollection* take a tender part,   5
Assuage the raging tortures of your heart,
Still the wild tempest of tumultuous grief,
And pour the heav'nly nectar of relief:
Suspend the sigh, dear Sir, and check the groan,
Divinely bright your daughter's *Virtues* shone: 10
How free from scornful pride her gentle mind,
Which ne'er its aid to indigence declin'd!
Expanding free, it sought the means to prove
Unfailing charity, unbounded love!

  She unreluctant flies to see no more   15
Her dear-lov'd parents on earth's dusky shore:
Impatient heav'n's resplendent goal to gain,
She with swift progress cuts the azure plain,
Where grief subsides, where changes are no more,
And life's tumultuous billows cease to roar;   20
She leaves her earthly mansion for the skies,
Where new creations feast her wond'ring eyes.

  To heav'n's high mandate chearfully resign'd
She mounts, and leaves the rolling globe behind;
She, who late wish'd that *Leonard* might return,   25
Has ceas'd to languish, and forgot to mourn;
To the same high empyreal mansions come,
She joins her spouse, and smiles upon the tomb:
And thus I hear her from the realms above:
"Lo! this the kingdom of celestial love!   30
"Could ye, fond parents, see our present bliss,
"How soon would you each sigh, each fear dismiss?
"Amidst unutter'd pleasures whilst I play
"In the fair sunshine of celestial day,
"As far as grief affects an happy soul   35
"So far doth grief my better mind controul,
"To see on earth my aged parents mourn,
"And secret wish for T—l to return:
"Let brighter scenes your ev'ning-hours employ:
"Converse with heav'n, and taste the promis'd joy."   40

[29nn]

NIOBE in Distress for her Children slain by APOLLO, from *Ovid's* Metamorphoses, Book VI. and from a view of the Painting of Mr. *Richard Wilson.*

APOLLO'S wrath to man the dreadful spring
Of ills innum'rous, tuneful goddess, sing!
Thou who did'st first th' ideal pencil give,
And taught'st the painter in his works to live,
Inspire with glowing energy of thought,   5
What *Wilson* painted, and what *Ovid* wrote.
Muse! lend thy aid, nor let me sue in vain,
Tho' last and meanest of the rhyming train!
O guide my pen in lofty strains to show
The *Phrygian* queen, all beautiful in woe.   10

'Twas where *Maeonia* spreads her wide domain
Niobe dwelt, and held her potent reign:
See in her hand the regal sceptre shine,
The wealthy heir of *Tantalus* divine,
He most distinguish'd by *Dodonean Jove*,   15
To approach the tables of the gods above:
Her grandsire *Atlas*, who with mighty pains
Th' ethereal axis on his neck sustains:
Her other gran sire on the throne on high
Rolls the loud-pealing thunder thro' the sky.   20

Her spouse, *Amphion*, who from *Jove* too springs,
Divinely taught to sweep the sounding strings.

Seven sprightly sons the royal bed adorn,
Seven daughters beauteous as the op'ning morn,
As when *Aurora* fills the ravish'd sight,   25
And decks the orient realms with rosy light
From their bright eyes the living splendors play,
Nor can beholders bear the flashing ray.

Wherever, *Niobe*, thou turn'st thine eyes,
New beauties kindle, and new joys arise!   30

But thou had'st far the happier mother prov'd,
If this fair offspring had been less belov'd:
What if their charms exceed *Aurora's* teint,
No words could tell them, and no pencil paint,
Thy love too vehement hastens to destroy   35
Each blooming maid, and each celestial boy.

Now *Manto* comes, endu'd with mighty skill,
The past to explore, the future to reveal.
Thro' *Thebes'* wide streets *Tiresia's* daughter came,
Divine *Latona's* mandate to proclaim: 40
The *Theban* maids to hear the orders ran,
When thus *Maeonia's* prophetess began:

"Go *Thebans*! great *Latona's* will obey,
"And pious tribute at her altars pay:
"With rights divine, the goddess be implor'd,   45
"Nor be her sacred offspring unador'd."
Thus *Manto* spoke. The *Theban* maids obey,
And pious tribute to the goddess pay.
The rich perfumes ascend in waving spires,
And altars blaze with consecrated fires;   50
The fair assembly moves with graceful air,
And leaves of laurel bind the flowing hair.

Niobe comes with all her royal race,
With charms unnumber'd, and superior grace:
Her *Phrygian* garments of delightful hue,   55
Inwove with gold, refulgent to the view,
Beyond description beautiful she moves
Like heav'nly *Venus*, 'midst her smiles and loves:
She views around the supplicating train,
And shakes her graceful head with stern disdain,   60
Proudly she turns around her lofty eyes,
And thus reviles celestial deities:
"What madness drives the *Theban* ladies fair
"To give their incense to surrounding air?
"Say why this new sprung deity preferr'd?   65
"Why vainly fancy your petitions heard?
"Or say why *Coeus'* offspring is obey'd,
"While to my goddesship no tribute's paid?
"For me no altars blaze with living fires,

"No bullock bleeds, no frankincense transpires,   70
"Tho' *Cadmus*' palace, not unknown to fame,
"And *Phrygian* nations all revere my name.
"Where'er I turn my eyes vast wealth I find.
"Lo! here an empress with a goddess join'd.
"What, shall a *Titaness* be deify'd,   75
"To whom the spacious earth a couch deny'd?
"Nor heav'n, nor earth, nor sea receiv'd your queen,
"'Till pitying *Delos* took the wand'rer in.
"Round me what a large progeny is spread!
"No frowns of fortune has my soul to dread.   80
"What if indignant she decrease my train
"More than *Latona's* number will remain?
"Then hence, ye *Theban* dames, hence haste away,
"Nor longer off'rings to *Latona* pay;
"Regard the orders of *Amphion's* spouse,   85
"And take the leaves of laurel from your brows."
Niobe spoke. The *Theban* maids obey'd,
Their brows unbound, and left the rights unpaid.

    The angry goddess heard, then silence broke
On *Cynthus*' summit, and indignant spoke;   90
"*Phoebus*! behold, thy mother in disgrace,
"Who to no goddess yields the prior place
"Except to Juno's self, who reigns above,
"The spouse and sister of the thund'ring *Jove*.
"*Niobe* sprung from *Tantalus* inspires   95
"Each *Theban* bosom with rebellious fires;
"No reason her imperious temper quells,
"But all her father in her tongue rebels;
"Wrap her own sons for her blaspheming breath,
"Apollo! wrap them in the shades of death."   100
Latona ceas'd and ardent thus replies,
The God, whose glory decks th' expanded skies.

    "Cease thy complaints, mine be the task assign'd
"To punish pride, and scourge the rebel mind."
This *Phoebe* join'd.—They wing their instant flight;   105
Thebes trembled as th' immortal pow'rs alight.

    With clouds incompass'd glorious *Phoebus* stands;
The feather'd vengeance quiv'ring in his hands.

Near *Cadmus'* walls a plain extended lay,
Where *Thebes'* young princes pass'd in sport the day: 110
There the bold coursers bounded o'er the plains,
While their great masters held the golden reins.
Ismenus first the racing pastime led,
And rul'd the fury of his flying steed.
"Ah me," he sudden cries, with shrieking breath,   115
While in his breast he feels the shaft of death;
He drops the bridle on his courser's mane,
Before his eyes in shadows swims the plain,
He, the first-born of great *Amphion's* bed,
Was struck the first, first mingled with the dead.   120

Then didst thou, *Sipylus*, the language hear
Of fate portentous whistling in the air:
As when th' impending storm the sailor sees
He spreads his canvas to the fav'ring breeze,
So to thine horse thou gav'st the golden reins,   125
Gav'st him to rush impetuous o'er the plains:
But ah! a fatal shaft from *Phoebus'* hand
Smites through thy neck, and sinks thee on the sand.

Two other brothers were at *wrestling* found,
And in their pastime claspt each other round: 130
A shaft that instant from *Apollo's* hand
Transfixt them both, and stretcht them on the sand:
Together they their cruel fate bemoan'd,
Together languish'd, and together groan'd:
Together too th'unbodied spirits fled,   135
And sought the gloomy mansions of the dead.

Alphenor saw, and trembling at the view,
Beat his torn breast, that chang'd its snowy hue.
He flies to raise them in a kind embrace;
A brother's fondness triumphs in his face: 140
Alphenor fails in this fraternal deed,
A dart dispatch'd him (so the fates decreed:)
Soon as the arrow left the deadly wound,
His issuing entrails smoak'd upon the ground.

What woes on blooming *Damasichon* wait!   145
His sighs portend his near impending fate.

Just where the well-made leg begins to be,
And the soft sinews form the supple knee,
The youth sore wounded by the *Delian* god
Attempts t'extract the crime-avenging rod,   150
But, whilst he strives the will of fate t'avert,
Divine *Apollo* sends a second dart;
Swift thro' his throat the feather'd mischief flies,
Bereft of sense, he drops his head, and dies.

    Young *Ilioneus*, the last, directs his pray'r,   155
And cries, "My life, ye gods celestial! spare."
Apollo heard, and pity touch'd his heart,
But ah! too late, for he had sent the dart:
Thou too, O *Ilioneus*, art doom'd to fall,
The fates refuse that arrow to recal.   160

    On the swift wings of ever-flying *Fame*
To *Cadmus*' palace soon the tidings came:
Niobe heard, and with indignant eyes
She thus express'd her anger and surprize:
"Why is such privilege to them allow'd?   165
"Why thus insulted by the *Delian* god?
"Dwells there such mischief in the pow'rs above?
"Why sleeps the vengeance of immortal *Jove*"
For now *Amphion* too, with grief oppress'd,
Had plung'd the deadly dagger in his breast.   170
Niobe now, less haughty than before,
With lofty head directs her steps no more.
She, who late told her pedigree divine,
And drove the *Thebans* from *Latona's* shrine,
How strangely chang'd!—yet beautiful in woe,   175
She weeps, nor weeps unpity'd by the foe.
On each pale corse the wretched mother spread
Lay overwhelm'd with grief, and kiss'd her dead,
Then rais'd her arms, and thus, in accents slow,
"Be sated cruel *Goddess*! with my woe;   180
"If I've offended, let these streaming eyes,
"And let this sev'nfold funeral suffice:
"Ah! take this wretched life you deign'd to save,
"With them I too am carried to the grave.
"Rejoice triumphant, my victorious foe,   185

"But show the cause from whence your triumphs flow?
"Tho' I unhappy mourn these children slain,
"Yet greater numbers to my lot remain."
She ceas'd, the bow string twang'd with awful sound,
Which struck with terror all th'assembly round,   190
Except the queen, who stood unmov'd alone,
By her distresses more presumptuous grown.
Near the pale corses stood their sisters fair
In sable vestures and dishevell'd hair;
One, while she draws the fatal shaft away,   195
Faints, falls, and sickens at the light of day.
To sooth her mother, lo! another flies,
And blames the fury of inclement skies,
And, while her words a filial pity show,
Struck dumb—indignant seeks the shades below.   200
Now from the fatal place another flies,
Falls in her flight, and languishes, and dies.
Another on her sister drops in death;
A fifth in trembling terrors yields her breath;
While the sixth seeks some gloomy cave in vain,   205
Struck with the rest, and mingled with the slain.

    One only daughter lives, and she the least;
The queen close clasp'd the daughter to her breast:
"Ye heav'nly pow'rs, ah spare me one," she cry'd,
"Ah! spare me one," the vocal hills reply'd: 210
In vain she begs, the Fates her suit deny,
In her embrace she sees her daughter die.

    *"The queen of all her family bereft,
"Without or husband, son, or daughter left,
"Grew stupid at the shock. The passing air   215
"Made no impression on her stiff'ning hair.
"The blood forsook her face: amidst the flood
"Pour'd from her cheeks, quite fix'd her eye-balls stood.
"Her tongue, her palate both obdurate grew,
"Her curdled veins no longer motion knew;   220
"The use of neck, and arms, and feet was gone,
"And ev'n her bowels hard'ned into stone:
"A marble statue now the queen appears,
"But from the marble steal the silent tears."

*This Verse to the End is the Work of another Hand.

[2900]

To S.M. a young *African* Painter, on seeing his Works.

TO show the lab'ring bosom's deep intent,
And thought in living characters to paint,
When first thy pencil did those beauties give,
And breathing figures learnt from thee to live,
How did those prospects give my soul delight,   5
A new creation rushing on my sight?
Still, wond'rous youth! each noble path pursue,
On deathless glories fix thine ardent view:
Still may the painter's and the poet's fire
To aid thy pencil, and thy verse conspire!   10
And may the charms of each seraphic theme
Conduct thy footsteps to immortal fame!
High to the blissful wonders of the skies
Elate thy soul, and raise thy wishful eyes.
Thrice happy, when exalted to survey   15
That splendid city, crown'd with endless day,
Whose twice six gates on radiant hinges ring:
Celestial *Salem* blooms in endless spring.

Calm and serene thy moments glide along,
And may the muse inspire each future song!   20
Still, with the sweets of contemplation bless'd,
May peace with balmy wings your soul invest!
But when these shades of time are chas'd away,
And darkness ends in everlasting day,
On what seraphic pinions shall we move,   25
And view the landscapes in the realms above?
There shall thy tongue in heav'nly murmurs flow,
And there my muse with heav'nly transport glow:
No more to tell of *Damon's* tender sighs,
Or rising radiance of *Aurora's* eyes,   30
For nobler themes demand a nobler strain,
And purer language on th' ethereal plain.
Cease, gentle muse! the solemn gloom of night
Now seals the fair creation from my sight.

[29pp]

To His Honour the Lieutenant-Governor, on the Death of his Lady. *March* 24, 1773.

ALL-conquering Death! by thy resistless pow'r,
Hope's tow'ring plumage falls to rise no more!
Of scenes terrestrial how the glories fly,
Forget their splendors, and submit to die!
Who ere escap'd thee, but the saint* of old   5
Beyond the flood in sacred annals told,
And the great sage,* whom fiery courses drew
To heav'n's bright portals from *Elisha's* view;
Wond'ring he gaz'd at the refulgent car,
Then snatch'd the mantle floating on the air.   10
From *Death* these only could exemption boast,
And without dying gain'd th' immortal coast.
Not falling millions sate the tyrant's mind,
Nor can the victor's progress be confin'd.
But cease thy strife with *Death*, fond *Nature*, cease: 15
He leads the *virtuous* to the realms of peace;
His to conduct to the immortal plains,
Where heav'n's Supreme in bliss and glory reigns.

There sits, illustrious Sir, thy beauteous spouse;
A gem-blaz'd circle beaming on her brows.   20
Hail'd with acclaim among the heav'nly choirs,
Her soul new-kindling with seraphic fires,
To notes divine she tunes the vocal strings,
While heav'n's high concave with the music rings.
Virtue's rewards can mortal pencil paint?   25
No—all descriptive arts, and eloquence are faint;
Nor canst thou, *Oliver*, assent refuse
To heav'nly tidings from the *Afric* muse.

As soon may change thy laws, eternal *fate*,
As the saint miss the glories I relate;   30
Or her *Benevolence* forgotten lie,
Which wip'd the trick'ling tear from *Mis'ry's* eye.
Whene'er the adverse winds were known to blow,
When loss to loss* ensu'd, and woe to woe,

Calm and serene beneath her father's hand   35
She sat resign'd to the divine command.

No longer then, great Sir, her death deplore,
And let us hear the mournful sigh no more,
Restrain the sorrow streaming from thine eye,
Be all thy future moments crown'd with joy!   40
Nor let thy wishes be to earth confin'd,
But soaring high pursue th'unbodied mind.
Forgive the muse, forgive th'advent'rous lays,
That fain thy soul to heav'nly scenes would raise.

*Enoch
*Elijah
*Three amiable Daughters who died when just arrived to Womens Estate.

[29qq]
A Farewel to AMERICA. To Mrs. S.W.

I.
ADIEU, *New-England's* smiling meads,
   Adieu, the flow'ry plain:
I leave thine op'ning charms, O spring,
   And tempt the roaring main.

II.
In vain for me the flow'rets rise,   5
   And boast their gaudy pride,
While here beneath the northern skies
   I mourn for *health* deny'd.

III.
Celestial maid of rosy hue,
   O let me feel thy reign!   10
I languish till thy face I view,
   Thy vanish'd joys regain.

IV.
Susannah mourns, nor can I bear
   To see the crystal show'r,
Or mark the tender falling tear   15
   At sad departure's hour;

V.

Nor unregarding can I see
   Her soul with grief opprest:
But let no sighs, no groans for me,
   Steal from her pensive breast.   20

VI.

In vain the feather'd warblers sing,
   In vain the garden blooms,
And on the bosom of the spring
   Breathes out her sweet perfumes,

VII.

While for *Britannia's* distant shore   25
   We sweep the liquid plain,
And with astonish'd eyes explore
   The wide-extended main.

VIII.

Lo! *Health* appears! celestial dame!
   Complacent and serene,   30
With *Hebe's* mantle o'er her Frame,
   With soul-delighting mein.

IX.

To mark the vale where *London* lies
   With misty vapours crown'd,
Which cloud *Aurora's* thousand dyes,   35
   And veil her charms around.

X.

Why, *Phoebus*, moves thy car so slow?
   So slow thy rising ray?
Give us the famous town to view
   Thou glorious king of day!   40

XI.

For thee, *Britannia*, I resign
   New-England's smiling fields;
To view again her charms divine,
   What joy the prospect yields!

XII.

But thou! Temptation hence away, 45
    With all thy fatal train
Nor once seduce my soul away,
    By thine enchanting strain.

XIII.

Thrice happy they, whose heav'nly shield
    Secures their souls from harms, 50
And fell *Temptation* on the field
    Of all its pow'r disarms!

Boston, May 7, 1773.

[29rr]
A REBUS, by *I.B.*

I.

A BIRD delicious to the taste,
On which an army once did feast,
    Sent by an hand unseen;
A creature of the horned race,
Which *Britain's* royal standards grace; 5
    A gem of vivid green;

II.

A town of gaiety and sport,
Where beaux and beauteous nymphs resort,
    And gallantry doth reign;
A *Dardan* hero fam'd of old 10
For youth and beauty, as we're told,
    And by a monarch slain;

III.

A peer of popular applause,
Who doth our violated laws,
    And grievances proclaim. 15
Th'initials show a vanquish'd town,
That adds fresh glory and renown
    To old *Britannia's* fame.

[29ss]

An ANSWER to the *Rebus*, by the Author of these POEMS.

THE poet asks, and *Phillis* can't refuse
To shew th'obedience of the Infant muse.
She knows the *Quail* of most inviting taste
Fed *Israel's* army in the dreary waste;
And what's on *Britain's* royal standard borne,   5
But the tall, graceful, rampant *Unicorn?*
The *Emerald* with a vivid verdure glows
Among the gems which regal crowns compose;
Boston's a town, polite and debonair,
To which the beaux and beauteous nymphs repair,   10
Each *Helen* strikes the mind with sweet surprise,
While living lightning flashes from her eyes.
See young *Euphorbus* of the *Dardan* line
By *Menelaus*' hand to death resign:
The well known peer of popular applause   15
Is *C—m* zealous to support our laws.
   Quebec now vanquish'd must obey,
   She too must annual tribute pay
   To *Britain* of immortal fame,
   And add new glory to her name.   20

FINIS.

[30]

The Right Honourable The Countess of Huntington [*sic*], At Talgarth South Wales.—

Madam   London June 27th.. 1773

It is with pleasure I acquaint your Ladyship of my safe arrival in London after a fine passage of 5 weeks, in the Ship London, with my young Master; (advis'd by my Physicians for my Health.) have Brought a letter from Rich[d]. Carey Esq[r]. but was disappointed by your absence of the honour of waiting upon your Ladyship with it. I would have inclos'd it, but was doubtful of the safety of the conveyance.

I should think my self very happy in seeing your Ladyship, and if you was so desirous of the Image of the Author as to propose it for a Frontispiece I flatter myself that you would accept the Reality.

I conclude with thanking your Ladyship for permitting the Dedication of my Poems to you; and am not insensible, that, under the patronage of your Ladyship, not more eminent in the Station of Life than in your exemplary Piety and Virtue, my feeble efforts will be Shielded from the Severe trials of unpitying Criticism and, being encourage'd by your Ladyship's Indulgence, I the more freely resign to the world these Juvenile productions, And Am, Madam, with greatest humility, your Dutiful Hum[l] Ser.[t] Phillis Wheatley

[31]

The Right Hon'ble The Countess of Huntingdon

Madam,

I rec'd with mixed sensations of pleasure & disappointment your Ladiship's message favored by M[r]. Rien Acquainting us with your pleasure that my Master & I Should wait upon you in S[o][uth]. Wales, delighted with your Ladiship['s] Condescention to me so unworthy of it. Am sorry [to a]cquaint your Ladiship that the Ship is certainly to Sail next Thurs[day on] which I must return to America. I long to see my Friends there. [I am ex]tremely reluctant to go without having first Seen your Ladiship.

It gives me very great satisfaction to hear of an African soworthy to be honour'd with your Ladiship's approbation & Friendship as him ^whom^ you call your Brother. I rejoice with your Ladiship in that Fund of mental

Felicity which you cannot but be possessed of, in the consideration of your exceeding great reward. My great opinion of your Ladiship's goodness, leads to believe, I have an interest in your most happy hours of communion, with your most indulgent Father and our great and common Benefactor. With greatest humility I am,

> most dutifully
> your Ladiship's Obed^t. Sert
> Phillis Wheatley.

London July 17 ⎱
1773   ⎰

My master is yet undetermined about going home, and sends his dutiful respects to your Ladiship.

[32]
"Ocean"

Now muse divine, thy heav'nly aid impart,
The feast of Genius, and the play of Art.
From high Parnassus' radiant top repair,
Celestial Nine! propitious to my pray'r.
In vain my Eyes explore the wat'ry reign,   5
By you unaided with the flowing strain.
    When first old Chaos of tyrannic soul
Wav'd his dread Sceptre o'er the boundless whole,
Confusion reign'd till the divine Command
On floating azure fix'd the Solid Land,   10
Till first he call'd the latent seeds of light,
And gave dominion o'er eternal Night.
From deepest glooms he rais'd this ample Ball,
And round its walls he bade its surges roll;
With instant haste the new made seas complyd,   15
And the globe rolls impervious to the Tide;
Yet when the mighty Sire of Ocean frownd
"His awful trident shook the solid Ground."
The King of Tempests thunders o'er the plain,
And scorns the azure monarch of the main,   20
He sweeps the surface, makes the billows rore,
And furious, lash the loud resounding shore.

His pinion'd race his dread commands obey,
Syb's, Eurus, Boreas, drive the foaming sea!
See the whole stormy progeny descend!   25
And waves on waves devolving without End,
But cease Eolus, all thy winds restrain,
And let us view the wonders of the main
Where the proud Courser paws the blue abode,
Impetuous bounds, and mocks the driver's rod.   30
There, too, the Heifer fair as that which bore
Divine Europa to the Cretan shore.
With guileless mein the gentle Creature strays[,]
Quaffs the pure stream, and crops ambrosial Grass[.]
     Again with recent wonder I survey   35
The finny sov'reign bask in hideous play[.]
(So fancy sees) he makes a tempest rise
And intercept the azure vaulted skies[.]
Such is his sport:—but if his anger glow
What kindling vengeance boils the deep below!   40
     Twas but e'er now an Eagle young and gay
Pursu'd his passage thro' the aierial way[.]
He aim'd his piece, would C[ale]f's hand do more[?]
Yes, him he brought to pluto's dreary shore[.]
Slow breathed his last, the painful minutes move   45
With lingring pace his rashness to reprove;
Perhaps his father's Just commands he bore
To fix dominion on some distant shore[.]
["]Ah! me unblest," he cries[.] ["] Oh! had I staid
Or swift my Father's mandate had obey['d.]   50
But ah! too late. ["]—Old Ocean heard his cries[.]
He stroakes his hoary tresses and replies[:]
["]What mean these plaints so near our wat'ry throne,
And what the Cause of this distressful moan?
Confess[,] Iscarius, let thy words be true   55
Nor let me find a faithless Bird in you[."]
His voice struck terror thro' the whole domain[.]
Aw'd by his frowns the royal youth began,
["]Saw you not[,] Sire, a tall and Gallant ship
Which proudly skims the surface of the deep[?]   60
With pompous form from Boston's port she came[,]
She flies, and London her resounding name[.]
O'er the rough surge the dauntless Chief prevails

For partial Aura fills his swelling sails[.]
His fatal musket shortens thus my day   65
And thus the victor takes my life away[."]
    Faint with his wound Iscarius said no more[,]
His Spirit sought Oblivion's sable shore.
This Neptune saw, and with a hollow groan
Resum'd the azure honours of his Throne.   70

[Written in another hand on page four of the manuscript:]

  OCEAN
A poem by Phillis
in her handwriting
made on her return from
England in Capt Calef
Sept. 1773—

[33]

To Col. David Worcester in New Haven, Connecticut. favour'd by
Mr. Badcock's Servant.

Sir,

    Having an opportunity by a Servant of M^r. Badcock's who lives near
you, I am glad to hear you and your Family are well, I take the Freedom to
transmit to you, a short Sketch of my voyage and return from London
where I went for the recovery of my health as advisd by my Physician.
I was receiv'd in England with such kindness[,] Complaisance, and so
many marks of esteem and real Friendship as astonishes me on the reflec-
tion, for I was no more than 6 weeks there.—Was introduced to Lord
Dartmouth and had near half an hour's conversation with his Lordship,
with whom was Alderman Kirkman,—Then to Lord Lincoln, who visited
me at my own Lodgings with the Famous D^r. Solander, who accompany'd
M^r. Banks in his late expedition round the World.
    Then to Lady Cavendish, and Lady Carteret Webb,—Mrs. Palmer
a Poetess, an accomplished Lady.—[To] D^r. Thos. Gibbons, Rhetoric
Proffesor, To Israel Mauduit Esqr[,] Benjamin Franklin Esqr F[ellow].
R[oyal]. S[ociety]., Grenville [*sic*] Sharp Esqr who attended me to the
Tower & show'd the Lions, Panthers, Tigers, &^{c}. The Horse Armoury,
Sma[ll] Armoury, the Crowns, Sceptres, Diadems, the Font for christineng

the Royal Family. Saw Westminster Abbey, British Museum[,] Coxe's Museum, Saddler's wells, Greenwich Hospital, Park and Chapel, the royal Observatory at Greenwich, &c. &c. too many things and Places to trouble you with in a Letter.—The Earl of Dartmouth made me a Compliment of 5 guineas, and desir'd me to get the whole of Mr. Pope's Works, as the best he could recommend to my perusal, this I did, also got Hudibrass, Don Quixot, & Gay's Fables—was presented with a Folio Edition of Milton's Paradise Lost, printed on a Silver Type, so call'd from its elegance, (I suppose) By Mr. Brook Watson Merch.t[,] whose Coat of Arms is prefix'd.— Since my return to America my Master, has at the desire of my friends in England given me my freedom. The Instrument is drawn, so as to secure me and my property from the hands of Exectut.rs[,] administrators, &c. of my master, and secure whatsoever Should be given me as my Own. A Copy is Sent to Isra. Mauduit Esq.r F[ellow]. [of the] R[oyal]. S[ociety].

I expect my Books which are publishd in London in [the vessel commanded by] Capt. Hall, who will be here I believe in 8 or 10 days. I beg the favour that you would honour the enclos'd Proposals, & use your interest with Gentlemen & Ladies of your acquaintance to subscribe also, for the more subscribers there are, the more it will be for my advantage as I am to have half the Sale of the Books. This I am the more Solicitous for, as I am now upon my own footing and whatever I get by this is entirely mine, & it is the Chief I have to depend upon. I must also request you would desire the Printers in New Haven, not to reprint that Book, as it will be a great hurt to me, preventing any further Benefit that I might receive from the Sale of my Copies from England. The price is 2/6d [two shillings, six pence] Bound or 2 [shillings]/Sterling Sewed.—If any should be so ungenerous as to reprint them the Genuine Copy may be known, for it is sign'd in my own handwriting. My dutiful respects attend your Lady and Children and I am

ever respectfully your oblig'd Huml Ser.t
Phillis Wheatley

Boston October
18th 1773

I found my mistress very sick on my return
But she is somewhat better. We wish we could depend on it. She gives her Compliments to you & your Lady.

[34]

To Obour Tanner in New Port

Boston Oct. 30, 1773

Dear Obour,

I rec'd your most kind Epistles of Augt. 27, & Oct. 13th by a young man of your Acquaintance, for which I am obligd to you. I hear of your welfare with pleasure; but this acquaints you that I am at present indisposd by a cold, & Since my arrival have been visited by the asthma.—

Your observations on our dependence on the Deity, & your hopes that my wants will be supply'd from his fulness which is in Christ Jesus, is truely worthy of your self—I can't say but my voyage to England has conduced to the recovery (in a great measure) of my Health. The Friends I found there among the Nobility and Gentry, Their Benevolent conduct towards me, the unexpected, and unmerited civility and Complaisance with which I was treated by all, fills me with astonishment, I can scarcely Realize it,—This I humbly hope has the happy Effect of lessning me in my own Esteem. Your Reflections on the Sufferings of the Son of God, & the inestimable price of our immortal Souls, Plainly dem[on]strate the sensations of a Soul united to Jesus. What you observe of Esau is true of all mankind, who, (left to themselves) would sell their heavenly Birth Rights for a few moments of sensual pleasure whose wages at last (dreadful wages!) is eternal condemnation. Dear Obour let us not sell our Birth right for a thousand worlds, which indeed would be as dust upon the Balance.—The God of the Seas and dry Land, has graciously Brought me home in safety. Join with me in thanks to him for so great a mercy, & that it may excite me to praise him with cheerfulness, to Persevere in Grace & Faith, & in the Knowledge of our Creator and Redeemer,—that my heart may be filld with gratitude. I should have been pleasd greatly to see Miss West, as I imagine she knew you. I have been very Busy ever since my arrival or should have, now wrote a more particular account of my voyage, But must submit that satisfaction to some other Opportunity. I am Dear friend,

most affectionately ever yours,
Phillis Wheatley

my mistress has been very sick above 14 weeks & confined to her Bed the whole time, but is I hope s[om]e what Better, now.

The young man by whom this is handed you seems to me to be a very clever man, knows you very well, & is very Complaisant: accommodating and agreable.—

P.W

I enclose Proposals for my Book, and beg you[d] use your interest to get Subscriptions as it is for my Benefit.

[35]

To John Thornton Esqre. Merchant London

Hon'd Sir

It is with great satisfaction, I acquaint you with my experience of the goodness of God in safely conducting my passage over the mighty waters, and returning me in safety to my American Friends. I presume you will join with them and me in praise to God for so distinguishing a favour, it was amazing Mercy, altogether unmerited by me: and if possible it is augmented by the consideration of the bitter reverse, which is the deserved wages of my evil doings. The Apostle Paul, tells us that the wages of Sin is death. I don't imagine he excepted any sin whatsoever, being equally hateful in its nature in the sight of God, who is essential Purity.

Should we not sink hon'd Sir, under this Sentence of Death, pronounced on every Sin, from the comparatively least to the greatest, were not this blessed Contrast annexed to it, "But the Gift of God is eternal Life, through Jesus Christ our Lord?" It is his Gift. O let us be thankful for it! What a load is taken from the Sinner's Shoulder when he thinks that Jesus has done that work for him which he could never have done, and Suffer'd, that punishment of his imputed Rebellions, for which a long Eternity of Torments could not have made sufficient expiation. O that I could meditate continually on this work of wonder in Deity itself. This, which Kings & Prophets have desir'd to see, & have not See[n.] This, which Angels are continually exploring, yet are not equal to the search,—Millions of Ages shall roll away, and they may try in vain to find out to perfection, the sublime mysteries of Christ's Incarnation. Nor will this desir[e] to look into the deep things of God, cease, in the Breasts of glorified Saints & Angels. It's duration will be coeval with Eternity. This Eternity how dreadfu[l,] how delightful! Delightful to those who have an interest in the Crucified Saviour, who has dignified our Nature, by seating it at the Right Hand of the divine Majesty.—They alone who are thus interested have Cause to rejoice even on the brink of that Bottomless Profound: and I doubt not (without the least Adulation) that you are one of that happy number. O pray that I may be one also, who Shall Join with you in Songs of praise at the Throne of him, who is no respecter of Persons: being equally the great Maker of all:—Therefor disdain not to be called the Father of Humble Africans and Indians; though despisd on earth on account of our colour, we have this Consolation, if he enables us to deserve it. "That God dwells in the humble & contrite heart." O that I were more & more possess'd of this inestimable blessing; to be directed by the immediate influence of the divine Spirit in my daily walk & Conversation.

Do you, my hon'd Sir, who have abundant Reason to be thankful for the great Share you possess of it, be always mindful in your Closet, of those who want it—of me in particular.—

When I first arrived at home my mistress was so bad as not to be expected to live above two or three days, but through the goodness of God She is still alive but remains in a very weak & languishing Condition. She begs a continued interest in your most earnest prayers, that she may be duely prepar'd for that great Change which [she] is likely Soon to undergo; She intreats you, as her Son is Still in England, that you would take all opportunities to advise & counsel him; ^She says she is going to leave him & desires you'd be a Spiritual Father to h[im].^ She will take it very kind. She thanks you heartily for the kind notice you took of me while in England. Please to give my best Respects to M^{rs}. & miss Thorton, and masters Henry and Robert who held with me a long conversation on many subjects which M^{rs}. Drinkwater knows very well. I hope she is in better Health than when I left her. Please to remember me to your whole family & I thank them for their kindness to me. begging still an interest in your best hours

I am Hon'd Sir

most respectfully your Humble Servt.

Boston Dec: 1. 1773}   Phillis Wheatley

I have written to Mrs. Wilberforce, sometime since please to give my duty to her; Since writing the above the Rev'd M^{r}. Moorhead has made his Exit from this world, in whom we lament the loss of the Zealous Pious & true christian.

[36]

An ELEGY To Miss. Mary Moorhead, on the DEATH of her Father, The Rev. Mr. JOHN MOORHEAD.

INVOLV'D in Clouds of Wo, *Maria* mourns,
And various Anguish wracks her Soul by turns;
See thy lov'd Parent languishing in Death,
His Exit watch, and catch his flying Breath;
"Stay happy Shade," distress'd *Maria* cries;   5
"Stay happy Shade," the hapless Church replies;
"Suspend a while, suspend thy rapid flight,
"Still with thy Friendship, chear our sullen Night;
"The sullen Night of Error, Sin, and Pain;
"See Earth astonish'd at the Loss, complain;"   10
Thine, and the Church's Sorrows I deplore;
Moorhead is dead, and Friendship is no more;
From Earth she flies, nor mingles with our Wo,
Since cold the Breast, where once she deign'd to glow;
Here shone the heavenly Virtue, there confess'd,   15
Celestial Love, reign'd joyous in his Breast;
Till Death grown jealous for his drear Domain,
Sent his dread Offspring, unrelenting Pain.
With hasty Wing, the Son of Terror flies,
Lest *Moorhead* find the Portal of the Skies;   20
Without a Passage through the Shades below,
Like great *Elijah*, Death's triumphant Foe;
Death follows soon, nor leaves the Prophet long,
His Eyes are seal'd, and every Nerve unstrung;
Forever silent is the stiff'ning Clay,   25
While the rapt Soul, explores the Realms of Day.
Oft has he strove to raise the Soul from Earth,
Oft has he travail'd in the heavenly Birth;
Till JESUS took possession of the Soul,
Till the new Creature liv'd throughout the whole.   30

When the fierce conviction seiz'd the Sinner's Mind,
The Law-loud thundering he to Death consign'd;
JEHOVAH'S Wrath revolving, he surveys,
The Fancy's terror, and the Soul's amaze.

Say, what is Death? The Gloom of endless Night, 35
Which from the Sinner, bars the Gates of Light:
Say, what is Hell? In Horrors passing strange;
His Vengeance views, who seals his final Change;
The winged Hours, the final Judgment brings,
Decides his Fate, and that of Gods and Kings; 40
Tremendous Doom! And dreadful to be told,
To dwell in Tophet 'stead of shrines of Gold.
"Gods! Ye shall die like Men," the Herald cries,
"And stil'd no more the Children of the Skies."

   Trembling he sees the horrid Gulf appear, 45
Creation quakes, and no Deliverer near;
With Heart relenting to his Feelings kind,
See *Moorhead* hasten to relieve his Mind.
See him the Gospel's healing Balm impart,
To sooth the Anguish of his tortur'd Heart. 50
He points the trembling Mountain, and the Tree,
Which bent beneath th' incarnate Deity,
How God descended, wonderous to relate,
To bear our Crimes, a dread enormous Weight;
Seraphic Strains too feeble to repeat, 55
Half the dread Punishment the GOD-HEAD meet.
Suspended there, (till Heaven was reconcil'd,)
Like MOSES' Serpent in the Desert wild.
The Mind appeas'd what new Devotion glows,
With Joy unknown, the raptur'd Soul o'erflows; 60
While on his GOD-like Savior's Glory bent,
His Life proves witness of his Heart's intent.
Lament ye indigent the Friendly Mind,
Which oft relented, to your Mis'ry kind.

   With humble Gratitude he render'd Praise, 65
To Him whose Spirit had inspir'd his Lays;
To Him whose Guidance gave his Words to flow,
Divine instruction, and the Balm of Wo:
To you his Offspring, and his Church, be given,
A triple Portion of his Thirst for Heaven; 70
Such was the Prophet; we the Stroke deplore,
Which let's us hear his warning Voice no more.
But cease complaining, hush each murm'ring Tongue,

Pursue the Example which inspires my Song.
Let his Example in your Conduct shine;   75
Own the afflicting Providence, divine;
So shall bright Periods grace your joyful Days,
And heavenly Anthems swell your Songs of Praise.

Boston, Decem. 15 1773. Phillis Wheatley.

Printed from the Original Manuscript, and Sold by WILLIAM
M'ALPINE, at his Shop in *Marlborough-Street*, 1773.

[37]

John Thornton holograph copy of letter he sent to PW, *c.*February 1774

Ph.

I have to thank you for your Letter of 1ˢᵗ of Decʳ which I perused with
pleasure. Your adoration of the Divine protection over you, while crossing
the great Atlantic, is worthy a creature & a Christian. Your transition from
these wonders, to the wonderful depths of redeeming Love, gave me much
satisfaction. For, surely, what good and wise men, prior to Christ's appear-
ing, have desired to see; what every believer in every age, since that memo-
rable period, have delighted to dwell upon in their meditations; what
the angels are represented as desirous to look into; and what will be the
increasing wonder of glorified spirits, thro' the succeeding ages of eternity;
is a subject worthy our deepest meditation, our most exalted reflections:
and the upshot at last must be, with the Apostle, "O the depth!" and with
Nehemiah, "The Name of the Lord our God is exalted above all blessing &
praise." You request my prayers: you shall have them. Two blessings I will
ask of God for you: that you may have increasing views of redeeming love;
and that you may have more humbling views of yourself. If, upon examination of yourself, you find things thus in your soul, I hope you may conclude, that the grace of God is in you of a truth. I generally judge of myself
and others by these Two marks. But, as in every thing else, so in these there
may be danger. When I want you to have increasing views of redeeming
Love, I do not mean, that you should be able to talk more exactly about it:
because ideas and language of this kind may be greatly enriched by reading the scriptures, and joining in the conversation of the righteous; and I
too well know, it is very possible to talk excellently of divine things, even so
as to raise the admiration of others, and at the same time, the heart not be
affected by them. This is too common a deception among the people of

God. The kingdom of heaven is not in word, but in power. How many extol free grace, whose walk is very far from what it should be! When I wish you to have increasing views of redeeming love, I would have you thrown into silent wonders and adoration of the wisdom and goodness of God. Look at yourself; look at Jesus; look at the Law, look at the world; look at your own peculiar situation: these are all wonderful subjects. Then, with Mary, ponder them in your heart. This will always make you thankful and humble. Many a good man is a snare to another, by too openly commending his good qualities, and not aware how undesignedly he spreads a net for the feet of his friend. Your present situation and the kindness you meet with from many good people, and the respect that is paid to your uncommon genius, extort this friendly hint from me. I have no reason to charge you with any indiscretions of this kind: I mean only to apprize you of the danger. I feared for you when here, least the notice many took of you, should prove a snare. For half of our religious folks kill one another with kindness: that is, they get into a religious gossiping, they commend each others good qualities; praise is agreeable to corrupt nature; and the consequence is, we begin to be of the same opinion, are off our guard, become proud of our graces, the power of grace gradually dwindles away, and little more than the empty name and profession remains. Dear M.ʳˢ W. wanted me to speak a word in the religious way to her son: I will give you my sentiments on this subject.—It is a settled point with me, that none can touch the heart to purpose, but God; and for a person to suppose he can, by word or deed, make another a convert, seems to me to sacrifice to his own net, to seek his own glory, and to infringe upon the divine prerogative. When a door opens, I would go in; I would use no violence. To walk and work with God (viz. to go his pace) are not so easy as some imagine. Moses at 40 was willing to deliver Israel; at 80 he was full of excuses. A young, raw Christian fears no man, thinks he can convert all; when he comes to better experience, he sees conversion work is of God. To speak to a harden'd sinner of the things of God, and the salvation of Christ would be like casting pearls before swine. To tell him of the terrors of God, serves only to irritate his passions the more. This is not the effect of the fear of man, however some may deem it so, but I trust, the result of solid judgement and experience. I have often observed, that mankind will not be bullied into religion; and tho' they may be silenced by scripture-authority, yet they cannot be convinced of their danger without divine grace. I will go a step farther: Suppose a person has really had some religious impressions and expressed a liking to the things of God; while this approbation is visible, I would strike in, and give the best advice I could: but, if the same person had cooled in his desires, and was afraid of the cross, or a nick-name, I would then pray for him in secret, but by no means aggravate his conduct, least I should forever lose him. People in such a situation are to be borne with: their experience is small, their temptations strong, and the children of God should shew them compassion; not to lull them asleep, for that would be wrong, but for fear of overdriving them, and they begin to have a dislike to the way of God. When they are upon their return to God, I would then lay before them the danger of their coldness and backsliding: for, when a person is recovering from sickness, you may shew him the danger he has been in, which would not have been so seasonable when he was really ill: the case is the same in spiritual sickness and recovery. I will give you another case: Suppose a person is a professor of religion, and has been for some time, and yet gives into some of the vanities of the age; what is to be done with such a one? Restraint won't do, while the heart is hankering after vanity. This professor is in danger, you see it clearly; but the person concerned sees his danger in no such point of view. The only thing in such a case is to wait. If there be real grace in the heart, it will by degrees make the conscience tender, and beget a dislike to the vanities of the age in time. Nothing but experience can teach a person in these matters. When such a one finds he cannot have fellowship with God, returns of prayer, nor sensible communications of Grace, in the pursuit of such vanities, he will grow restless and uneasy. Then, I take it, is the proper time to speak to such a person, and apprize him of his danger. Then, probably, he will listen, and all will be well. Whereas to interpose when his head is filled with vanity, he will count you his enemy.—How far my method is justifiable in all respects, I will not say: but I am sure it is the way to keep our own souls humble, to acknowledge the power of divine grace, and our insufficiency; and a christian friendship begun and carried on thus, is most lasting & comfortable.

[38]

The Rev'd M.ʳ Sam.ˡ Hopkins
p[e]ʳ Post Newport Rhode Island

Boston Feb: 9ᵗʰ 1774.

Rev'd Sir,

I take with pleasure the opportunity by the Post, to acquaint you of the arr[iva]ˡ of my books from London. I have Seal'd up a package, containing 17 for you 2 for Mʳ. Tanner and one for Mʳˢ. Mason, and only wait for you to appoint some proper person by whom I may convey them to you. I rec[eive]ᵈ some time ago 20/sterling upon them by the hands of your Son, in a Letter from Obour Tanner. I rec[eive]ᵈ at the same time a paper by which I understand there are two Negro men who are desirous of returning to their native Country, to preach the Gospel; But being much indispos'd by the return of my Asthmatic complaint, besides, the sickness of my mistress who has been long confin'd to her bed, & is not expected to live above a great while; all these things render it impracticable for me to do any thing at present with regard to that paper, but what I can do in influencing my Christian friends and acquaintance, to promote this laudable design shall not be wanting. Methinks Rev'd Sir, this is the beginning of that happy period foretold by the Prophets, when all shall know the Lord from the least to the greatest, and that without the assistance of human Art & Eloquence. my heart expands with sympathetic Joy to see at distant time the thick cloud of ignorance dispersing from the face of my benighted Country; Europe and America have long been fed with the heavenly provision, and I fear they loathe it, while Africa is perishing with a Spiritual Famine. O that they could partake of the crumbs, the precious crumbs, Which fall from the table, of these distinguishd children of the Kingdome[.]

Their minds are unprejudiced against the truth therefore tis to be hoped they wouᵈ recieve it with their Whole heart. I hope that which the divine royal Psalmist Says by inspiration is now on the point of being Accomplish'd, namely, Ethiopia Shall Soon Stretch forth her hands Unto God. of this, Obour Tanner (and I trust many others within your knowledge are living witnesses[)]. Please to give my love to her & I intend to write her soon. my best respects attend every kind inquirer after your obligd Humble Servant.

Phillis Wheatley

[39]

The following is an extract of a Letter from Phillis, a Negro Girl of Mr. Wheatley's, in Boston, to the Rev. Samson Occom, which we are desired to insert as a Specimen of her Ingenuity.—It is dated 11th Feb., 1774.

"Rev'd and honor'd Sir,

I have this Day received your obliging kind Epistle, and am greatly satisfied with your Reasons respecting the Negroes, and think highly reasonable what you offer in Vindication of their natural Rights: Those that invade them cannot be insensible that the divine Light is chasing away the thick Darkness which broods over the Land of Africa; and the Chaos which has reign'd so long, is converting into beautiful Order, and [r]eveals more and more clearly, the glorious Dispensation of civil and religious Liberty, which are so inseparably united, that there is little or no Enjoyment of one without the other: Otherwise, perhaps, the Israelites had been less solicitous for their Freedom from Egyptian Slavery; I do not say they would have been contented without it, by no means, for in every human Breast, God has implanted a Principle, which we call Love of Freedom; it is impatient of Oppression, and pants for Deliverance; and by the Leave of our Modern Egyptians I will assert, that the same Principle lives in us. God grant Deliverance in his own Way and Time, and get him honour upon all those whose Avarice impels them to countenance and help forward the Calamities of their Fellow Creatures. This I desire not for their Hurt, but to convince them of the strange Absurdity of their Conduct whose Words and Actions are so diametrically opposite. How well the Cry for Liberty, and the reverse Disposition for the Exercise of oppressive Power over others agree,—I humbly think it does not require the Penetration of a Philosopher to determine."—

[40]

To Miss Obour Tanner Newport

Dear Obour,

I rec^d. your obliging Letter, enclosd, in your rev.^{d} Pastor's & handed me by his Son. I have lately met with a great trial in the death of my mistress, let us imagine the loss of a Parent, Sister or Brother the tenderness of all these were united in her.—I was a poor little outcast & a stranger when she took me in, not only into her house but I presently became, a sharer in her most tender affections. I was treated by her more like her child than her Servant, no opportunity was left unimprov'd, of giving me the best of advice, but in terms how tender! how engaging! this I hope ever to keep in remembrance. Her exemplaly [sic] life was a greater monitor than all her precepts and Instructions, thus we may observe of how much greater force example is than Instruction. To alleviate our sorrows we had the satisfaction to see her depart in inexpresible raptures, earnest longings & impatient thirstings for the upper Courts of the Lord. Do, my dear friend, remember me & this family in your Closet, that this afflicting dispensation may be sanctify'd to us. I am very sorry to hear that you are indispos[d] but hope this will find you in better health. I have been unwell the greater Part of the winter, but am much better as the Spring approaches. Pray excuse my not writing to you so long before, for I have been so busy lately, that I could not find liezure. I shall send the 5 Books you wrote for, the first convenient Opportunity. if you want more, they Shall be ready for you I am very affectionately your Friend

Phillis Wheatley

Boston March 21. 1774.

[41]

John Thornton Esq[r]. Merchant at Clapham Near London P[e]r Capt Hood

Much honoured Sir,

I should not so soon have troubled you with the 2[d]. Letter, but the mournful Occasion will sufficiently Apologize. It is the death of M[rs]. Wheatley. She has been labouring under a languishing illness for many months past and has at length took her flight from hence to those blissful regions, which need not the light of any, but the Sun of Righteousness. O could you have been present, to See how She long'd to drop the tabernacle of Clay, and to be freed from the cumbrous Shackles of a mortal Body, which had so many Times retarded her desires when Soaring upward. She has often told me how your Letters hav[e] quicken'd her in her Spiritual Course: when She has been in darkness of mind they have rais'd and enliven'd her insomuch, that She went on, with chearfuln[ess] and alacrity in the path of her duty. She did truely, run with patience the race that was Set before her, and hath, at length obtained the celestial Goal. She is now Sure, that the afflictions of this present time, were not worthy to be compared to the Glory, which is now, revealed in her, Seeing they have wrought out for her, a far more exceeding and eternal weight of Glory. This, Sure, is sufficient encouragement under the bitterest Sufferings, which we can endure.—About half an hour before her Death, She Spoke with a more audible voice, than She had for 3 months before. She call[d]. her friends & relations around her, and charg'd them not to leave their great work undone till that hour, but to fear God, and keep his Commandments. being ask'd if her faith faild her She answer'd, No. Then Spr[ead] out her arms crying come! come quickly! come, come! O pray for an eas[y] and quick Passage! She eagerly longed to depart to be with Christ. She retain[d] her Senses till the very last moment

when "fare well, fare well" with a very low voice, were the last words She utter'd. I sat the whole time by her bed Side, and Saw with Grief and Wonder, the Effects of Sin on the human race. Had not Christ taken away the envenom'd Sting, where had been our hopes? what might we not have fear'd, what might we not ^have^ expect^d^ from the dreadful King of Terrors? But <u>this</u> is matter of endless praise, to the King eternal immortal, invisible, that, <u>it is finished</u>. I hope her Son will be interested in Your Closet duties, & that the prayers which she was continually putting up, & wch. are recorded before God, in the Book of his remembrance for her Son & for me may be answer'd. I can Scarcely think that an Object of so many prayers, will fail of the Blessings implor'd for him ever Since he was born. I intreat the same Interest in your best thoughts for my Self, that her prayers, in my behalf, may be favour'd with an Answer of <u>Peace</u>. We received and forwarded your Letter to the rev'd M^r. Occom, but first, took the freedom to peruse it, and am exceeding glad, that you have order'd him to draw immediately for £25. for I really think he is in absolute necessity for that and as much more, he is so loth to run in debt for fear he Shall not be able to repay, that he has not the least Shelter for his Creatures ^to defend them^ from the inclemencies of the weather, and he has lost some already for want of it. His hay is quite as defenceless, thus the former are in a fair way of being lost, and the latter to be wasted; It were to be wished that his <u>dwelling house</u> was like the Ark, with appartments, to contain the beasts and their provision; He Said M^{rs}. Wheatley and the rev'd M^r. Moorhead were his best friends in Boston. But alass! they are gone. I trust ^gone^ to recieve the rewards promis'd to those, who Offer a Cup of cold water in the name ^& for the sake^ of Jesus—They have both been very instrum[ental in meetin]g the wants of that child of God, M^r. Occom—but I fear your [patience has been] exhausted, it remains only that we thank you for your kind Letter to my mistress it came above a fortnight after her Death.—Hoping for an interest in your prayers for these Sanctificiation [*sic*] of this bereaving Providence, I am hon'd Sir with dutiful respect ever your obliged
and devoted Humble Servant Phillis Wheatley

Boston
N[ew] England March 29th
1774.
John Thornton Esqr.

Phillis Wheatley
Boston 29th March 1774
Rec^d 25 May
Ans^d 2 Aug^t

[42]

To Miss Obour Tanner New Port Rhode Island
Fav^d by Mr. Pemberton

Dear Obour,

I rec^d. last evening your kind & friendly Letter, and am <u>not</u> a little animated thereby. I hope ever to follow your good advices and be resignd to the afflicting hand of a Seemingly frowning Providence. I have rec^d. the money you sent for the 5 books & 2/6 [2 shillings, six pence] more for another, which I now send & wish Safe to hand. Your tenderness for my welfare demands my gratitu[de]. Assist me, dear Obour! to Praise our great benefactor, for the innumerable Benefits continually pour'd upon me, that while he strikes one Comfort <u>dead</u> he raises up another. But O, that I could dwell on, & delight in him alone above every other Object! While the world hangs loose about us we shall not be in painful <u>anxiety</u> in giving up to God, that which he first gave to us. Your letter came by M^r. Pemberton who brings you the book you wrote for. I shall wait upon M^r. Whitwell with your Letter, and am,

Dear Sister, ever Affectionately, your
Phillis Wheatley

I have rec^d by ^some of^ the last Ships 300 more of my Poems.
Boston May 6, 1774

[43]

To the Rev'd M^r. Saml Hopkins New Port Rhode Island fav'^d. by M^r. Pemberton

Rev'd Sir

I recieved your kind letter last Evening by M^r. Pemberton, by whom also this is to be handed you. I have also rec.^d the money for the 5 Books I sent Obour, & 2/6 more for another. She has wrote me, but the date is 29 April. I am very sorry to hear, that Philip Quaque has very little or no <u>apparent</u> Success in his mission—Yet, I wish that what you hear respecting him, may be only a misrepresentation—Let us not be discouraged, but still hope that God will bring about his great work. tho' Philip may <u>not</u> be the Instrument in the divine Hand to perform this work of wonder, turning the Africans "from darkness to light." Possibly, if Philip would introduce himself properly to them, (I don't know the reverse) he might be more Successful; and in setting a good example which is more powerfully winning than Instruction. I Observe your Reference to the Maps of Guinea & Salmon's Gazetteer, and shall consult them. I have rec.^d in some of the last ships from London 300 more copies of my Poems, and wish to dispose of them as soon as Possible. If you know of any being wanted I flatter myself you will be pleas'd to let me know it, which will be adding one more to the many Obligations already confer'd on her, who is, with a due Sense of your kindness,

Your most humble,
And Obedient Servant
Phillis Wheatley

Boston
May 6, 1774
The revd S. Hopkins

[44]

To John Thornton Esqr. Merchant London

Much hon^d. Sir,

I have the honour of your obliging favour of August 1st. by M^r. Wheatley who arriv'd not before the 27th. Ultimo after a tedious passage of near two months; the obligations I am under to the family I desire to retain a grateful Sense of, And consequently rejoice in the bountiful dealings of providence towards him—

By the great loss I have Sustain'd of my best friend, I feel like One [fo]rsaken by her parent in a desolate wilderness, for Such the world appears to [me], wandring thus without ^my^ friendly guide. I fear lest every step should lead me [in]to error and confusion. She gave me many precepts and instructions; which I hope I shall never forget. Hon'd sir, pardon me if after the retrospect of such uncommon tenderness for thirteen years from my earliest youth—such unwearied diligence to instruct me in the principles of the true Religion, this in some degree Justifies me while I deplore my misery—^If^ I readily Join with you in wishing that you could in these respects Supply her place, but this does not seem probable from the great distance of your residence. However I will endeavour to compensate it by a Strict Observance of hers and your good advice from time ^to^ time, which you have given me encouragement to hope for—What a Blessed Source of consolation that our greatest friend is an immortal God whose friendship is invariable! from whom I have all that is ^in me^ praise worthy in ^mental^ possession. This Consideration humbles me much under encomiums on the gifts of God, the fear that I should not improve them to his glory and the good of mankind, it almost hinders a commendable self estimation (at times) but quite beats down the boldness of presumption. The world is a severe Schoolmaster, for its frowns are less dang'rous than its Smiles and flatteries, and it is a difficult task to keep in the path of Wisdom. I attended, and find exactly true your thoughts on the behaviour of those who seem'd to respect me while under my mistresses patronage: you said right, for Some of those have already put on a reserve; but I submit while God rules; who never forsakes any till they have ungratefully forsaken him—. My old master's generous behaviour in granting me my freedom, and still so kind to me I delight to acknowledge my great obligations to him, this he did about 3 months before the death of my dear mistress & at her desire, as well as his own humanity, ^of wch. I hope ever to retain a grateful Sense, and treat ^him^ with that respect which is ever due to a paternal friendship—If this had not been the Case, yet I hope I should willingly Submit to Servitude to be free in Christ.—But since it is thus—Let me be a Servant of Christ and that is the most perfect freedom.—

You propose my returning to Africa with Bristol yamma and John Quamine if either of them upon Strict enquiry is such, as I dare give my heart and hand to, I believe they are either of them good enough if not too good for me, or they would not be fit for missionaries; but why do you hon'd Sir, wish those poor men so much trouble as to carry me So long a voyage? Upon my arrival, how like a Barbarian Shoul^d I look to the Natives; I can promise that my tongue shall be quiet ^for a strong reason indeed^ being an utter stranger to the Language of Anamaboe. Now to be Serious, This undertaking appears too hazardous, and not sufficiently Eligible, to go—and leave my British & American Friends—I am also unacquainted with those Missionaries in Person. The reverend gentleman who unde[r] [ta]kes their Education has repeatedly inform^d. me by Letters of their pro[gress] in Learning also an Account of John Quamine's family and Kingdo[m.] But be that as it will I resign it all to God's all wise governance; I thank you heartily for your generous Offer—With sincerity—

I am hon^d. Sir

most gratefully your Devoted Servt.
Phillis Wheatley

Boston October 30th 1774

Phillis Wheatley
Boston 30 Octr 1774
Rec^d 4 Jany 1775
Ans^d 28 April

[45]

Thomas Wallcut to Phillis Wheatley
Canada Montreal Novr 17 1774
Much Esteem'd Madam,

According to Your Desire and my Promise of Writing I now Com[p]ly & fulfil—Not without Reluctance tho You Excused me with only Giving You 2 or three Lines as what I write will hardly bear reading much more Critisising but I have Just thought that You said You Don't Like Apolygies therefore Desist However I hope You Will be so Good as not to Expect it but if any Body Should read this Letter besides Yourself Perhaps they would say Why I should think that one Who is in another Country and Nation Would find Matter of Subject or the Contrey for a Letter to such a one I would Reply that Every one has not the Gift of Letter Writing

To Miss Phillis Wheatly
but I beg that no one May have the Advantage but Your self—I belive You are by this Time tired of Reading such Nonsense therefore with being Remmembered to all Your Dear Family I subscribe my Self

Your Sincere & Obliged Friend
Thomas Wallcut

Please to Indulge me with an Answer and that will Convince me that You have not got out of Conceit of me

[46]
["To a Gentleman of the Navy"]

For the *ROYAL AMERICAN MAGAZINE* [December 1774].

By particular request we insert the following Poem addressed, by Philis [sic], (a young African, of surprising genius) to a gentleman of the navy, with his reply. By this single instance may be seen, the importance of education.—Uncultivated nature is much the same in every part of the globe. It is probable Europe and Africa would be alike savage or polite in the same circumstances; though, it may be questioned, whether men who have no artificial wants, are capable

of becoming so ferocious as those, who by faring sumptuously every day,
are reduced to a habit of thinking it necessary to their happiness, to plunder the
whole human race.

Celestial muse! for sweetness fam'd inspire
My wondrous theme with true poetic fire,
Rochfort, for thee! And Greaves deserve my lays
The sacred tribute of ingenuous praise.
For here, true merit shuns the glare of light,   5
She loves oblivion, and evades the sight.
At sight of her, see dawning genius rise
And stretch her pinions to her native skies.

Paris, for Helen's bright resistless charms,
Made Illion bleed and set the world in arms.   10
Had you appear'd on the Achaian shore
Troy now had stood, and Helen charm'd no more.
The Phrygian hero had resign'd the dame
For purer joys in friendship's sacred flame,
The noblest gift, and of immortal kind,   15
That brightens, dignifies the manly mind.

Calliope, half gracious to my prayer,
Grants but the half and scatters half in air.

Far in the space where ancient Albion keeps
Amidst the roarings of the sacred deeps,   20
Where willing forests leave their native plain,
Descend, and instant, plough the wat'ry main.
Strange to relate! with canvas wings they speed
To distant worlds; of distant worlds the dread.
The trembling natives of the peaceful plain,   25
Astonish'd view the heroes of the main,
Wond'ring to see two chiefs of matchless grace,
Of generous bosom, and ingenuous face,
From ocean sprung, like ocean foes to rest,
The thirst of glory burns each youthful breast.   30

In virtue's cause, the muse implores for grace,
These blooming sons of Neptune's royal race;
Cerulean youths! your joint assent declare,
Virtue to rev'rence, more than mortal fair,

A crown of glory, which the muse will twine,   35
Immortal trophy! Rochfort shall be thine!
Thine too O Greaves! for virtue's offspring share,
Celestial friendship and the muse's care.
Yours is the song, and your's the honest praise,
Lo! Rochfort smiles, and Greaves approves my lays.   40

BOSTON; October 30th. 1774.

[47]
"PHILIS'S [*sic*] Reply to the Answer in our last by the Gentleman in the Navy"

For one bright moment, heavenly goddess! shine,
Inspire my song and form the lays divine.
Rochford, attend. Beloved of Phoebus! hear,
A truer sentence never reach'd thine ear;
Struck with thy song, each vain conceit resign'd   5
A soft affection seiz'd my grateful mind,
While I each golden sentiment admire
In thee, the muse's bright celestial fire.
The generous plaudit 'tis not mine to claim,
A muse untutor'd, and unknown to fame.   10

The heavenly sisters pour thy notes along
And crown their bard with every grace of song.
My pen, least favour'd by the tuneful nine,
Can never rival, never equal thine;
Then fix the humble Afric muse's seat   15
At British Homer's and Sir Isaac's feet.
Those bards whose fame in deathless strains arise
Creation's boast, and fav'rites of the skies.

In fair description are thy powers display'd
In artless grottos, and the sylvan shade;   20
Charm'd with thy painting, how my bosom burns!
And pleasing Gambia on my soul returns,
With native grace in spring's luxuriant reign,
Smiles the gay mead, and Eden blooms again,
The various bower, the tuneful flowing stream,   25

The soft retreats, the lovers golden dream,
Her soil spontaneous, yields exhaustless stores;
For phoebus revels on her verdant shores.
Whose flowery births, a fragrant train appear,
And crown the youth throughout the smiling year,   30

There, as in Britain's favour'd isle, behold
The bending harvest ripen into gold!
Just are thy views of Afric's blissful plain,
On the warm limits of the land and main.

Pleas'd with the theme, see sportive fancy play,   35
In realms devoted to the God of day!
Europa's bard, who the great depth explor'd,
Of nature, and thro' boundless systems soar'd,
Thro' earth, thro' heaven, and hell's profound domain,
Where night eternal holds her awful reign.   40
But, lo! in him Britania's prophet dies,
And whence, ah! whence, shall other *Newton's* rise?
Muse, bid thy Rochford's matchless pen display
The charms of friendship in the sprightly lay.
Queen of his song, thro' all his numbers shine,   45
And plausive glories, goddess! shall be thine.
With partial grace thou mak'st his verse excel,
And *his* the glory to describe so well.
Cerulean bard! to thee these strains belong,
The Muse's darling and the prince of song.   50

DECEMBER 5th, 1774.

[48]
"To His Excellency General Washington"

The following LETTER *and* VERSES, *were written by the famous* Phillis
Wheatley, *the African Poetess, and presented to his Excellency Gen.*
Washington.

SIR,

I Have taken the freedom to address your Excellency in the enclosed poem,
and entreat your acceptance, though I am not insensible of its inaccuracies.

Your being appointed by the Grand Continental Congress to be Generalissimo of the armies of North America, together with the fame of your virtues, excite sensations not easy to suppress. Your generosity, therefore, I presume, will pardon the attempt. Wishing your Excellency all possible success in the great cause you are so generously engaged in. I am,

Your Excellency's most obedient humble servant, PHILLIS WHEATLEY. *Providence, Oct. 26, 1775. His Excellency Gen. Washington.*

> Celestial choir! enthron'd in realms of light,
> Columbia's scenes of glorious toils I write.
> While freedom's cause her anxious breast alarms,
> She flashes dreadful in refulgent arms.
> See mother earth her offspring's fate bemoan,   5
> And nations gaze at scenes before unknown!
> See the bright beams of heaven's revolving light
> Involved in sorrows and the veil of night!
>
> The goddess comes, she moves divinely fair,
> Olive and laurel binds her golden hair: 10
> Wherever shines this native of the skies,
> Unnumber'd charms and recent graces rise.
>
> Muse! bow propitious while my pen relates
> How pour her armies through a thousand gates:
> As when Eolus heaven's fair face deforms,   15
> Enwrapp'd in tempest and a night of storms;
> Astonish'd ocean feels the wild uproar,
> The refluent surges beat the sounding shore;
> Or thick as leaves in Autumn's golden reign,
> Such, and so many, moves the warrior's train.   20
> In bright array they seek the work of war,
> Where high unfurl'd the ensign waves in air.
> Shall I to Washington their praise recite?
> Enough thou know'st them in the fields of fight.
> Thee, first in place and honours,—we demand   25
> The grace and glory of thy martial band.
> Fam'd for thy valour, for thy virtues more,
> Hear every tongue thy guardian aid implore!
>
> One century scarce perform'd its destin'd round,
> When Gallic powers Columbia's fury found;   30

And so may you, whoever dares disgrace
The land of freedom's heaven-defended race!
Fix'd are the eyes of nations on the scales,
For in their hopes Columbia's arm prevails.
Anon Britannia droops the pensive head,   35
While round increase the rising hills of dead.
Ah! cruel blindness to Columbia's state!
Lament thy thirst of boundless power too late.

    Proceed, great chief, with virtue on thy side,
Thy ev'ry action let the goddess guide.   40
A crown, a mansion, and a throne that shine,
With gold unfading, WASHINGTON! be thine.

[49]

Miss Obour Tanner
Fav^d by}
M^r. Zingo} Newport

Dear Obour

I rec.^d your kind Letter of the 17th ultimo by Cato Coggeshall; had not the opportunity to see him. I doubt not that your present situation is extremely unhappy; nor that you with wonder exclaim on the proceedings of nations that are fav.^d with the divine revelation of the Gospel. Even I a mere spectator am in anxious suspence concerning the fortune of this unnatural civil Contest—

Possibly the Ambition & thirst of dominion in some, is design'd as the punishment of the national vices of others, tho' it bears the appearance of greater Barbarity than that of the unciviliz'd part of mankind. But Let us leave the Event to him whose wisdom alone can bring good out of Evil. & he is infinitely superior to all the Craftiness of the enemies of this seemingly devoted Country. This is handed you by M^r. Zingo, with whom and M^r. Quamine I passd the last evening very agreably.

    Dutiful respects to M^r. Hopkins & family
    And believe me to be your affectionate
        P. Wheatley
Providence feb^y 14,
1776

[50]
George Washington to Phillis Wheatley

M^rs. Phillis,   Cambridge February 28th 1776.

Your favour of the 26th of October did not reach my hands 'till the middle of December. Time enough, you will say, to have given an answer ere this. Granted. But a variety of important occurences, continually interposing to distract the mind and withdraw the attention, I hope will apologize for the delay, and plead my excuse for the seeming, but not real, neglect.

I thank you most sincerely for your polite notice of me, in the elegant Lines you enclosed; and however undeserving I may be of such encomium and panegyrick, the style and manner exhibit a striking proof of your great poetical Talents. In honour of which, and as a tribute justly due to you, I would have published the Poem, had I not been apprehensive, that, while I only meant to give the World this new instance of your genius, I might have incurred the imputation of vanity. This, and nothing else, determined me not to give it place in the public prints.

If you should ever come to Cambridge, or near Head Quarters, I shall be happy to see a person so favoured by the Muses, and to whom nature has been so liberal and beneficent in her dispensations.

I am, with great Respect,
Your obed^t humble servant,
G. Washington.

[51]
"On the Capture of General Lee"

The following thoughts on his Excellency Major General Lee being betray'd into the hands of the Enemy by the treachery of a pretended Friend; To the Honourable James Bowdoin Esqr are most respectfully Inscrib'd, By his most obedient and devoted humble Servant.

> The deed perfidious, and the Hero's fate,
> In tender strains, celestial Muse! relate.
> The latent foe to friendship makes pretence
> The name assumes without the sacred sense!

He, with a rapture well dissembl'd, press'd 5
The hero's hand, and fraudful, thus address'd.

"O friend belov'd! may heaven its aid afford,
"And spread yon troops beneath thy conquering sword!
"Grant to America's united prayer
"A glorious conquest on the field of war. 10
"But thou indulgent to my warm request
"Vouchsafe thy presence as my honour'd guest:
"From martial cares a space unbend thy soul
"In social banquet, and the sprightly bowl."
Thus spoke the foe; and warlike Lee reply'd, 15
"Ill fits it me, who such an army guide;
"To whom his conduct each brave soldier owes
"To waste an hour in banquets or repose:
"This day important, with loud voice demands
"Our wisest Counsels, and our bravest hands." 20
Thus having said he heav'd a boding sigh.
The hour approach'd that damps Columbia's Joy.
Inform'd, conducted, by the treach'rous friend
With winged speed the adverse train attend
Ascend the Dome, and seize with frantic air 25
The self surrender'd glorious prize of war!
On sixty coursers, swifter than the wind
They fly, and reach the British camp assign'd.
Arriv'd, what transport touch'd their leader's breast!
Who thus deriding, the brave Chief address'd. 30
"Say, art thou he, beneath whose vengeful hands
"Our best of heroes grasp'd in death the sands?
"One fierce regard of thine indignant eye
"Turn'd Brittain pale, and made her armies fly;
"But Oh! how chang'd! a prisoner in our arms 35
"Till martial honour, dreadful in her charms,
"Shall grace Britannia at her sons' return,
"And widow'd thousands in our triumphs mourn."
While thus he spoke, the hero of renown
Survey'd the boaster with a gloomy frown 40
And stern reply'd. "Oh arrogance of tongue!
"And wild ambition, ever prone to wrong!
"Believ'st thou Chief, that armies such as thine
"Can stretch in dust that heaven-defended line?

"In vain allies may swarm from distant lands   45
"And demons aid in formidable bands.
"Great as thou art, thou shun'st the field of fame
"Disgrace to Brittain, and the British name!
"When offer'd combat by the noble foe,
"(Foe to mis-rule,) why did thy sword forgo   50
"The easy conquest of the rebel-land?
"Perhaps <u>too</u> easy for thy martial hand.
"What various causes to the field invite!
"For plunder <u>you</u>, and we for freedom fight:
"Her cause divine with generous ardor fires,   55
"And every bosom glows as she inspires!
"Already, thousands of your troops are fled
"To the drear mansions of the silent dead:
"Columbia too, beholds with streaming eyes
"Her heroes fall—'tis freedom's sacrifice!   60
"So wills the Power who with convulsive storms
"Shakes impious realms, and nature's face deforms.
"Yet those brave troops innum'rous as the sands
"One soul inspires, one General Chief commands
"Find in your train of boasted heroes, one   65
"To match the praise of Godlike Washington.
"Thrice happy Chief! in whom the virtues join,
"And heaven-taught prudence speaks the man divine!"

    He ceas'd. Amazement struck the warrior-train,
And doubt of conquest, on the hostile plain.   70

                    BOSTON. Dec.ʳ 30, 1776

                    [52]

Miss Obour Tanner Worcester

                    Boston May 29th '78

Dear Obour,

    I am exceedingly glad to hear from you by Mʳˢ. Tanner, and wish you had timely notice of her departure, so as to have wrote me; next to that is the pleasure of hearing that you are well. The vast variety of Scenes that have pass'd before us these 3 years past will to a reasonable mind serve to convince us of the uncertain duration of all things Temporal, and the proper result of such a consideration is an ardent desire of, & preparation for, a State and enjoyments which are more Suitable to the immortal mind;—You will do me a great favour if you'll write me by every Opp'y [opportunity].—Direct your letters under cover to Mr. John Peters in Queen Street. I have but half an hour's notice; and must apologize for this hasty scrawl. I am most affectionately, my dear Obour, your sincere friend

Phillis Wheatley

[53]
"On the Death of General Wooster"

Madam [Mary Wooster],

I recd. your favour by Mr Dennison inclosing a paper containing the Character of the truely worthy General Wooster. It was with the most sensible regret that I heard of his fall in battle, but the pain of so afflicting a dispensation of Providence must be greatly alleviated to you and all his friends in the consideration that he fell a martyr in the Cause of Freedom—

<blockquote>

From this the muse rich consolation draws
He nobly perish'd in his Country's cause
His Country's Cause that ever fir'd his mind
Where martial flames, and Christian virtues join'd.
How shall my pen his warlike deeds proclaim   5
Or paint them fairer on the list of Fame—
Enough great Chief—now wrapt in shades around
Thy grateful Country shall thy praise resound
Tho' not with mortals' empty praise elate
That vainest vapour to th' immortal State   10
Inly serene the expiring hero lies
And thus (while heav'nward roll his swimming eyes)[:]
["]Permit, great power while yet my fleeting breath
And Spirits wander to the verge of Death—
Permit me yet to paint fair freedom's charms   15
For her the Continent shines bright in arms
By thy high will, celestial prize she came—

</blockquote>

For her we combat on the feild of fame
Without her presence vice maintains full sway
And social love and virtue wing their way   20
O still propitious be thy guardian care
And lead <u>Columbia</u> thro' the toils of war.
With thine own hand conduct them and defend
And bring the dreadful contest to an end—
For ever grateful let them live to thee   25
And keep them ever Virtuous, brave, and free—
But how, presumptuous shall we hope to find
Divine acceptance with th' Almighty mind—
While yet (O deed ungenerous!) they disgrace
And hold in bondage Afric's blameless race[?]   30
Let Virtue reign—And thou accord our prayers
Be victory our's, and generous freedom theirs.["]
The hero pray'd—the wond'ring Spirit fled
And Sought the unknown regions of the dead—
Tis thine fair partner of his life, to find   35
His virtuous path and follow close behind—
A little moment steals him from thy Sight
He waits thy coming to the realms of light
Freed from his labours in the ethereal Skies
Where in Succession endless pleasures rise!   40

you will do me a great favour by returning to me by the first opp^y those books that remain unsold and remitting the money for those that are sold—I can easily dispose of them here for 12/Lm.° each—I am greatly obliged to you for the care you show me, and your condescention in taking so much pains for my Interest—I am extremely Sorry not to have been honour'd with a personal acquaintance with you—if the foregoing lines meet with your acceptance and approbation I shall think them highly honour'd. I hope you will pardon the length of my letter, when the reason is apparent—fondness of the Subject &—the highest respect for the deceas'd—I sincerely sympathize with you in the great loss you and your family Sustain and am Sincerely

Your friend & very humble Servt Phillis Wheatley Queenstreet Boston July—15<u>th</u> 1778

Phillis Wheatley

[54]

Miss Obour Tanner Worcester
Fav^d by Cumberland

D^r. Obour,

By this opportunity I have the pleasure to inform You that I am well and hope you are so; tho' I have been Silent, I have not been unmindful of you but a variety of hindrances was the cause of my not writing to you—But in time to Come I hope our correspondence will revive—and revive in better times—pray write me soon, for I long to hear from you—you may depend on constant replies—I wish you much happiness, and am

D^r. Obour, your friend & sister
Phillis Peters
Boston May 10. 1779.

[55]

Proposals

For Printing By Subscription a Volume of Poems And Letters on Various Subjects, Dedicated to the Right Honourable Benjamin Franklin Esq: One of the Ambassadors of the United States at the Court of France, By Phillis Peters

Poems

Thoughts on the Times.
On the Capture of General Lee, to I.B. Esq.
To his Excellency General Washington.
On the death of General Wooster.
An Address to Dr—.
To Lieut R— of the Royal Navy.
To the same.
To T.M. Esq. of Granada.
To Sophia of South Carolina.
To Mr. A. M'B— of the Navy.
To Lieut R— D— of the Navy.
Ocean.

The choice and advantages of a Friend; to Mr. T— M—
Farewell to England 1773.
To Mrs. W—ms on Anna Eliza.
To Mr. A McB—d.
Epithalamium to Mrs. H—
To P.N.S. & Lady on the death of their infant son.
To Mr. El—y on the death of his Lady.
On the death of Lieut. L—ds.
To Penelope.
To Mr. & Mrs. L— on the death of their daughter.
A Complaint.
To Mr. A.I.M. on Virtue.
To Dr. L—d and Lady on the death of their son aged 5 years
To Mr. L—g on the death of his son.
To Capt. F—r on the death of his granddaughter.
To Philandra an Elegy.
Niagara.
Chloe to Calliope.
To Musidora on Florello.
To Sir E.L— Esq.
To the Hon. John Montague Esq. Rear Admiral of the Blue.

Letters

1. To the Right Hon. Wm E. of Dartmouth, Sec. of State for N. America.
2. To the Rev. Mr. T.P. Farmington.
3. To Mr. T.W.—Dartmouth College.
4. To the Hon. T. H. Esq.
5. To Dr. B. Rush, Phila.
6. To the Rev. Dr. Thomas, London.
7. To the Right Hon. Countess of H—.
8. To I.M.—Esq. London.
9. To Mrs. W—e in the County of Surrey.
10. To Mr. T.M. Homerton, near London.
11. To Mrs. S. W—
12. To the Rt. Hon. the Countess of H—.
13. To the same.

Messieurs Printers,—The above collection of Poems and Letters was put into my hands by the desire of the ingenious author, in order to be introduced to public View.

The subjects are various and curious, and the author a *Female African*, whose lot it was to fall into the hands of a *generous* master and *great* benefactor. The learned and ingenuous as well as those who are pleased with novelty, are invited to incourage the publication by a generous subscription—the former, that they may fan the sacred fire which, is self-enkindled in the breast of this *young* African—The ingenuous that they may by reading this collection, have a large play for their imaginations, and be ex[c]ited to please and benefit mankind, by some brilliant production of their own pens.—Those who are *always* in search of some *new* thing, that they may obtain a sight of this *rara avis in terra* [Latin for "rare bird upon the earth"]—And every one, that the ingenious author may be encouraged to improve her own mind, benefit and please mankind.

CONDITIONS

They will be printed on good paper and a neat Type, and will contain about 300 Pages in Octavo.

The price to Subscribers will be *Twelve Pounds*, neatly Bound & Lettered, and *Nine Pounds* sew'd in blue paper, one Half to be paid on Subscribing, the other Half on delivery of the Books.

The Work will be put to the Press as soon as a sufficient Number of Encouragers offer.

Those who subscribe for Six [books] will have a Seventh Gratis.

Subscriptions are taken by White and Adams, the Publishers, in School-Street, *Boston*.

[56]

AN ELEGY, SACRED TO THE MEMORY OF THAT GREAT DIVINE, THE REVEREND AND LEARNED DR. SAMUEL COOPER, *Who departed this Life December* 29, 1783, AETATIS 59.

BY PHILLIS PETERS. BOSTON: *Printed and Sold by E. Russell, in Essex-Street, near Liberty-Pole*, M,DCC,LXXXIV [1784].

To the CHURCH *and* CONGREGATION *assembling in Brattle-Street, the following*, ELEGY, *Sacred to the* MEMORY *of their late Reverend and Worthy* PASTOR, *Dr.* SAMUEL COOPER, *is, with the greatest Sympathy, most respectfully inscribed by their Obedient,*

Humble Servant,
PHILLIS PETERS.

BOSTON, Jan. 1784.

O THOU whose exit wraps in boundless woe,
    For Thee the tears of various Nations flow:
For Thee the floods of virtuous sorrows rise
From the full heart and burst from streaming eyes,
Far from our view to Heaven's eternal height,   5
The Seat of bliss divine, and glory bright;
Far from the restless turbulence of life,
The war of factions, and impassion'd strife.
From every ill mortality endur'd,
Safe in celestial *Salem*'s walls secur'd.   10

E'ER yet from this terrestrial state retir'd,
The Virtuous lov'd Thee, and the Wise admir'd.
The gay approv'd Thee, and the grave rever'd;
And all thy words with rapt attention heard!
The Sons of Learning on thy lessons hung,   15
While soft persuasion mov'd th' illit'rate throng.
Who, drawn by rhetoric's commanding laws,
Comply'd obedient, nor conceiv'd the cause.
Thy every sentence was with grace inspir'd,
And every period with devotion fir'd;   20
Bright Truth thy guide without a dark disguise,
And penetration's all-discerning eyes.

THY COUNTRY mourn's th' afflicting Hand divine
That now forbids thy radiant lamp to shine,
Which, like the sun, resplendent source of light   25
Diffus'd its beams, and chear'd our gloom of night.

WHAT deep-felt sorrow in each *Kindred* breast
With keen sensation rends the heart distress'd!
Fraternal love sustains a tenderer part,
And mourns a BROTHER with a BROTHER'S heart.   30

THY CHURCH laments her faithful PASTOR fled
To the cold mansions of the silent dead.
There hush'd forever, cease the heavenly strain,
That wak'd the soul, but here resounds in vain.
Still live thy merits, where thy name is known,   35
As the sweet Rose, its blooming beauty gone
Retains its fragrance with a long perfume:
Thus COOPER! thus thy death-less name shall bloom

Unfading, in thy *Church* and *Country*'s love,
While Winter frowns, or spring renews the grove.   40
The hapless Muse, her loss in COOPER mourns,
And as she sits, she writes, and weeps, by turns;
A Friend sincere, whose mild indulgent grace
Encourag'd oft, and oft approv'd her lays.

WITH all their charms, terrestrial objects strove,   45
But vain their pleasures to attract his love.
Such COOPER was—at Heaven's high call he flies;
His task well finish'd, to his native skies.
Yet to his fate reluctant we resign,
Tho' our's to copy conduct such as thine: 50
Such was thy wish, th' observant Muse survey'd
Thy latest breath, and this advice convey'd.

[57]

LIBERTY AND PEACE, A POEM. *By* PHILLIS PETERS.
BOSTON: *Printed by* WARDEN *and* RUSSELL, *At Their Office in
Marlborough-Street.* M,DCC,LXXXIV [1784].

LO! Freedom comes. Th' prescient Muse foretold,
All Eyes th' accomplish'd Prophecy behold:
Her Port describ'd, "*She moves divinely fair,*
"*Olive and Laurel bind her golden Hair.*"
She, the bright Progeny of Heaven, descends,   5
And every Grace her sovereign Step attends;
For now kind Heaven, indulgent to our Prayer,
In smiling *Peace* resolves the Din of *War.*
Fix'd in *Columbia* her illustrious Line,
And bids in thee her future Councils shine.   10
To every Realm her Portals open'd wide,
Receives from each the full commercial Tide.
Each Art and Science now with rising Charms
Th' expanding Heart with Emulation warms.
E'en great *Britannia* sees with dread Surprize,   15
And from the dazzl'ing Splendors turns her Eyes!
Britain, whose Navies swept th' *Atlantic* o'er,
And Thunder sent to every distant Shore:
E'en thou, in Manners cruel as thou art,

The Sword resign'd, resume the friendly Part!   20
For *Galia's* Power espous'd *Columbia's* Cause,
And new-born *Rome* shall give *Britannia* Law,
Nor unremember'd in the grateful Strain,
Shall princely *Louis'* friendly Deeds remain;
The generous Prince th' impending Vengeance eye's,   25
Sees the fierce Wrong, and to the rescue flies.
Perish that Thirst of boundless Power, that drew
On *Albion's* Head the Curse to Tyrants due.
But thou appeas'd submit to Heaven's decree,
That bids this Realm of Freedom rival thee!   30
Now sheathe the Sword that bade the Brave attone
With guiltless Blood for Madness not their own.
Sent from th' Enjoyment of their native Shore
Ill-fated—never to behold her more!
From every Kingdom on *Europa's* Coast   35
Throng'd various Troops, their Glory, Strength and Boast.
With heart-felt pity fair *Hibernia* saw
Columbia menac'd by the Tyrant's Law:
On hostile Fields fraternal Arms engage,
And mutual Deaths, all dealt with mutual Rage;   40
The Muse's Ear hears mother Earth deplore
Her ample Surface smoak with kindred Gore:
The hostile Field destroys the social Ties,
And ever-lasting Slumber seals their Eyes.
Columbia mourns, the haughty Foes deride,   45
Her Treasures plunder'd, and her Towns destroy'd:
Witness how *Charlestown's* curling Smoaks arise,
In sable Columns to the clouded Skies!
The ample Dome, high-wrought with curious Toil,
In one sad Hour the savage Troops despoil.   50
Descending *Peace* the Power of War confounds;
From every Tongue celestial *Peace* resounds:
As from the East th' illustrious King of Day,
With rising Radiance drives the Shades away,
So Freedom comes array'd with Charms divine,   55
And in her Train Commerce and Plenty shine.
Britannia owns her Independent Reign,
Hibernia, *Scotia*, and the Realms of *Spain*;
And great *Germania's* ample Coast admires
The generous Spirit that *Columbia* fires.   60

Auspicious Heaven shall fill with fav'ring Gales,
Where e'er *Columbia* spreads her swelling Sails:
To every Realm shall *Peace* her Charms display,
And Heavenly *Freedom* spread her golden Ray.

[58]
Wheatley's Final Proposal

The Poem ["To Mr. and Mrs.—, On the Death of Their Infant Son,"
(59)], in page 488, of this Number, was selected from a manuscript Volume
of Poems, written by PHILLIS PETERS, formerly PHILLIS
WHEATLEY—and is inserted as a Specimen of her Work; should this
gain the approbation of the Publick and sufficient encouragement be
given, a Volume will be shortly Published, by the Printers hereof, who
received subscriptions for said Work.

[59]
To Mr. and Mrs.—, on the Death of their
Infant Son, By Phillis Wheatly [*sic*].

O DEATH! whose sceptre, trembling realms obey,
And weeping millions mourn thy savage sway;
Say, shall we call thee by the name of friend,
Who blasts our joys, and bids our glories end?
Behold, a child who rivals op'ning morn,   5
When its first beams the eastern hills adorn;
So sweetly blooming once that lovely boy,
His father's hope, his mother's only joy,
Nor charms nor innocence prevail to save,
From the grim monarch of the gloomy grave!   10
Two moons revolve when lo! among the dead
The beauteous infant lays his weary head:
For long he strove the tyrant to withstand,
And the dread terrors of his iron hand;
Vain was his strife, with the relentless power,   15
His efforts weak; and this his mortal hour;
He sinks—he dies—celestial muse, relate,
His spirit's entrance at the sacred gate.

Methinks I hear the heav'nly courts resound,
The recent theme inspires the choirs around.   20
His guardian angel with delight unknown,
Hails his bless'd charge on his immortal throne;
His heart expands at scenes unknown before,
Dominions praise, and prostrate thrones adore;
Before the Eternal's feet their crowns are laid,   25
The glowing seraph vails his sacred head.
Spirits redeem'd, that more than angels shine,
For nobler praises tune their harps divine:
These saw his entrance; his soft hand they press'd,
Sat on his throne, and smiling thus address'd,   30
"Hail: thou! thrice welcome to this happy shore,
"Born to new life where changes are no more;
"Glad heaven receives thee, and thy God bestows,
"Immortal youth exempt from pain and woes.
"Sorrow and sin, those foes to human rest,   35
"Forever banish'd from thy happy breast."
Gazing they spoke, and raptur'd thus replies,
The beauteous stranger in the etherial skies.
"Thus safe conducted to your bless'd abodes,
"With sweet surprize I mix among the Gods;   40
"The vast profound of this amazing grace,
"Beyond your search, immortal powers, I praise;
"Great Sire, I sing thy boundless love divine,
"Mine is the bliss, but all the glory thine."

    All heav'n rejoices as your . . . sings,   45
To heavenly airs he tunes the sounding strings;
Mean time on earth the hapless parents mourn,
"Too quickly fled, ah! never to return."
Thee, the vain visions of the night restore,
Illusive fancy paints the phantom o'er;   50
Fain would we clasp him, but he wings his flight;
Deceives our arms, and mixes with the night;
But oh! suppress the clouds of grief that roll,
Invading peace, and dark'ning all the soul.
Should heaven restore him to your arms again,   55
Oppress'd with woes, a painful endless train,
How would your prayers, your ardent wishes, rise,
Safe to repose him in his native skies.

TEXTUAL AND EXPLANATORY NOTES

[1]

Untitled handwritten transcriptions in Reverend Jeremy Belknap's diary, interleaved in *Bickerstaff's Boston Almanack. For the Year of Our Lord, 1773* (Boston, [1772]). Massachusetts Historical Society (Jeremy Belknap Papers, 1773 Diary).

Not included in Wheatley's 1772 "Proposals" [18].

Phillis Wheatley's earliest known piece of writing is the untitled four-line poem written on the last page of the 1773 diary of Reverend Jeremy Belknap (1744–98), pastor of a Congregationalist church in Dover, New Hampshire (1767–86). Belknap identifies the poem as "Phillis Wheatley's first Effort——A.D. 1765. AE [aged] 11."

Belknap transcribes Phillis Wheatley's text twice, first, in three lines, as if he could not decide whether it is prose or poetry. The two-word phrase "Unto Salvation" is written above the first line. A caret below the line indicates in the manuscript where the phrase should be inserted. Belknap's second transcription, immediately following the first, presents the text as a four-line poem, framed in the manuscript by an opening bracket. Belknap made the two transcriptions at different times. The three-line version is written in dark ink. The four-line poem and the "Unto Salvation" added to the three-line version are written in a lighter-colored ink.

Before the twentieth century, amateur authors, particularly women, often circulated their writings in manuscript before, or instead of, having them printed. Pride in their slave's precocious efforts may have motivated the Wheatleys to share them with members of the Boston literati. Belknap's attribution of the verses on the deaths of Mr. and Mrs. Thacher, Jr., to a young Phillis Wheatley makes it the first of her nineteen extant elegies (not including variants of several of those). It is also the first of her many occasional poems—that is, ones written in response to a recent event.

The Thachers had been one of the most distinguished Congregationalist families in Massachusetts for generations. Wheatley's Mrs. Thacher (d. 30 January 1776), the former Bathsheba Doggett, was the widow of John Kent of Boston when she became the second wife of Oxenbridge Thacher, Sr. (1681–1772), a widower, in 1740. Bathsheba's seventeen-year-old daughter, Sarah (1724–64), married Oxenbridge's twenty-one-year-old son, Oxenbridge Thacher, Jr. (1719–65), in 1741. Consequently, Oxenbridge Thacher, Jr., was the "Son" of Mrs. Oxenbridge Thacher, Sr., in two senses: he was her stepson, as well as her son-in-law. Oxenbridge Thacher, Jr., and his wife lived in central Boston, several streets west of the home of John Wheatley and his family. Oxenbridge Thacher, Jr., a well-respected Boston lawyer, was also a prominent and promising local politician. Like

John Wheatley before him and Nathaniel Wheatley after, Oxenbridge Thacher, Jr., held various town offices. He was an early proponent of colonial rights, and he was one of Boston's four representatives in the Massachusetts General Assembly when he died in 1765. He argued in *Sentiments of a British American* (1764) that direct taxation of the colonies by the British Parliament was unconstitutional.

Sarah Kent Thacher died on 4 July 1764 at her father-in-law's house in Milton, Massachusetts. The *Boston Gazette and Country Journal* reported on 9 July 1764 that she was a victim of the same smallpox epidemic in 1764 that caused the English evangelist George Whitefield (1714–70) to hesitate before entering Boston (cf. [14]). Oxenbridge Thacher, Jr., was indirectly a victim of the same epidemic the following year. The *Massachusetts Gazette and Boston News-Letter* announced on 11 July 1765 that he had died in Boston two days earlier, "after a long languishment." He had never recovered from the side effects of having been inoculated against the disease.

At a time when composing verses was much more frequent than now, would-be poets often attempted to write elegies. So common were elegies during the period that Philip Freneau (1752–1832), an elegist himself, observed in his "On Funeral Elogiums" in 1790, "No species of poetry is more frequently attempted" than poems on death. (Philip M. Marsh, ed., *The Prose of Philip Freneau* [New Brunswick, NJ: Scarecrow Press, 1955], 268.) Contemporaneous satires and parodies of elegies also attested to the popularity of the genre. In 1722 Benjamin Franklin (1706–90) mocked the formulaic quality of elegies in one of his Silence Dogood letters. But Franklin later admitted in his *Autobiography* that his own earliest attempt at poetry was an elegy written in 1718 that has not survived.

Belknap knew Wheatley, or at least knew of her, before 1773. Belknap was living in New Hampshire in 1765, when the lines on the Thachers were most likely composed, as well as in 1773, when he transcribed them. But he frequently visited Boston, his hometown, during that period. Wheatley sent him, probably in 1769, a variant manuscript version of her elegy on the death of Reverend Sewall (1688–1769) [11], which is now at Dartmouth College. Belknap's uncle, Reverend Mather Byles (1707–88), a major published colonial poet who resided in Boston, may have first brought Wheatley to Belknap's attention. Belknap imitated Byles in his own early attempts at poetry. Byles may also have served as a model for Wheatley, whom he encouraged as a poet. He is one of the eighteen Boston worthies who attested in print to the authenticity of her *Poems on Various Subjects, Religious and Moral*, published in London in 1773. The publication of Wheatley's *Poems* and Belknap's familiarity with at least one of her earlier elegies probably prompted him to seek more information about her in 1773. Byles was clearly in a position to inform Belknap about Phillis Wheatley's progress as an aspiring author.

The brevity, style, genre, content, and allusions of the poem on the Thachers all point to Phillis Wheatley as its author in 1765. The succession of brief clauses, staccato rhythm, and nearly successful attempt to write couplets are typical of juvenilia, especially by someone who had been living in an English-speaking environment for only four years. As a brief occasional elegy on the death of a

Boston notable, the lines in Belknap's diary anticipate the most common type of poem found among Wheatley's later works. Not surprisingly, the emphasis on private and domestic loss in the poem contrasts with the concentration on public and political loss found in fourteen lines titled "Written Extempore, on hearing of the Death of Oxenbridge Thacher, Esq.; on a supposed View of the Corps" that "S.Y." published in the *Boston News-Letter and New England Chronicle* on 18 July 1765.

As one might expect from a young girl, the pious sentiment expressed in the piece that Belknap attributes to Wheatley concerns only the surviving mother and her late children. Although Oxenbridge Thacher, Sr., was still alive when the poem was written, he is not mentioned. Wheatley may have ignored the father because he had been living in Milton for several years, and thus was unfamiliar to her. Sarah and Oxenbridge Thacher, Jr., on the other hand, were members of the Old South Church, which Phillis Wheatley formally joined in 1771. Writing an elegy on their deaths effectively highlighted the spiritual community the author shared with them.

[2] "Atheism—"

Library Company of Philadelphia manuscript at the Historical Society of Pennsylvania (Rush Family Papers, Series IV. Miscellaneous Documents, Box 14/ Folder 27). Not included in Wheatley's 1772 "Proposals" [18]. An early draft of the "An Address to the Atheist, by P. Wheatley at the Age of 14 Years—1767—" [3].

Circulation of manuscript versions of this and other poems brought Wheatley to the attention of women beyond Boston. For example, among the Library Company of Philadelphia's undated "Mss. of Hannah Griffitts," on deposit at the Historical Society of Pennsylvania, is the "rough Copy" by the Philadelphia Quaker poet Hannah Griffitts (1727–1817) of Wheatley's "Atheism," entitled "On Atheism." Griffitts attributes it to "Africania." Griffitts's headnote suggests that she recorded the poem soon after it was written: "The following Lines are said to be Composed by a Native of Africa, about 15 years of age,—& who a few Years ago Could not Speak one word of English, she belong'd to John Wheatley of Boston."

3:9 Julian D. Mason, Jr., *The Poems of Phillis Wheatley* (Chapel Hill: University of North Carolina Press, 1989), 118, misreads "my" as "any."

3:11 "preterperfect": more than perfect.

4:44 "Minerva": goddess of wisdom, invention, martial prowess, and the arts.

4:45 "Pluto": god of the underworld.

4:53 "Pheobus" [*sic*]: Phoebus Apollo, god of the sun.

4:55 "Cynthia": Diana or Phoebe or Artemis, goddess of the moon.

[2a] "Atheism— Boston July 1769"

Holograph copy at Massachusetts Historical Society (Whitwell Autograph Collection). Not included in Wheatley's 1772 "Proposals" [18]. Despite its title, apparently an intermediate stage between [2] above and [3] below.

[3] "An Address to the Atheist, by P. Wheatley at the Age of 14 Years—1767"

Manuscript at the Massachusetts Historical Society (Robie-Sewall Family Papers). Included in Wheatley's 1772 "Proposals" [18]. "An Address to the Atheist, by P. Wheatley at the Age of 14 Years—1767—" is a more concise revision of the earlier draft entitled "Atheism" [2].

Wheatley employs the poetic convention of invoking the classical muse to open her poem, as well as the equally conventional assertion of poetic inadequacy, only to have the poem itself undermine both conventions. For a fourteen-year-old girl to try her hand at what was considered the most serious possible subject was an extraordinary assumption and expression of poetic authority. The poem's sophisticated combination of evidence from design with biblical authority to create an argument in support of theism is an impressive advance from the simple expression of faith found in her verses on the deaths of Oxenbridge and Sarah Thacher written only two years earlier [1].

Wheatley's unoriginal argument in "An Address" reveals her familiarity with orthodox Congregationalist Christian theology. She bases her argument on the belief that God is the author of two books, the book of nature and the book of revelation, which when "read," or interpreted, together correctly demonstrate the benevolence and omnipotence of the Christian God. Although Wheatley begins her poem by invoking the classical "Muse," and including a reference to the "Sol" worshipped by contemporaneous pagans, she concludes by carefully rejecting non-Christian gods. They are merely poetic ornaments, and the sun's circuit is significant only as part of a transcendent plan.

[4] "Deism"

Library Company of Philadelphia manuscript at the Historical Society of Pennsylvania (Pierre Eugène du Simitière Collection, Series X. Miscellaneous Papers from du Simitière [Scraps], 1740–83, Box 6/Folder 42). An early draft of "An Address to the Deist—1767" [cf. 5]. Not included in Wheatley's "Proposals" [18]. Unpublished.

8:23 "Who trod the wine press of Jehovahs wrath": cf. "I have trodden the winepress alone; and of the people *there was* none with me: for I will tread them in mine anger, and trample them in my fury; and their blood shall be sprinkled upon my garments, and I will stain all my raiment" (Isaiah 63:3, *King James Version*). Cf. [5], [29w].

[5] "An Address to the Deist—1767"

Manuscript at the Massachusetts Historical Society (Robie-Sewall Family Papers). Included in Wheatley's 1772 "Proposals" [18]. Unpublished. Cf. [4].

Wheatley's unpublished "Deism" and "An Address to the Deist—1767—," are at least as sophisticated as "An Address to the Atheist" [3]. Eighteenth-century deists generally believed in a discrete (unitary) rational God who was bound by the same laws of nature that applied to the world He had created. Deists were consequently dubious about the orthodox belief that the Bible was of supernatural origin. They also questioned biblical accounts of miraculous events, as well as the post-biblical doctrine formulated in the fourth century of the mystery of the Trinity of three consubstantial beings (Father, Son, and Holy Ghost) in one triune God. To an orthodox Trinitarian Calvinist, a deist was little better than an atheist, and orthodox Christians often equated them during the period. Hence, the theological position Wheatley embraces in "An Address to the Deist" was not extraordinary for her day. Extraordinary, however, is the rhetorical position Wheatley assumes in the poem in relation to the imaginary deist she addresses in it, as well as to the external reader of the poem. She significantly begins the poem, "Must Ethiopians be employ'd for you? | Much I rejoice if any good I do." The term "Ethiopians" does much more than simply reveal Wheatley's complexion, ethnicity, and probable status to her readers. By calling herself an Ethiopian rather than an African or a black in a religious poem she claims an identity that grants her biblical authority to speak to her readers. Wheatley surely expected her readers to recall that Moses had married an Ethiopian (Numbers 12:1), and that Psalm 68:31 predicts that "Ethiopia shall soon stretch out her hands unto God."

[6] "To the University of Cambridge, wrote in 1767—"

Manuscript at the American Antiquarian Society (MSS Misc. Boxes W Phillis Wheatley Poems [manuscript], 1767; 1769). Cf. variant [29i]. Included in Wheatley's 1772 "Proposals" [18].

Harvard College was frequently referred to simply as Cambridge because of its location near Boston. During the eighteenth and nineteenth centuries the enslaved condition of Africans in America was often likened to the Egyptian bondage of the ancient Hebrews. *Ethiop* or *Ethiopian* was a name frequently applied to anyone from Africa (cf. [5]).

Wheatley's "To the University of Cambridge, wrote in 1767—" is essentially a commencement address, in which she appropriates the persona of authority or power normally associated with men and her social superiors. Like a teacher to his students, or a minister to his flock, Wheatley counsels the young men of what was to become Harvard University, many of whom were being trained there to become ministers themselves.

Comparison of the initial verse paragraph in "To the University of Cambridge, wrote in 1767—," to the corresponding paragraph in the later "To the University of Cambridge, in New-England" published in *Poems on Various Subjects, Religious and Moral* shows how carefully and rapidly Wheatley improved her craft. The differences in versification, diction, concision, and specificity of metaphors are striking. Wheatley made significant theological changes between the manuscript and print versions. She revised line four of the former—"The sable Land of error's darkest night"—to read "The land of errors, and *Egyptian* gloom" in the published version. Wheatley's substitution of "*Egyptian* gloom" to refer to her spiritual condition in Africa associates her and her fellow Africans with God's chosen people, the Israelites, before their Exodus from Egypt. As anyone who has faith in an omnipotent, omniscient, and benevolent God must, Wheatley believes that the evil of enslavement that caused her exodus from Africa has to serve an ultimately positive purpose that may as yet be unknowable to humankind. Hence, she can say without irony, "Father of mercy, 'twas thy gracious hand | Brought me in safety from those dark abodes" (cf. 29k). Wheatley revised "Powerfull" in line six of "To the University of Cambridge, wrote in 1767—" to read "gracious" in line five of "To the University of Cambridge, in New-England" to emphasize the free and unmerited generosity of God, rather than His strength.

[7] "On Messrs. Hussey and Coffin."

As Mason (115) notes, this is the poem "On two friends, who were cast away" listed (and misdated) in Wheatley's 1772 "Proposals" [18].

Phillis Wheatley's first published work appeared in the 14–21 December 1767 issue of the *Newport Mercury*. The headnote for "On Messrs. Hussey and Coffin," addressed "To the Printer" of the *Newport Mercury*, identifies the occasion for the poem. Captain Coffin's schooner, with its cargo of whale-oil, was one of several vessels cast ashore during the most "terrible Gale" ever experienced by "the oldest Seamen" (*Boston News-Letter and New-England Chronicle*, 1 October 1767). "On Messrs Hussey and Coffin" was never again published after its appearance in the *Newport Mercury*. The poem's combination of Christian piety and classical allusions anticipates the themes and expression found in many of Wheatley's subsequent poems.

Wheatley's poem was probably published through Susanna Wheatley's support and contacts. Her most likely contact in Rhode Island was Sarah Haggar Wheaton Osborn (1714–96), a member of the First Congregationalist Church in Newport and instrumental in the evangelical Newport revival of 1766–7. She and Susanna Wheatley shared a mutual correspondent in the Mohegan Presbyterian evangelical minister Samson Occom (1732–92). Cf. [29e]. Osborn was inspired by Reverend Gilbert Tennent (1703–64), a Presbyterian evangelist, as well as by the Huntingdonian Methodist minister George Whitefield. Cf. [14].

Osborn helped to create a female prayer society that met weekly in her home from the 1740s until her death. She also held ecumenical meetings attended by a wide spectrum of society. More than three hundred people attended her meetings in July 1766. The number reached 525 by January 1767. Osborn played a major role in having Phillis Wheatley's future correspondent, Reverend Samuel Hopkins (1721–1803), installed as pastor of the First Congregationalist Church in Newport in 1770 (cf. [21], [38]). From the late 1750s Osborn ran a boarding school in her home that enrolled nearly seventy students, rich and poor, male and female, black and white. From 1766 an "Ethiopian Society," probably composed of free people of African descent, attended revival meetings at her house to sing, pray, read, and discuss religious issues. They were joined by as many as forty-two slaves, who attended with the permission of their masters.

11:3 "Boreas": the north wind.
12:7 "Eolus": Aeolus, king of the winds.
12:11 "Gulph": gulf, Cape Cod Bay.

[8] "America"

Library Company of Philadelphia manuscript at the Historical Society of Pennsylvania (Rush Family Papers, Series IV. Miscellaneous Documents, Box 14/ Folder 27). Included in Wheatley's 1772 "Proposals" [18]. Unpublished.

Wheatley responded to the growing tension between Britain and its colonies in several poems, only one of which was published during her lifetime. "America" is more subversive than her published work on the Stamp Act crisis and Britain's other efforts to tax the colonies. "America" is no doubt a draft version of "On America, 1768," listed in her 1772 "Proposals." "America" is a brief allegorical history of New England from its founding to the crisis of relations between "A certain lady" [i.e., Britannia] and her "only son" [i.e., America]. The poem calls for reconciliation between the mother and son before the child grows strong enough to overpower the parent. The invocation of "Liberty" in a work by an enslaved person of African descent, who identifies herself as such—"Thy Power, O Liberty, makes strong the weak | And (wond'rous instinct) Ethiopians speak" (ll. 5–6)—as well as her mention of "scourges" (l. 15) and "rebel" (l. 23), and her comment that "[America] weeps afresh to feel this Iron chain" (l. 31), introduce the subtext of slavery to the poem.

13:33 "Riecho": probably re-echo.
13:35 "Agenoria": In light of "Indolence" (line 34) and "Industry" (line 40), cf. *An Universal, Historical, Geographic, Chronological and Poetical Dictionary* (London, 1703), 2 vols.: "*Agenoria*, or *Agenora*, the Goddess of Industry, that makes Men *Active*"; Society of Gentlemen, *A New and Complete Dictionary of Arts and Sciences* (London, 1754), 1: 68: "AGENORIA, in mythology, the goddess of courage and industry, as Vacuna was of indolence."

[9] "To The King's Most Excellent Majesty on His Repealing the American Stamp Act"

Manuscript at the Historical Society of Pennsylvania (Simon Gratz Collection, Case 6, Folder 40). Included in Wheatley's 1772 "Proposals" as "On the King" [18]. Cf. variant [29j].

Like many colonists, Wheatley wanted to believe that by approving the repeal of the 1765 Stamp Act in 1766, George III (1738–1820) was expressing sympathy with colonial resistance to the principle of external taxation. "To the King's Most Excellent Majesty on His Repealing the American Stamp Act 1768" is a draft of "To the King's Most Excellent Majesty. 1768" [29j] in *Poems on Various Subjects, Religious and Moral*. Even more than the draft, the published version celebrates the King as a parental figure who has freed his children from the tyranny of

Parliament and the politicians in his ministry. Coming from an enslaved person of African descent, the last line is also a not-so-subtle reminder that not only taxed colonists should be set free.

Wheatley's argument and choice of imagery indicate that she was very familiar with contemporaneous political rhetoric. Despite evidence to the contrary, colonists clung to the belief that George III was their potential, if not their actual, ally against what they saw as threats by Parliament to the British constitution and its guarantees of freedom. Wheatley's reference to a familial relationship between Britain and America underscores the allegedly abnormal treatment America received.

14:5 "resent": to take revenge on.

[10] "To the Hon.ᵇˡᵉ Commodore Hood on his pardoning a deserter"

Library Company of Philadelphia manuscript at the Historical Society of Pennsylvania (Rush Family Papers, Series IV. Miscellaneous Documents, Box 14/ Folder 27).

Included in Wheatley's 1772 "Proposals" [18], dated 1769.

The *Boston Post-Boy & Advertiser* reported the occasion for Wheatley's poem on 5 December 1768, under the heading "Boston, December 2":

A few days ago a court martial was held on board his Majesty's ship Mermaid for the trial of some sailors for desertion; two were sentenced to be flogg'd from ship to ship, and another was condemned to be hanged[.] And last Friday being the Day appointed for his Execution, he was brought on Deck, and just going to be turn'd off, when a Pardon was read to him by Order of Commodore Hood.

Commodore Samuel Hood (1724–1816) was commander of the North American station, 1767–70.

[11] "On the Decease of the Rev'd Doctʳ Sewall"

Manuscript at the Dartmouth College Library (Rauner Ticknor 7669940.2). Sent "To the Revd. Mr. Jeremy Belknap In Dover New Hampshire." Given the general lack of punctuation, and the subsequent substantive revisions, the Dartmouth holograph is probably the earliest known version of this poem. Included in Wheatley's 1772 "Proposals" [18]. Cf. variants [11a], [11b], [29l].

Reverend Joseph Sewall (1688–1769) was the son of Samuel Sewall (1652–1730), Chief Justice of Massachusetts. Samuel Sewall was the author of *The Selling of Joseph* (Boston, 1700), one of the earliest American writings against the mistreatment of slaves. Joseph Sewall declined election to the presidency of Harvard College in 1726 in order to continue as pastor of the Congregationalist Old South Church, into which Phillis Wheatley was baptized in 1771. Sewall served in that capacity for fifty-six years. He died on 27 June 1769.

Spelling, including that of proper names—Sewall, Sewell—was not standardized in North America before the publication of Noah Webster's *American Dictionary of the English Language* in 1828.

[11a] "On the Decease of the rev'd Dr. Sewell—"

Manuscript in the Huntingdon Papers at the Cheshunt Foundation, Cambridge, United Kingdom (A3/1/29). Another manuscript version in the Huntingdon Papers, with slight differences in punctuation, lacks lines 36–7 of [11b].

[11b] "On the Death of the Rev'd D.ʳ Sewall. 1769—"

Manuscript at the American Antiquarian Society (MSS Misc. Boxes W Phillis Wheatley Poems [manuscript], 1767; 1769). Cf. [11], [11a].

[12] "On Friendship"

Manuscript at the Moorland-Spingarn Research Center, Howard University (Thomas Montgomery Gregory Papers Collection, Box 37-12/Folder 362). Included in Wheatley's 1772 "Proposals" [18], dated 1768. Unpublished.

20:1 "amicitia": Latin for friendship.
20:4 "Amor": Latin for love.

[13] "On the Death of Mʳ Snider Murder'd by Richardson"

Library Company of Philadelphia manuscript at the Historical Society of Pennsylvania (Pierre Eugène du Simitière Collection, Series X. Miscellaneous Papers from du Simitière [Scraps], 1740–83, Box 6/Folder 44). Included in Wheatley's 1772 "Proposals" [18], dated 1770. Unpublished.

The continuing unrest in Boston (cf. [8], [9]) led the British government in 1768 to send Royal Governor Francis Bernard (1712–79) the four thousand troops he requested to try to keep the peace. Their presence had the opposite effect because there were so many of them that the residents of Boston were forced to house them. The occupation appeared to confirm fears of a design to impose tyrannical rule on the colonies. The formation of the self-described "Sons of Liberty" and subsequent acts of resistance in turn appeared to confirm British fears of a colonial rebellion.

Boston merchant Theophilus Lillie (1730–76), saying that he would rather be governed by one tyrant than by many, refused to participate in the boycott of British goods. In response, some self-styled patriots erected an effigy of him in front of his store to warn others to avoid doing business with him. When Ebenezer Richardson (1722–83), a loyalist like Lillie, tried to remove the effigy on 22 February 1770, he was confronted by a rock-throwing crowd composed mainly of boys, who chased him back to his own house. Richardson fired randomly into the crowd from his window to keep them from breaking into his house. He killed ten-year-old Christopher Snider (1759–70), and wounded another. Only the intervention of British soldiers, who had heard the shots, saved Richardson from the crowd when they arrested him. The boy's funeral became a political event. Richardson was convicted of murder, but sentencing was delayed in expectation of a pardon from London, which came two years later.

Snider, sometimes spelled Seider (proper names were often spelled in various ways during the eighteenth century), was only about two years younger than Wheatley when she commemorated him as the "the first martyr for the [colonial] cause" (l. 2). Although Wheatley uses her poetic license to elevate young Snider to the status of a potential "Achilles" cut down "in his mid career" (l. 6), he may have simply been at the wrong place at the wrong time. Wheatley portrays Richardson as satanic, "The grand Usurpers bravely vaunted Heir" (l. 22). Speeches denouncing tyranny and calling for Richardson's execution accompanied the massive burial parade for the boy Wheatley calls "their young champion" (l. 10), and "this young martial genius" (l. 15). Wheatley considers Snider's death "In heavens eternal court...decreed" (l. 1) as part of God's providential design.

Snider's death would probably be far better known today had it not been quickly overshadowed by the Boston Massacre on 5 March 1770, when British soldiers killed five civilians, including Crispus Attucks (1723–70), "the first martyr for the cause" of African descent. The Boston Massacre was the subject of Wheatley's now-lost "On the Affray in King-Street, on the Evening of the 5th of March" advertised in her 1772 Proposals. Either Wheatley or her London publisher, or both, wisely chose to exclude from her 1773 *Poems* both "On the Affray" and the equally politically provocative "On the Death of Mr Snider Murder'd by Richardson."

William H. Robinson, *Phillis Wheatley and Her Writings* (New York: Garland, 1984), 455, attributes twelve lines of verse published in the *Boston Evening Post* on 12 March 1770 to Wheatley "because the style, sentiment, and vocabulary are very much like Phillis's, and may be part of" the lost poem. Antonio T. Bly, "Wheatley's 'On the Affray in King Street,'" *Explicator* 56:4 (Summer 1998), 177, asserts that "[t]he author of the anonymous lines is unquestionably Phillis Wheatley." The attribution to Wheatley of the lines, however, remains to be proven.

20:2 "martyr for the cause": cf. "a martyr in the Cause" [53].
20:6 "Achilles": the hero of Homer's *Iliad*.

[14] An Elegiac Poem, On the Death of that celebrated Divine, and eminent Servant of Jesus Christ, the late Reverend, and pious George Whitefield, Chaplain to the Right Honourable the Countess of Huntingdon, &c &c.

Broadside in the Library Company of Philadelphia. Included in Wheatley's 1772 "Proposals" [18]. Cf. [29m].

This is probably the version of the now-lost copy that Wheatley sent to the Countess of Huntingdon with [15]. Because the copy of the poem that Wheatley sent to the Countess with her cover letter is missing, we do not know whether it was a copy of the printed broadside or a manuscript copy.

Selina Hastings (1707–91), Countess of Huntingdon, was the most socially prominent Methodist leader in England. She was the correspondent, as well as patron, of many writers besides Wheatley, including the African Britons James Albert Ukawsaw Gronniosaw (*c.*1710–75), John Marrant (1755–91), and Olaudah Equiano (1745?–97). In 1748 the Countess chose the Reverend George Whitefield to be one of her personal chaplains. She promoted his brand of Calvinist Methodism, especially through the missionary associations known as the "Huntingdonian Connexion," conceived as mediating between the Church of England and the Dissenting sects.

Methodism, so-called because its adherents sought to methodize the principles and practice of Anglicanism by establishing a routine of personal devotion and charitable acts, was the evangelical reform movement within the Church of England. Whitefield, together with the Wesley brothers, Charles (1707–88) and John (1703–91), founded Methodism in the 1730s. Conservative Anglicans looked with suspicion on the "enthusiastic" Methodists, whom they considered potential Dissenting separatists from the Church. Methodist ministers tended to be more evangelical, energetic, and emotional in their style of preaching than most of their fellow Anglicans. Methodists often addressed audiences that were socially very inclusive, preaching outside of churches, as well as within them, to bring religion to the poor. Methodism was especially attractive during the eighteenth century to people of African descent. Except for the Huntingdonians, Methodists did not separate from the Church of England until after John Wesley's death. Forced by the Church of England in 1779 to register her chapels as Dissenting meeting-houses, the Countess and her Connexion left the Church of England in 1782.

The Countess sent members of her "Connexion" to America to proselytize. She maintained an extensive transatlantic correspondence with them, as well as with other evangelical Christians, including Susanna Wheatley. Whitefield visited Boston during his second (1739–41), sixth (1763–5), and last (1769–70) tours of America. Since Susanna Wheatley greatly admired Whitefield and corresponded with the Countess of Huntingdon, Whitefield likely stayed at the Wheatley residence when he was in Boston. Although Phillis was probably already familiar with Whitefield through his publications, she may have first seen him when he came to Boston in 1764. No known record survives, however, of Phillis Wheatley's having heard Whitefield preach at her Old South Church. During his seventh and last tour of North America, Whitefield preached in Philadelphia and New York before reaching Boston in August 1770. He preached there three times in Old South, as well as once in the Congregationalist New North Church, whose minister was Reverend Andrew Eliot (1718–78), one of the signers of the attestation that prefaces Wheatley's *Poems*. From Boston Whitefield proceeded farther north to Newbury-Port, Massachusetts, where he died on 30 September 1770. (*Massachusetts Spy*, 14–16, 25–8 August, 17 September 1770.)

Unlike the Wesleys, whose Arminian doctrine held that all who believed in Christ and repented of their sins could be saved, Whitefield preached the doctrine of John Calvin (1509–64), who taught that very few Christians were among the elect—predestined, or elected, by the grace of God to be saved. Everyone else was a reprobate, doomed to eternal damnation, despite their faith or acts of charity.

Grace could only be freely given by God, and could not be earned by the good works of professed believers. Whitefield's position was consistent with Article 17, the most Calvinistic of the Thirty-Nine Articles of the Church of England that loosely constituted its creed.

Wheatley's poem was one of two elegies about Whitefield advertised in the *Boston News-Letter* on 11 October 1770. The *Massachusetts Spy* also advertised Wheatley's poem as "this day published" on 11 October 1770. Many other elegies on Whitefield's death soon appeared. The speed with which Wheatley produced the elegy, as well as its content and quality, indicate the astounding progress she had made as a poet since the elegy on the Thachers, as well as how familiar she was with Whitefield's cultural significance as a religious and political figure. In just the eleven days immediately following Whitefield's death on 30 September 1770, Wheatley had written the poem and (presumably) her owners had arranged to have it printed and sold by Ezekiel Russell (1743–96), in Queen-Street, and John Boyles, in Marlboro-Street, for "7 Coppers." It was "Embellished with a Plate, representing the Posture, in which Mr. Whitefield lay, before and after his Interment at Newbury-Port."

On 12 November 1770, Henry Pelham (1749–1806) wrote from Boston to his older brother Charles Pelham in Newton, Massachusetts, about the composition of Wheatley's elegy: "I send you a new Specimen of the Abilitys of our Boston Poetess Phillis, which has undergone no Corrections what ever. Mr. [Joseph?] Green, who examen'd her Poem on the death of Mr. Whitfield before it went to the Press altered but one Word in the Whole, and that was the Word Stars instead of star [l. 25]." (*Letters and Papers of John Singleton Copley and Henry Pelham 1739–1776. Massachusetts Historical Society Collections*. Vol. 71 [Cambridge, MA: Riverside Press, 1914], 96–7.) "Mr. Green" may have been the Joseph Green who signed the "Attestation" appended to Wheatley's *Poems* in 1773 [29f].

Wheatley opens her elegy by acknowledging Whitefield's popularity, eloquence, and exemplary piety. Whitefield's beliefs and practices allowed Wheatley to represent him as a religious figure who transcended narrow sectarianism. Claiming the "whole world" as his parish, Whitefield preached to non-Anglican as well as Anglican congregations. (*The Works of the Rev. George Whitefield, M.A. Late of Pembroke College, Oxford, and Chaplain to the Rt. Hon. The Countess of Huntingdon, Containing All his Sermons and Tracts Which Have Been Already Published with a Selected Collection of Letters*, ed. John Gillies [London: Printed for Edward and Charles Dilly; and Messrs. Kincaid and Bell, at Edinburgh, 1771–2], 1: 105). Whitefield promoted an ecumenical ideal of a universal Christianity: "It is very remarkable, there are but two sorts of people mentioned in Scripture: it does not say the Baptists and Independents, nor the Methodists and Presbyterians, no[,] Jesus Christ divides the whole world into but two classes, sheep and goats." ("The Good Shepherd," in *Eighteen Sermons Preached by the Late Rev. George Whitefield* [London: Printed for and sold by Joseph Gurney, 1771], 434.) "Glow'd," "inflame," and "captivate" emphasize Whitefield's successful use of emotional appeals in his preaching.

Wheatley reflects the widespread conviction in the colonies that Whitefield was as concerned about the liberties of Americans as he was about their souls. There was ample reason for such conviction. As he was ending his visit in April 1764 to Portsmouth, New Hampshire, Whitefield warned two Congregationalist ministers, "I can't in conscience leave the town without acquainting you with a secret. My heart bleeds for *America*. O poor *New England*! There is a deep laid plot against both your civil and religious liberties. Your golden days are at an end. You have nothing but troubles before you. My information comes from the best authority in *Great Britain*. I was allowed to speak of the affair in general, but enjoined not to mention particulars." (Quoted in William Gordon, *The History of the Rise, Progress, and Establishment, of the Independence of the United States of America* [London: Printed for the author; and sold by Charles Dilly; and James Buckland, 1788], 4 vols., 1: 143–4; emphases in original.) According to Samuel Adams (1722–1803), Whitefield assured New Englanders that he would "serve our civil as well as religious Interests." (Samuel Adams, *Writings of Samuel Adams*, ed. Harry Alonzo Cushing [New York: G.P. Putnam's Sons, 1904–8], 4 vols., 1: 26.) Whitefield was as concerned about a reported attempt to impose an Anglican bishop on the American colonies as he was about British plans to tax them. Colonial politics made strange bedfellows: Whitefield and Congregationalist Reverend Charles Chauncy (1705–87), his theological antagonist since the 1740s, joined forces to oppose the plan to assign an Anglican bishop to America.

When the Stamp Act was repealed in 1766, Whitefield exclaimed, "Stamp Act repealed, Gloria Deo." (John Gillies, "Memoirs of the Life of the Reverend George Whitefield," in *Works*, 7: 248.) Just before leaving London for his final American tour, Whitefield preached against "the great mischiefs the poor pious people [of Boston] suffered lately through the town's being disturbed by the [British] soldiers." (Whitefield, *Eighteen Sermons*, 388.) And in the last letter that Whitefield wrote before his death he expressed his sympathy for the people of Massachusetts, whose charter the British government sought to retract: "Poor *New-England* is much to be pitied; *Boston* people most of all. How falsely misrepresented! What a mercy, that our *Christian charter* cannot be dissolved!" (Whitefield, *Works*, 3: 426; emphases in original.) Wheatley was not alone in depicting the late Whitefield as America's friend and defender. He also appears as such, for example, in the anonymously published *An Elegiac Poem Sacred to the Memory of the Rev. George Whitefield* (Boston: Isaiah Thomas, 1770), as well as in the *Massachusetts Gazette and the Boston Weekly News-Letter*, 4 October 1770. Wheatley represents Whitefield as a heroic transatlantic figure who resists alleged British attempts to impose tyranny on a proto-national American community.

Wheatley's vision of the capaciousness of an American community goes far beyond Whitefield's. Here, as elsewhere in her works, Wheatley employs ventriloquism to speak through the dead to give her viewpoint an authority that transcends the mundane. Wheatley's Whitefield addresses his message of salvation through Christ to two separate audiences in her poem: " 'my dear AMERICANS' " (l. 39), and "ye *Africans*" (l. 41). The ultimate source of Whitefield's prophecy in the poem to "ye Africans" that "You shall be sons, and kings, and priests to GOD" (l. 44) is Christ's promise to Christians in Revelation 1:6: "And [Jesus Christ] hath made us kings and priests unto God and his Father." Wheatley's phrasing of the prophecy suggests that she was familiar with Samuel Bourn, *Lectures to Children and Young People in a Catechetical Method, Consisting of Three Catechisms* (London, 1738). According to Bourn, human happiness is found by establishing "*New Relations* to God, as Sons, as Kings and Priests" (101).

Prominently identified in the poem's headnote as being of African descent, Wheatley consistently uses the first-person plural *we* to render people of both European and African descent equally American. Although Wheatley may never have read Whitefield's undated "A Prayer for a poor Negroe," in which he creates a contented slave, her writings through 1770 offer an interesting gloss on it. Wheatley shared some of the desires expressed by Whitefield's fictional "Negroe." But more significantly, by writing and publishing, Wheatley repeatedly refuses to join Whitefield's "Negroe," who prays, "Lord, keep the door of my lips, that I may not offend with my tongue." Her elegy effectively rejects Whitefield's endorsement of passive acceptance of slavery by the enslaved. Wheatley opens the closing paragraph of her eulogy on Whitefield with a direct address to Whitefield's patron, as if she is bidding for her patronage as well.

Wheatley's poem brought her intercolonial and transatlantic fame very soon after it first appeared on 11 October 1770. The *New-Hampshire Gazette, and Historical Chronicle* advertised the poem on 19 October 1770, recommending that "[t]his excellent Piece ought to be preserved…on Account of its being [written] by a Native of Africa, and yet would have done Honor to a Pope or Shakespere [*sic*]." Wheatley's elegy was republished before the end of the year with minor changes as a broadside in New York, Philadelphia, and Newport, Rhode Island, as well as four more times in Boston, with varying visual embellishments.

At a time when a voyage across the Atlantic normally took at least five weeks, the *Gazeteer and New Daily Advertiser* in London advertised a version of the elegy on 16 November 1770 as "An Ode of Verses, composed in America by a Negro Girl seventeen years of age, and sent over to a gentleman of character in London. Now made public for the benefit of a family that has lately been reduced by fire, near Shoreditch church." The deletion of Wheatley's dozen lines (45–56) that associate Whitefield with the Countess of Huntingdon, as well as the addition of two four-line stanzas and a six-line "Conclusion," appropriately renders this charitable appeal even more nondenominational than Wheatley's original. Wheatley's poem was also republished in London in 1771, appended to *Heaven the Residence of the Saints*, a funeral sermon for Whitefield by Reverend Ebenezer Pemberton (1705–77), minister of Boston's Congregationalist New Brick Church. Pemberton was among those who authenticated Wheatley's *Poems on Various Subjects, Religious and Moral* in "To the Publick" [29f].

Wheatley's eulogy expanded her community of women supporters beyond her American and English patrons to include her fellow Bostonian poet Jane Dunlap. In her *Poems Upon Several Sermons Preached by the Rev'd and Renowned George*

Whitefield While in Boston... A New Year's Gift (Boston, 1771), Dunlap styles herself "a Daughter of Liberty and Lover of Truth," who sees the publication of Wheatley's poem as an incentive for her own.

[15] Letter to the Countess of Huntingdon (25 October 1770)

Manuscript in the Huntingdon Papers at the Cheshunt Foundation, Cambridge, United Kingdom (A3/5/1). Cf. [14].

Wheatley sent this letter to the Countess of Huntingdon to accompany a non-extant copy of her poem on the death of Whitefield. Two weeks after Wheatley's elegy on Whitefield was advertised in the *Boston News-Letter* she sent her appeal to the Countess with a copy of her poem. Wheatley may have corresponded with the Countess earlier. Among the Countess of Huntingdon's papers is a manuscript copy of Wheatley's elegy on Reverend Joseph Sewall [11a], who had died in June 1769. Wheatley certainly knew that both her poem on Whitefield and her accompanying letter obviously contradicted her self-deprecating reference to herself in the latter as an "untutor'd African." She also knew that the significance of ending her letter "With great humility your Ladiship's most Obedient Humble Servant" was formulaic. Thomas Jefferson (1743–1826), for example, signed a letter that he sent in 1791 to Benjamin Banneker, a free man of African descent, "I am with great esteem, Sir, Your most obedient Humble Servant."

Although determining the amount of agency, or control, Wheatley exercised in the publication and distribution of her poems while she was a slave is impossible, they could never have been produced without her active cooperation. For an adolescent slave to conduct an apparently unsolicited correspondence with a noblewoman was indeed the act of "boldness" that Wheatley acknowledges in her letter to the Countess.

[16] To Mrs. Leonard, on the Death of her Husband.

Published in Boston as a broadside soon after the death of Dr. Thomas Leonard (1744–71) on 21 June 1771. Included in Wheatley's 1772 "Proposals" [18]. Cf. [29p].

Thankfull Hubbard Leonard (1745–72) was the daughter of Thomas Hubbard (1702–73) [cf. 26]. She had been married for less than nine months. Phillis knew the Hubbard family because they had been neighbors of the Wheatleys on King Street. Thankfull Hubbard Leonard's own death soon became the subject of Wheatley's *To the Hon'ble* Thomas Hubbard, *Esq.; On the Death of Mrs.* Thankfull Leonard. *Boston, January 2. 1773* [cf. 26].

[17] "On the Death of Dr. Samuel Marshall"

Manuscript at the Connecticut Historical Society (MS 09172, Phillis Wheatley poems). Included in Wheatley's 1772 "Proposals" [18]. Cf. variants [17a], [29hh].

Phillis may have known Susanna Wheatley's relative Samuel Marshall (1735–71) through his wife, the former Lucy Tyler, whom Phillis names in the poem, as well as through Susanna. Lucy Tyler Marshall and Phillis joined the Old South Church on the same day, 18 August 1771. Phillis's elegy appeared unsigned in the *Boston Evening-Post* on 7 October 1771. Marshall had died on 29 September, one week before the anniversary of his marriage in 1765. Marshall was a prominent physician who returned to Boston in 1764 from London, where he had studied medicine after graduating from Harvard, in 1754. His obituary in the *Boston Evening-Post* and the *Boston Post-Boy* on 30 September reports that he had been "suddenly seized with an Apoplectic Fit and died in a few minutes." He was "a very skillful Physician, Surgeon, and Man Midwife," possessed of "many social Virtues, and [an] agreeable, obliging Disposition," which "rendered him peculiarly endearing." To Phillis Wheatley he was "the universal freind."

25:13 "on Tyler's Soul": Lucy Tyler.
25:19 "Esculapius": Roman god of medicine, often said to be the son of Apollo.

[17a] On the Death of Doctor *Samuel Marshall.*

Published in the *Boston Evening-Post*, 14 October 1771.

[18] "Proposals for Printing by Subscription" (29 February 1772)

Published in the *Boston Censor*, 29 February, 14 March, 18 April 1772.

Wheatley had written so many poems by the beginning of 1772 that she and her owners confidently sought subscribers for a rather expensive book. They probably turned to Ezekiel Russell to produce the book because he had been one of the publishers of her elegy on the death of Whitefield in 1770 (cf. [15]). We do not know who wrote the "Proposals," but as one of the editors of Wheatley's writings observes, if she did not write it, "[c]ertainly she cooperated in [its] conception and contents." (Mason 35.) The *Boston Censor*'s readers were accustomed to seeing people of African descent mentioned in print, usually unnamed, in advertisements for selling them, in advertisements for runaway slaves, or in accounts of domestic and foreign resistance to slavery. But they must have been startled by the elaborate appeal published on Wheatley's behalf.

Wheatley and Ezekiel Russell, the most likely publisher of Wheatley's book if the public demonstrated sufficient interest in it, hoped to profit from the growing interest during the later eighteenth century in temporally, geographically, socially, and ethnically exotic origins of literary works. Examples include the Ossianic forgeries of ancient oral Gaelic epics (1762) of James Macpherson (1736–96), or the poems (1785) of the uneducated "Journeyman Shoemaker" John Bennet, of the milkwoman Ann Yearsley (*c.*1753–1806), published in 1785, and of the supposedly unlettered Scot Robert Burns (1759–96) published in 1786. References in the "Proposals" to Wheatley, "a Negro Girl," as having recently been "an uncultivated

Barbarian from *Africa*," who has written "POEMS, wrote at several times, and upon various occasions... from the strength of her own Genius" were clearly intended to appeal to this interest in exotic authors.

But works by women and anyone else whose status raised questions about whether they were capable of producing the promised work were also especially risky for a bookseller like Russell. He anticipated concern about the authenticity of Wheatley's poetry: "The Poems have been seen and read by the best judges, who think them well worthy of the Publick View; and upon critical examination, they find that the declared Author was capable of writing them." Similar attestations of authenticity also commonly prefaced contemporaneous works by improbable authors of European descent. Wheatley's "Proposals" is noteworthy, however, because it was only the second in what would soon become a tradition of having white commentators or editors attest to the authenticity of works by people of African descent. The first was *A Narrative of the Most Remarkable Particulars in the Life of James Albert Ukawsaw Gronniosaw, an African Prince, as Related by Himself*. Gronniosaw's as-told-to narrative, published in Bath at the end of 1772, includes a preface addressed "To the Reader" by the Countess of Huntingdon's cousin Walter Shirley (1725–86). Shirley, a clergyman, writer, collector and publisher of hymns, assures the reader that "This account of the Life and spiritual Experience of JAMES ALBERT was taken from his own Mouth." Like Wheatley, Gronniosaw corresponded with the Countess of Huntingdon.

ON THE DEATH OF THE REV. DR. *Sewell*, WHEN SICK, 1765—

Non-extant. Sewell recovered from his illness in 1765: cf. "On the Death of Reverend Dr. *Sewell*, do.—;" below.

ON VIRTUE, [17]66—

Cf. [29h].

ON TWO FRIENDS, WHO WERE CAST AWAY, D[ITT]O,—

Cf. [7]. Not included in the 1773 *Poems*.

TO THE UNIVERSITY OF CAMBRIDGE, 1767—

Cf. [6], [29i].

AN ADDRESS TO THE ATHEIST, DO.—

Cf. [2], [3]. Not included in the 1773 *Poems*.

AN ADDRESS TO THE DEIST, DO.—

Cf. [4]. Not included in the 1773 *Poems*.

ON AMERICA, 1768—

Cf. [8]. Not included in the 1773 *Poems*.

ON THE KING, DO.—

Cf. [9], [29j].

ON FRIENDSHIP, DO.—

Cf. [12]. Not included in the 1773 *Poems*.

THOUGHTS ON BEING BROUGHT FROM AFRICA TO AMERICA, DO.—

Cf. [29k].

ON THE NUPTIALS OF MR. *Spence* TO MISS *Hooper*, DO.—

Non-extant. The *Boston Chronicle*, 1–8 February 1768, announced: "Tuesday last, was married John Russel Spence Esq; of London merchant, to Miss Mary Hooper, only daughter of the late Rev. Doctor William Hooper of Trinity church in this place.— The ceremony was performed in church, which was crouded [*sic*] with spectators."

ON THE HON. COMMODORE HOOD,
ON HIS PARDONING A DESERTER, 1769—

Cf. [10].

ON THE DEATH OF REVEREND DR. *Sewell*, DO.—

Cf. [11], [11a], [11b], [29l].

ON THE DEATH OF MASTER *Seider*, WHO WAS KILLED
BY *Ebenezer Richardson*, 1770.—

Cf. [13]. Not included in the 1773 *Poems*.

ON THE DEATH OF THE REV. *George Whitefield*, DO.—

Cf. [15].

ON THE DEATH OF A YOUNG MISS, AGED 5 YEARS, DO.—

Cf. [29n].

ON THE ARRIVAL OF THE SHIPS OF WAR, AND LANDING
OF THE TROOPS. [UNDATED]—

Non-extant. The British troops landed in 1770 to try to quell the growing unrest in Boston.

ON THE AFFRAY IN KING-STREET, ON THE EVENING
OF THE 5TH OF MARCH. [UNDATED]—

Non-extant. The "Affray" was the so-called Boston Massacre on 5 March 1770, when British troops killed several protestors in Boston, including Crispus Attucks, a man of African descent.

ON THE DEATH OF A YOUNG GENTLEMAN. [UNDATED]—

Cf. [29o].

TO *Samuel Quincy*, ESQ; A PANEGYRICK. [UNDATED]—

Non-extant. Samuel Quincy (1735–89) was one of the prosecuting attorneys in the trial at the end of 1770 of the civilians and British soldiers accused of murder in the Boston Massacre.

TO A LADY ON HER COMING TO AMERICA
FOR HER HEALTH. [UNDATED]—

Cf. [29dd].

TO MRS. *Leonard*, ON THE DEATH OF HER HUSBAND. [UNDATED]—

Cf. [16], [29p].

TO MRS. BOYLSTON AND CHILDREN ON
THE DEATH OF HER SON AND THEIR BROTHER.
[UNDATED]—

Nicholas Boylston (1716–1771), prominent Boston merchant, died 18 August 1771. He was the son of Thomas (d. 1739) and Sarah Moorcock Boylston (d. 1774), and brother of Thomas (1721–1798), Rebecca (1727–1798), Mary (b. 1722). Nicholas Boylston's business partner, Joseph Green, signed the "Attestation" prefacing Wheatley's 1773 Poems.

Cf. [29ff].

TO A GENTLEMAN AND LADY ON THE DEATH OF THEIR SON,
AGED 9 MONTHS. [UNDATED]—

Apparently non-extant, though possibly a variant of "To Mr. and Mrs.—, on the Death of their Infant Son, By Phillis Wheatly [*sic*]" [Cf. 59].

TO A LADY ON HER REMARKABLE DELIVERANCE
IN A HURRICANE. [UNDATED]—

Cf. [29ee].

TO *James Sullivan*, ESQ; AND LADY ON THE DEATH
OF HER BROTHER AND SISTER, AND A CHILD *Avis*,
AGED 12 MONTHS. [UNDATED]—

Cf. [29gg].

Goliah [*SIC* FOR GOLIATH] OF GATH. [UNDATED]—

Cf. [29q].

ON THE DEATH OF DR. *Samuel* MARSHALL. [UNDATED]—

Cf. [17], [17a], [29hh].

[19] "*Recollection, to Miss A—M—, humbly inscribed by the Authoress.*"

Published in *The London Magazine: Or Gentleman's Monthly Intelligencer* for March 1772 (41: 134–5). Reprinted in the *Massachusetts Gazette and Post Boy and Advertiser*, 1 March 1773, the *Essex Gazette*, 16–23 March 1773, and (without the accompanying letters) the *Annual Register, or a View of the History, Politics, and Literature for the Year 1772* (London, 1773, and subsequent editions). Cf. variant [29x].

Mason (141) suggests that the "L" who submitted the poem and accompanying prose pieces may have been either Reverend John Lathrop (1740–1816) or his wife, Mary Wheatley Lathrop (1743–78), the daughter of Phillis Wheatley's owners. Mason (141) also believes that the dedicatee, "A.M.," may have been Abigail May, Phillis's fellow congregant in Boston's Old South Church.

Publication of the "Proposals" in the *Boston Censor* [18] was apparently part of a sophisticated transatlantic publicity campaign. The "Poetical Essays" section in the March 1772 issue of the prestigious *London Magazine: Or, Gentleman's Monthly Intelligencer* includes "Recollection," Wheatley's most belletristic, or literary, poem to date. Commissioned as a performance piece, it is clearly intended to demonstrate the aesthetic value of her poetry more overtly than she had tried to do in her earlier work. Besides reminding readers of Wheatley's elegy on Whitefield, "L" assures readers that Wheatley "discovers [reveals] a most surprising genius." Readers also learn from "L" that in the Wheatley household Phillis has the status of "a compleat sempstress," an occupation much more respectable and far less arduous than that of a charwoman or washerwoman. She is worthy of "being in company with some young ladies of family." The exchange serves the same function as the attestation in the "Proposals" in the *Boston Censor*.

"Recollection" is a striking departure from Wheatley's previously published works, all of which had been occasional pieces written in response to contemporaneous events, as "L" cleverly reminds readers. The initial invocation of "Mneme" (or Mnemosyne) as her muse, references to "Maro" (Virgil) and "Menellian strains," and the absence of an overtly Christian context all serve to assert the claim of the "vent'rous *Afric*" to a place in the secular poetic tradition derived from the classical examples of the ancient Greeks and Romans.

29:1 "Mneme": Identified in Samuel Boyse, *A New Pantheon: or, Fabulous History of the Heathen Gods, Heroes, Goddesses, &c...*(London, 1753; republished 1758, 1760?, 1771, 1772, &c.), as the muse of memory, a daughter of Jupiter and Mnemosyne.

29:11 "he pours": Wheatley misidentifies the goddess Mneme as male, an error she corrects in the 1773 *Poems* [29x].

29:14 "*Phoebe's* realm": Phoebe, also known as Artemis, goddess of the moon, and her twin brother, Phoebus Apollo, were children of Zeus and Leto (Latona).

30:28 "Menellian strains": This obscure reference is revised in the 1773 *Poems* to read "entertaining strains."

30:42 "round the central sun": The same phrase is found earlier in Moses Brown, *Poems on Various Subjects* (London, 1739), John Wesley, *A Collection of Moral and Sacred Poems from the Most Celebrated English Authors* (London, 1744), Mather Byles, *Poems on Several Occasions* (Boston, 1744), Thomas Marriott, *Female Conduct: Being an Essay on the Art of Pleasing. To Be Practiced by the Fair Sex, before, and after Marriage. A Poem, in Two Parts* (London, 1759), and Isaac Hawkins Browne, *A Poem on the Immortality of the Soul* (Cambridge, England, 1765), among others.

[20] Letter to John Thornton (21 April 1772)

Manuscript at National Records of Scotland, Edinburgh (GD26/13/663/2).

John Thornton (1720–90) was a wealthy English merchant and philanthropist, an evangelical Anglican supporter of the Countess of Huntingdon's missionary activities, and a member of her circle. The Reverend Samson Occom had been his guest during his 1766–8 fundraising visit to England. Thornton sent money to John and Susanna Wheatley for Indian missions, and they kept him informed of their progress. Phillis Wheatley had apparently initiated a correspondence with him to request his guidance in religious matters.

Phillis Wheatley mentions her recurrent illness, especially during the winter, several more times in her later correspondence: cf. [21], [23], [33], [34], [38], [40].

[21] Letter to Arbour Tanner (19 May 1772)

Manuscript at Haverford College (Quaker and Special Collections, Charles Roberts Autograph Collection, American Poets 110).

Phillis Wheatley's correspondent was African-born Obour (also spelled Abour and Arbour) Tanner (1750?–1835), in Newport, Rhode Island. Although we do not know whether Wheatley and Obour Tanner ever met in person, Wheatley's surviving correspondence reveals that they developed an increasingly affectionate relationship. Phillis and Obour were united in their Christian faith and their consequent belief that their enslavement was part of God's providential design. They may have been taken from Africa on the same vessel, but evidence supporting that possibility remains lacking. Obour apparently initiated their correspondence in late 1771 or early 1772. She was Wheatley's only known correspondent of African descent. She may have been about three years older than Phillis: Obour was baptized and admitted in the First Congregationalist Church in Newport on 10 July 1768 as Obour Tanner, euphemistically identified as the "servant of James Tanner." Assuming that Obour Tanner was baptized when she was thought to have been eighteen years old, as was the usual Congregationalist practice, she was probably born around 1750. She and Phillis may have met because of James Tanner's link with Boston: having been dismissed from "South Church" in Boston, he had been admitted to membership in the First Congregationalist Church in Newport on

5 March 1758. Reverend Samuel Hopkins married Obour Tanner to Barra (also spelled Barry) Collins in the First Congregationalist Church in Newport on 4 November 1790. Obour died in Newport on 21 June 1835.

I thank Bertram Lipincott III, librarian at the Newport Historical Society, Rhode Island, for his help in finding the records relating to Obour Tanner: First Congregational Church, Newport, Rhode Island, Church record book #832, page 27, #200; Church record book #832, page 17, #59; Church record book #832, page 61; Parish Records book 814, page 71.

"we . . . Righteous": cf. Numbers 23:10: "Let me die the death of the righteous, and let my last end be like his!"

[22] "To the Rev. M^r. Pitkin, on the Death of his Lady."

Manuscript at the Connecticut Historical Society (MS 09172, Phillis Wheatley poems). Subsequently published as a broadside [22a]. Cf. [29t].

Temperance Clap Pitkin (1732–72) died in childbirth on 19 May 1772. She was a daughter of Reverend Thomas Clap (1703–67), president of Yale College (1740–66), and the only sister of Mary Clap Wooster (1729–1807). Mary Wooster was the wife, and later widow, of David Wooster (1711–77), and one of Phillis Wheatley's correspondents (cf. [33], [53]). Reverend Timothy Pitkin (1727–1811), son of the Governor of Connecticut, William Pitkin (1694–1769), was a Congregationalist minister in Farmington, Connecticut, from 1752 to 1785. He was a wealthy classical scholar, long associated with Yale College, his alma mater. He was also a trustee of Dartmouth College (1769–73), and a supporter of Christian Indian ministers, including Samson Occom. A letter from Wheatley to Reverend Pitkin was to be included in her proposed, but never-published, second volume of writings (cf. [55]).

[22a] To the Rev. Mr. Pitkin, on the Death of his Lady.

Published 1772, dated 16 June 1772. The printer probably made the few differences from MS [22] in accidentals (capitalizations and corrected spelling).

[23] Letter to Arbour Tanner (19 July 1772)

Manuscript at the Massachusetts Historical Society (Hugh Upham Clark Collection).

William Whitwell (1714—95), a prosperous Boston merchant, was also a member of the Old South Church.

[24] "A Poem on the death of Charles Eliot aged 12 m^o. To M^r. S Eliot."

Manuscript in Houghton Library at Harvard University (Autograph File W: Phillis Wheatley, 1). Addressed and sent by Wheatley to Samuel Eliot (1739–1820), dated 1 September 1772, two days after his son, Charles Eliot (1771–2), died of measles on 30 August 1772. Cf. [29z].

Charles Eliot was the second of the two children of Samuel and Elizabeth Eliot who died as infants. Samuel Eliot wrote to Mrs. Harrison, a friend in London, on 30 September 1772 to tell her of the death of Charles:

Previous to the disorder which tore our darling from us, he appeared in better health and spirits in the more early period of his life. But the pleasing prospect was soon removed, the measles appeared upon him and he is no more! Pity us, Mrs. Harrison, for the hand of God hath touched us. Mrs. Eliot is bowed down with affliction.... You have, enclosed, a few lines wrote by Phillis Wheatley. A former production of hers I sent you some time ago. ([Anna Eliot Ticknor], *Samuel Eliot* (Boston, 1869), 47)

Samuel Eliot was a prominent Boston merchant, an amateur poet, and a member of the network of people surrounding Phillis Wheatley. He was the nephew of Reverend Andrew Eliot (1718–78), one of the dignitaries who endorsed Wheatley's 1773 *Poems* (cf. [29f]). One of Samuel Eliot's sisters married Jeremy Belknap, to whom Wheatley sent manuscript copies of her poems (cf. [1], [24b]). Samuel Eliot married his first wife, Elizabeth Barrell (d. 1783), in 1765. Elizabeth Barrell Eliot was the sister of William Barrell, a Philadelphia merchant. William Barrell was the brother-in-law of John Andrews (1743–1822), a Boston lawyer. Andrews wrote to Barrell on 22 September 1772:

Dear Will

...

The 3^d Instant I wrote you by the post, acquainting you with the death of little Charles [Eliot], Ruthy [Ruth Barrell Andrews (1749–1831), William Barrell's sister, and John Andrews's wife,] has inclosd you by this opp: a Poem by P. Wheatly [*sic*] addressd to ye Father on this melancholy occasion, wch I think is a masterly performance...Flowry Language...runs through ye whole...(Massachusetts Historical Society: Andrews-Eliot MS N-1774, #12)

[24a] A Poem on the Death of Charles Eliot, aged 12 Months

A very slightly revised manuscript version of [24], at the Massachusetts Historical Society (MS N-25, Phillis Wheatley Papers). Wheatley has written on the outside of the manuscript: "Poem | On the Death of Charles | Eliot | My Dear Polly | I take this opport | unity to write to | you—." "Polly," a nickname for Mary, is perhaps Mary Wheatley Lathrop, who had left the Wheatley household when she married Reverend John Lathrop in 1771.

[24b] A Poem on the death of Charles Eliot aged 12 months

A third, very slightly revised, Wheatley holograph, which belonged to Jeremy Belknap (cf. [1]). In Dartmouth College Rauner Special Collections Library (Rauner Ticknor 772501.1).

[25] Letter to the Earl of Dartmouth, 10 October 1772, including
"To the Right Honourable WILLIAM, Earl of Dartmouth,
His Majesty's Principal Secretary of State for North America,
&c. &c. &c."

Manuscript in the Staffordshire Records Office in Stafford, United Kingdom
(D(W)1778/I/ii/835). Cf. [29bb].

Wheatley wrote her poem to William Legge (1731–1801), 2nd Earl of Dartmouth,
in October 1772 at the suggestion of Thomas Wooldridge (d. 1795), an Englishman
whom Dartmouth had sent to America to assess the state of the colonies. Dartmouth
had been appointed Secretary of State for the Colonies, and President of the Board
of Trade and Foreign Plantations in August 1772, during the ministry of Lord
North (1732–92). He held the position until November 1775. Wheatley expresses
in her poem and its accompanying letter the hopes that she and many other
colonists invested in Dartmouth, hopes that would soon be disappointed.

Wooldridge included his own account of the poem's genesis when he forwarded
it to Dartmouth in November 1772:

While in Boston, I heard of a very Extraordinary female Slave, who had made
some verses on our mutually dear deceased Friend [Whitefield]; I visited her mistress, and found by conversing with the African, that she was no Imposter; I asked
if she could write on any Subject; she said Yes; we had heard of your Lordships
appointment; I gave her your name, which she was well acquainted with. She,
immediately, wrote a rough Copy of the inclosed Address & Letter, which I promised to convey or deliver. I was astonishd, and could hardly believe my own Eyes.
I was present while she wrote, and can attest that it is her own production; she
shewd me her Letter to Lady Huntington [*sic*], which, I dare say, Your Lordship
has seen; I send you an Account signed by her master of her Importation, Education
&c. they are all wrote in her own hand. (Earl of Dartmouth Papers, Staffordshire
Record Office, Stafford, United Kingdom)

The "Account" that Wooldridge mentions was actually dictated to Phillis by
Nathaniel, not John, Wheatley. It became the basis of the first two paragraphs of
the statement attributed to John Wheatley that prefaces Phillis's *Poems* published
in 1773 [29e]. Wooldridge's mention of Phillis's letter to Huntingdon refers to the
common practice of correspondents keeping copies of letters they sent.

41 "To ... Dartmouth," line 3: "genial": generative
47:42 "Heav'ns refulgent fane": heaven's splendid temple.

While Phillis Wheatley was en route to London, the *New-York Journal; or, The
General Advertiser* (New York, New York) devoted its "Poet's Corner" on 3 June
1773 to an untitled version of her poem to Dartmouth, as well as to a copy of her
10 October 1772 letter to him. This printed version of her poem, which lacks lines
thirteen and fourteen, differs somewhat from the manuscript in both accidentals
and substantives. A preface introduces the poem and letter:

We have had several Specimens of the poetical Genius of an African Negro Girl, belonging to Mr. Wheatley of Boston, in New England, who was Authoress of the following Epistle and Verses, addressed to Lord Dartmouth—They were written, we are told on the following Occasion, viz. A Gentleman who had seen several of the Pieces ascribed to her, thought them so much superior to her Situation, and Opportunities of Knowledge, that he doubted their being genuine—And in order to be satisfied, went to her Master's House, told his Doubts, and to remove them, desired that she would write something before him. She told him she was then busy and engaged for the Day, but if he would propose a Subject, and call in the Morning, she would endeavour to satisfy him. Accordingly, he gave for a Subject, The Earl of Dartmouth, and calling the next Morning, she wrote in his Presence, as follows.

My Lord,

The joyful Occasion which has given me this Confidence in addressing your Lordship in the inclos'd Piece, will I hope sufficiently apologize for this Freedom in an African, who, with the now happy America, exults with equal Transport, in the View of one of its greatest Advocates presiding with equal Tenderness of a fatherly Heart over that Department.

Nor can they, my Lord, be insensible of the Friendship so much exemplified in your Endeavours in their Behalf, during the late unhappy Disturbances.—I sincerely wish your Lordship all possible Success in your Undertakings, for the Interest of North America.—That the united Blessings of Heaven and Earth may attend you here; and that the endless Felicity of the invisible State in the Presence of the divine Benefactor, may be your Portion hereafter, is the hearty Desire of,

> My LORD,
> Your Lordship's
> Most obedient humble Servant,
> Phillis Wheatley

TO THE RIGHT HONL. WILLIAM LEGGE, EARL OF DARTMOUTH, HIS MAJESTY'S SECRETARY OF STATE FOR NORTH AMERICA &.c &.c &.c

> HAIL! happy Day! when Smiling like the Morn,
> Fair *Freedom* rose, New England to adorn:
> The Northern Clime beneath her genial Ray
> Beholds, exulting, thy paternal Sway;
> For, big with Hopes, her Race no longer mourns; 5
> Each Soul expands, every Bosom burns:
> While in thy Hand, with Pleasure, we behold,
> The silken Reins, and *Freedom's* charms unfold!
> Long lost to Realms beneath the Northern skies,
> She shines supreme; while hated *Faction* dies: 10
> Soon as appear'd the Triumph long desir'd,

Sick at the View, he languish'd and expir'd.
　　　　No more, of Grievance unredress'd complain,
Or injur'd Rights, or groan beneath the Chain,
Which wanton Tyranny, with lawless Hand,　　　　　　　　15
Made to enslave, O *Liberty*! thy Land.—
My Soul rekindles, at thy glorious Name,
Thy Beams, essential to the vital Flame.—
　　　　The Patriots' Breast, what Heavenly Virtue warms,
And adds new Lustre to his mental Charms!　　　　　　　　20
While in thy Speech, the Graces all combine,
Apollo's too, with Sons of Thunder join.
Then shall the Race of injur'd Freedom bless,
The Sire, the Friend, and Messenger of Peace.
　　　　While you, my Lord, read o'er the advent'rous Song　　25
And wonder, whence such daring Boldness sprung;
Whence flow my Wishes for the common Good,
By feeling Hearts alone best understood?
　　　　From native Clime, when seeming cruel Fate
Me snatch'd from Afric's fancy'd happy Seat,　　　　　　　30
Impetuous.—Ah! what bitter pangs molest,
What Sorrows labour'd in the Parent breast?
That more than Stone, ne'er Soft compassion mov'd,
Who from its Father seiz'd his much belov'd.
Such once my Case.—Thus I deplore the Day,　　　　　　　35
When Britons weep beneath Tyrannic Sway.
To thee our Thanks for Favours past are due;
To thee we still solicit for the new:
Since in thy Pow'r as in thy will before,
To sooth the Griefs which thou di[d]st then deplore;　　　40
　　　　May Heav'nly Grace, the sacred Sanction give,
To all thy Works, and thou for ever live;
Not only on the Wing of fleeting Fame,
(Immortal Honours Grace the Patriot's Name,)
Thee to conduct to Heaven's refulgent Fane;　　　　　　　45
May fiery Courses sweep the ethereal Plain,
There, like the Prophet, find the bright Abode,
Where dwells thy Sire, the Everlasting GOD.

[26] To the Hon'ble Thomas Hubbard, *Esq; On the Death of Mrs.*
Thankfull Leonard. *Boston, January 2. 1773.*

Broadside. John Wesley published a variant version in his *Arminian Magazine* in
London in February 1784. Cf. [29mm].

Thomas Hubbard was a wealthy and eminent merchant, who for many years had been a deacon of Old South Church and treasurer of Harvard College. Hubbard was paradoxically a slave-trading philanthropist: at his death he left a substantial sum to be distributed to the poor. He was one of the endorsers of Wheatley's 1773 *Poems*. See *To Mrs. Leonard, on the Death of her Husband* [16].

[27] "Proposals" (16 April 1773)

Published in the *Massachusetts Gazette and the Boston Weekly News-Letter*, 16 April 1773.

[28] To the Empire of America, Beneath the Western Hemisphere. Farewell to America. To Mrs. S.W.

Dated 7 May 1773, published in the *Massachusetts Gazette and Boston Post-Boy and Advertiser*, 10 May 1773, as Wheatley sailed to London with her master's son, Nathaniel Wheatley. Phillis Wheatley's departure was announced in the *Boston News-Letter* (6 May), the *Connecticut Journal and New-Haven Post-Boy* (7 May), the *Providence Gazette* (8 May), the *Boston Evening Post* (10 May), the *Boston Gazette* (10 May), the *Boston Post-Boy* (10 May), the *Connecticut Courant* (11 May), the *Boston News-Letter* (13 May), the *Pennsylvania Chronicle* (17 May), the *Pennsylvania Packet* (24 May), and the *New York Gazette and Weekly Post-Boy* (27 May).

Phillis Wheatley's "Farewell" was reprinted in the *Boston Evening Post* (10 May), the *Boston News-Letter* (13 May), the *Essex Gazette* (18 May), the *Pennsylvania Packet* (24 May), the *Connecticut Courant* (25 May), the *Massachusetts Spy* (27 May), and the *New Hampshire Gazette* (18 June). The *London Chronicle* (3 June) also published Wheatley's "Farewell," with a letter from Boston telling readers that the poem was addressed to Susanna Wheatley. Cf. [28a].

"S.W." is Susanna Wheatley. Phillis Wheatley's "Farewell" has been called "both a parting tribute to America and an expression of regret for the coming separation from Susannah Wheatley." (Mukhtar Ali Isani, "Wheatley's Departure for London and Her 'Farewel to America,'" *South Atlantic Bulletin* 42 [1979], 123–9: 123.) But the poem is prospective as well as retrospective. The second half of the poem looks ahead, anticipating the speaker's arrival in England and the restoration of her health. Wheatley's reference in line 49 to "Temptation" may be her artful way of reminding her owner that the trip to London would offer her the opportunity to seize her freedom there. In June 1772 William Murray (1705–93), 1st Earl of Mansfield, as Lord Chief Justice of the King's Bench, the highest common law court in England, ruled that a slave brought to England from the colonies could not legally be forced to return to the colonies as a slave. Mansfield's ruling was widely reported in the press throughout the colonies within months of his decision, well before Phillis Wheatley's trip. Consequently, Mansfield's decision made England a very dangerous place for any colonial slave owner to send her human property.

45:26 "liquid": clear.

[28a] Farewell to America.

A copy of [28] with a slightly revised title. Published in the *Massachusetts Gazette and Boston Weekly News Letter*, 13 May 1773, as well as in the *Pennsylvania Packet and the General Advertiser* (Philadelphia), 24 May 1773, with a headnote: "Boston, May 10, 1773, Saturday last Capt. Calef sailed for London, in whom went Passengers Mr. Nathaniel Wheatley, Merchant; also, Phillis, the extraordinary Negro Poet, Servant to Mr. John Wheatley."

The publication of "Farewell to America" in the *Nova-Scotia Gazette and Weekly Chronicle* (Halifax, Canada) on 1 June 1773 initiated the transatlantic marketing campaign for Wheatley's *Poems* while she was still en route to England. A slightly revised headnote prefaces the poem: "Saturday last sailed for London, the ship London, Capt. Calef, in [with] whom went Passengers Mr. Nath. Wheatley, Merchant; also, Phillis, Servant to Mr. John Wheatley, the extraordinary Negro POET." The poem is followed by a version of Wheatley's 16 May 1773 "Proposals for Printing in *London* by Subscription, a Volume of Poems " [27]. Now, however, the subscriptions are to be received not in Boston, but in London and Halifax: "Subscriptions received at A. Bell's, Bookseller, No. 8, *Aldgate-street*; by E. Johnson, *Ave-Mary-Lane*; S. Leacroft, *Charing-Cross*; C. Davis, *Sackville-Street, Piccadilly*; Mess. Richardson and Urquart, *Royal-Exchange*; at the Bar of the *New-England* Coffee-House, and by Robert Fletcher, Merchant in *Halifax*."

Robert Fletcher (fl. 1766–85), a printer and bookseller in Halifax, published the *Nova-Scotia Gazette* from 1766 to 1770, when Anthony Henry (1734–1800) merged it with his own *Nova Scotia Chronicle and Weekly Advertiser* to form the *Nova-Scotia Gazette and Weekly Chronicle*. Fletcher's link to Phillis Wheatley may have been via John Boyles, one of the two Boston booksellers of her elegy on George Whitefield in October 1770 (see [14]). After Fletcher decided in the summer of 1770 to concentrate on the success of his bookshop, the first in Halifax, he sold his printing press to Boyles.

The extraordinary two-column advertisement in the *Nova Scotia Gazette* includes an address "To the PUBLIC":

THE Book here proposed to the Public for Subscription, displays perhaps, one of the greatest instances of pure unassisted Genius, that the World ever produced. The Author was born in *Africa*; and left not that dark part of the habitable system, 'till she was eight Years old; she is now no more than Nineteen; and many of the Poems were penned before she arrived at near that Age.

They are wrote upon a variety of interesting subjects, and in a stile rather to have been expected from those, who to a native genius, have had the happiness of a liberal education, than from one born in the Wilds of *Africa*.

But the Publisher means not, in these Proposals, to deliver any peculiar Eulogiums on the present publication; he rather desires to submit the striking beauties of its contents to the unbiased candour [generosity] of the impartial Public.

This address, which would subsequently be incorporated into the first advertisement for the book itself in the *London Chronicle or Universal Evening Post* on 9 September 1773, was followed in the *Nova Scotia Gazette* by variants of Wheatley's "Copy of a Letter [29e]" "To the Publick [29f]" and "Attestation [29f]" that would appear in her *Poems* [29] in early September 1773.

Less than two weeks after Phillis reached London, the *London Chronicle* (1–3 July) published her "Farewell to America" with a prefatory note dated Boston, 10 May, intended to stimulate interest in her soon-to-be-published volume. The London reprint expands the dedication to "S.W." to "Susanna W." The advertisement assumes that English readers already knew of Phillis:

Sir,

You have no doubt heard of Phillis the extraordinary negro girl here [i.e., Boston], who has by her own application, unassisted by others, cultivated her natural talents for poetry in such a manner as to write several pieces which (all circumstances considered) have great merit. This girl, who is a servant to Mr. John Wheatley of this place, sailed last Saturday for London, under the protection of Mr. Nathaniel Wheatley; since which the following little piece of her's [*sic*] has been published.

[29] Poems on Various Subjects, Religious and Moral.

Copy in the Library of Congress Rare Book and Special Collections Division (PS883 .W5 1773). Cf. "Editorial Note" in the present edition.

Phillis Wheatley's publisher, Archibald Bell, registered Phillis Wheatley's *Poems* at Stationers' Hall in London on 10 September 1773 in accordance with a condition of the 1709 Act of Copyright. Edition 1 probably comprised three hundred copies.

Wheatley told David Wooster on 18 October 1773 that Captain Hall would be bringing copies of her book from England [33]. Edition 1 arrived at Boston on 28 November 1773 aboard the *Dartmouth*, commanded by Captain James Hall (*Boston Evening Post*, 29 November 1773), and owned by the Quaker Rotch family in New Bedford, Massachusetts, headed by Joseph Rotch, Sr. (1704–84). He was one of the co-owners of the *London Packet*, which John and Nathaniel Wheatley frequently used to conduct trade between Boston and London. (Joseph Rotch, Jr. (1743–73) is the subject of one of the poems in Phillis Wheatley's book [29ii].) The copies of Wheatley's books remained aboard the *Dartmouth* for several weeks because of other goods on it. An assembly at the Old South Church voted to force Francis Rotch (1750–1822) to send the *Dartmouth* back to London (*Essex Gazette*, 30 November–7 December 1773). Francis Rotch, another son of Joseph Rotch, Sr., was a neighbor of the Wheatleys on King Street. The *Dartmouth*'s "pernicious Article"—"114 Chests of the much talked-of East India Company's Tea"— made it one of the three ships involved in the Boston Tea Party on 16 December 1773.

[29a] [Frontispiece]

Archibald Bell included the extraordinary "elegant engraved like-ness of the Author" at the urging of the Countess of Huntingdon. The inserted engraved frontispiece exists in two states because it had to be reworked during the printing of Edition 1, resulting in a recut print used in later issues of Edition 1, and in all copies of Edition 2 of *Poems*. State A lacks diagonal crosshatching behind the subject on the right side; in State B the copper plate was reworked for a second impression to add diagonal crosshatching to strengthen lines behind the subject on the right side. The frontispiece in the Library of Congress copy is State A.

Eighteenth-century books rarely included frontispiece-portraits of the author, especially not during the author's lifetime. Frontispieces were in effect status claims for authors as well as for the readers who could afford them. Phillis Wheatley was "the first colonial American woman of any race to have her portrait printed alongside her writings." (Gwendolyn DuBois Shaw, " 'On Deathless Glories Fix Thine Ardent View': Scipio Moorhead, Phillis Wheatley, and the Mythic Origins of Anglo-African Portraiture in New England," in *Portraits of a People: Picturing African Americans in the Nineteenth Century*, ed. Gwendolyn DuBois Shaw [Seattle: University of Washington Press, 2006], 26–43: 27.) A frontispiece-portrait of an identifiable woman of Wheatley's status and ethnicity was unprecedented.

Wheatley's frontispiece was probably designed in Boston, perhaps by Scipio Moorhead, a black artist to whom Wheatley apparently addresses one of the poems in her book [2900]. Moorhead may have been the artist who advertised in the *Boston News-Letter* on 7 January 1773: "At Mr. McLeans', Watch-Maker, near the Town Hall, is a Negro man whose extraordinary Genius has been assisted by one of the best Masters in London; he takes Faces at the lowest Rates." The frontispiece was engraved and inserted in Wheatley's *Poems* in London.

The frontispiece identifies the sitter as "Phillis Wheatley Negro Servant to Mr. John Wheatley, of Boston." The term *servant* was commonly used as a euphemism for *slave* when referring to domestic workers of African descent in Britain and its colonies in North America. Humbly dressed as a servant or domestic slave, the contemplative poet looks upward, as if seeking inspiration for the pen she holds. By doing so, as with most eighteenth-century representations of slaves or servants, she also deferentially avoids looking directly at the viewer. Wheatley is significantly shown with a book, perhaps intended to represent her own *Poems* to express her extraordinary talents, the Bible to reflect her piety, or as a more general indication that she is an educated as well as an inspired "native genius."

A frontispiece depicting an eighteenth-century black woman capable of writing poetry had revolutionary implications. Several elements in the frontispiece, however, seem designed to limit those implications. The artistic quality of Wheatley's frontispiece is as modest as her social status. The frontispiece emphasizes Wheatley's African heritage and her inferior social status by containing her likeness within an oval whose framing words appear to restrict the extent of her gaze. The Countess of Huntingdon obviously had no objection to Susanna

Wheatley's request that Phillis be dressed plainly, as befit her humble rank. The dark string around Wheatley's neck subtly reminded viewers of her enslaved colonial status. Slaves in earlier paintings were conventionally depicted wearing collars "to signifie [*sic*] whose Servant" they were. (*Athenian Mercury*, 24 October 1693.) The string may also have been intended to recall the common association during the period of favored slaves and collared pets. Shaw (29) assesses the portrait of Wheatley more positively.

[29b] [Title-page]

The full title of Wheatley's book indicated to prospective buyers that it was her first. Famous as well as obscure poets before and after Wheatley used similar titles for their initial books: Elizabeth Singer Rowe, *Poems on Several Occasions. Written by Philomela* (London, 1696); Alexander Pope, *Poems on Several Occasions* (London, 1717); William Shenstone (1714–63), *Poems on Various Occasions* (London, 1737); Sarah Dixon (fl. 1716–45), *Poems on Several Occasions* (Canterbury, 1740); Nicolas James, *Poems on Several Occasions* (Truro, 1742); Laurence Whyte (1700?–1755?), *Original Poems on Various Subjects, Serious, Moral, and Diverting* (Dublin, 1742); Samuel Wesley (1691–1739), *Poems on Several Occasions* (Cambridge, England, 1744); Wheatley's friend Mather Byles's *Poems on Several Occasions* (Boston, 1744); Wheatley's London acquaintance Thomas Gibbons's *Poems on Several Occasions* (London, 1743); Elizabeth Carter (1717–1806), *Poems on Several Occasions* (London, 1762); George Roberts, *Juvenile Poems on Various Subjects* (Limerick, 1763); Edward Cobden (1684–1764), *Poems on Several Occasions* (London, 1748); Mary Leapor, *Poems on Several Occasions* (London, 1748); Mary [Whateley] Darwall, *Original Poems on Several Occasions* (London, 1764); *Poems on Several Occasions. By John Bennet, a Journeyman Shoemaker* (London, 1774); and Samuel Taylor Coleridge (1772–1834), *Poems on Various Subjects* (London, 1796).

Wheatley's title also signaled to her readers that the volume contained juvenilia—works composed before she became an adult—that critics should judge leniently. The title of Wheatley's book was appropriate for a work intended to display a new poet's talents in various forms of verse, including an aubade, hymns, elegies, translations, philosophical poems, tales, and epyllia (short epics). The range of forms allowed her to display both her familiarity with tradition and her unique contribution to it. She wrote all of the works in her *Poems on Various Subjects, Religious and Moral* while she was still an adolescent. Perhaps only Alexander Pope (1688–1744) and John Keats (1795–1821) would still be considered major poets if judged by their juvenilia alone.

[29c] Dedication.

The Countess of Huntingdon did not respond directly to Phillis Wheatley about her elegy on Whitefield's death. Wheatley knew through intermediaries, however, that the Countess had received her letter and poem. The Countess was so intrigued by

Wheatley's writings that she turned to members of her Connexion to try to learn more about the young poet's Christian piety, as well as her authenticity. Richard Cary (1717–90), who lived in Charlestown, Massachusetts, reported to the Countess on 25 May 1772 that "The Negro Girl of Mrs Wheatley's, by her Virtuous Behaviour and Conversation in Life, gives Reason to believe, she's a Subject of Divine Grace—remarkable for her Piety, of an extraordinary Genius, and in full Communion with one of the Churches, the Family, & Girl, was affected at the kind enquiry Your Ladiship made after her." (Cheshunt Foundation, Westminster College, Cambridge, United Kingdom: A3/5/6.) Bernard Page, another of the Countess's American correspondents, soon corroborated Cary's account. On 19 March 1773, he wrote her,

I have dined at Mr Wheatley's and seen Phillis; whose Presence and Conversation demonstrate the written Performances, with her Signature, to be hers. M^r & Mrs Wheatley's due respects, together with this desire, wait on your Ladyship, That if you'll honor them with any of the itinerant Ministers taking up their abode at their house when in Boston, every thing to such, shall be equally agreeable with the most desirable home & further commissioned me to add That they beg an interest in your Ladyship's Prayers at the Throne of Grace. Mrs Wheatley I verily believe is a real Child of God and a better house in Boston, in all other respects, a Gospel Minister can't desire.

Phillis heartily desires, That her Duty together with her Request, whether Mr Whitefield's Elegy hath been duly received, might be humbly presented to your Ladyship.

…

Since I wrote thus far, I have again seen Phillis, who showed me a letter from a Minister to her and her Answer to the same. And I myself saw her write several lines and then took the opportunity to watch her narrowly; by which, I found she wrote a good & expeditious hand. She frequently made use of a quarto Dictionary: and well she deserves the use thereof: for I'll delineate her in few words: Her aspect, humble serene & graceful; her Thoughts, luminous & sepulchral, ethereal & evangelical and her Performances most excellent, yea almost inimitable. A WONDER of the Age indeed! (Cheshunt Foundation, Westminster College, Cambridge, United Kingdom: A3/5/17)

Shortly after Page had written to the Countess, Susanna Wheatley informed the Mohegan minister Samson Occom that the process of finding a publisher and patron in London had already been set in motion. Robert Calef sailed from Boston for London on 15 November 1772, arriving at the mouth of the River Thames on 17 December. (*Massachusetts Gazette, and the Boston Post Boy and Advertiser*, 16 November 1772; *London Chronicle*, 17 December 1772.)

On 29 March 1773 Susanna Wheatley sent Occom a copy of a 5 January letter she had received from Captain Calef, who, if the date of his letter is correct, had probably brought a copy of Phillis's manuscript to England with him on his previous voyage. (He had left Boston in early May 1772, reached London in mid-August, and returned to Boston in early October.)

Calef acted as Phillis Wheatley's literary agent in England. He enlisted Archibald Bell to publish her book if a patron could be found. Bell's bookshop was located in the City of London near the subsequently destroyed Saracens Head Inn, close to the eighteenth-century intersection of Whitechapel Street and Poor Jewry Lane (the present-day intersection of Aldgate High Street and Jewry Street). Although Bell was a relatively minor London printer, bookseller, and publisher, he was an appropriate choice to approach the Countess of Huntingdon. Bell specialized in the kind of evangelical religious works that appealed to her. For example, in 1771 he published William Mason's *The Best Improvement of the Much Lamented Death of that Eminent and Faithful Minister of the Gospel, The Rev^d Mr. George Whitefield, Chaplain to the Countess of Huntingdon.* Bell includes advertisements for other religious works on the last page of his edition of Wheatley's *Poems* in 1773: *The Memoirs of Miss Williams. A History Founded on Facts. In Two Volumes. By A.B.*, as well as *The Church-Member's Directory, or Every Christian's Companion.*

Susanna told Occom that Bell's mission as a go-between to gain Phillis her patron had been successful. Calef informed Susanna,

Mr Bell (the printer) Acquaints me that about 5 weeks ago he waited upon the Countess of Huntingdon with the Poems, who was greatly pleas'd with them, and pray'd him to Read them, and often would break in upon him and say, "is not this, or that, very fine! do read another," and then expressd herself, She found her heart to knit with her and Questiond him much, whether She was real without a deception? He then Convinc'd her by bringing my Name [Calef] in question. She is expected in Town in a Short time when we are both to wait upon her. I had like to forget to mention to you She is fond of having the Book dedicated to her; but one thing She desir'd which She said She hardly tho't would be denied her, that was to have Phillis' picture in the frontispiece. So that, if you can would get it done it can be Engrav'd here. I do imagine it can be Easily done, and think would contribute greatly to the Sale of the Book. I am impatient to hear what the Old Countess Says upon the Occasion, & shall take the Earliest Opp^y of waiting upon her when She comes to Town. (Connecticut Historical Society: Samson Occom Papers)

Phillis Wheatley was well aware of how useful a distinguished patron could be for a new author. She wrote to the Countess of Huntingdon on 27 June 1773, "I conclude with thanking your Ladyship for permitting the Dedication of my Poems to you; and am not insensible, that, under the patronage of your Ladyship, not more eminent in the Station of Life than in your exemplary Piety and Virtue, my feeble efforts will be Shielded from the Severe trials of unpitying Criticism and, being encourage'd by your Ladyship's Indulgence, I the more freely resign to the world these Juvenile productions" [30].

[29d] Preface.

New authors often disingenuously denied writing for publication. Equally disingenuous is the conventional claim that "[t]he following Poems were written originally for the Amusement of the Author, as they were the Products of her leisure Moments." Authors also frequently claimed that they agreed to allow their work to be published only at the urging of friends. Ample evidence demonstrates that Wheatley produced poems on demand, that she carefully revised her writings, and that several of the works included in *Poems* had been previously published.

[29e] The following is a Copy of a Letter sent by the
Author's Master to the Publisher.

The papers of Lord Dartmouth in the Staffordshire Record Office in Stafford, United Kingdom, include a one-paragraph draft in Phillis Wheatley's hand of this letter, dated 12 October 1772. The last sentence of the draft reads "Mistress," rather than "Master." Nathaniel Wheatley, rather than his father, John, dictated it to Phillis. The term *master* was used during the eighteenth century to mean *owner*, as well as *employer*.

The 1765 letter to Reverend Samson Occom has apparently not survived. He was a Native American member of the Mohegan people in Connecticut. He converted to Christianity at the age of seventeen during the Great Awakening. Three years later he entered a school founded by Congregationalist minister Eleazar Wheelock (1711–79) in Lebanon, Connecticut, to learn English and Christian theology. Phillis Wheatley may have first met Occom during Whitefield's visit to Boston in 1764. Whitefield had invited Occom to join him on his New England preaching tour. Occom subsequently corresponded with both Phillis and Susanna Wheatley, and he often stayed with the Wheatleys when he visited Boston. Occom and Presbyterian Reverend Nathaniel Whitaker (1732–95) of Norwich, Connecticut, began a nearly three-year-long fundraising tour of England and Scotland in 1766 to raise money for Wheelock's Indian Charity School in Lebanon, Connecticut, created to train Native American missionaries.

The date of the now-missing letter to Occom may be incorrect because he and Whitaker did not reach England until 3 February 1766. Occom delivered more than three hundred sermons during their stay. He was treated as a celebrity. He met the Earl of Dartmouth, the Countess of Huntingdon, and even King George III (1738–1820). People of many religious persuasions welcomed him. For example, on 26 February 1766 Occom and Whitaker "went to See Dr. [Thomas] Gibbons [1720–85] an Independent Minister, [who] received us kindly and promised to assist us according to his Influence, in our Great Business." (Joanna Brooks, ed., *The Collected Writings of Samson Occom, Mohegan* [New York: Oxford University Press, 2006], 269.) Occom also spent time in London as a sightseer, visiting the Tower of London, Parliament, and Westminster Abbey, among many other attractions. Occom and Whitaker's 1766–8 tour was so successful that they raised the astounding sum of £11,000, enabling Wheelock to move his school to Hanover, New Hampshire, and founded Dartmouth College in 1769. Occom suggested to Susanna Wheatley on 5 March 1771 that she send Phillis to Africa "as a Female Preacher to her kindred." (Brooks, ed., *The Collected Writings of Samson Occom*, 97.) Only part of one letter from Phillis Wheatley to Occom survives. Cf. [39].

Occom was also an author and occasional bookseller. His best-known published works are *A Sermon Preached at the Execution of Moses Paul, an Indian* (New Haven, 1772), and *A Choice Collection of Hymns and Sacred Songs* (New London, 1774). His most famous work today is his unpublished "Autobiographical Narrative" composed in 1768. An advertisement in the *Connecticut Gazette; and the Universal Intelligencer* (New London, Connecticut), 17 June 1774 for Edition 2 of Wheatley's *Poems* notes that "*A few of the above are likewise to be be* [*sic*] *sold by* SAMSON OCCOM."

The sentence, "She has a great Inclination to learn the Latin Tongue, and has made some Progress in it" was added between the 12 October 1772 date of the draft of the "Copy of a Letter" and the 14 November 1772 date in *Poems*. The question of how much "Progress" Wheatley had made in the study of Latin before the publication of *Poems* is vexed. The only other known affirmation of Wheatley's knowledge of Latin comes from one of her correspondents, John Thornton, with whom she stayed in London for about a week in 1773. A year later Thornton told a friend that Wheatley "understands Latin," though whether he is speaking from personal observation rather than merely recalling the comment in the "Copy of a Letter" is unclear. Also unclear is what precisely Thornton means by "understands." (John Thornton to Reverend William Richardson, 2 June 1774 [Cambridge University Library: Thornton Family Papers, GB 012 MS. Add. 7826].)

Phillis Wheatley's Latin instructor in Boston may have been Lewis Delile, who had been educated in France at the University of Bordeaux. Delile migrated from Hispaniola (modern-day Haiti and the Dominican Republic) to New England in 1771 at the age of twenty-three, settling first in Newport, Rhode Island, where he advertised himself as a teacher of French, Latin, and fencing (*Newport Mercury*, 18 November 1771). Delile taught both male and female students in his school, and also offered to teach students in their homes. By 30 March 1772 he had moved to Boston and opened his school on King Street, where the Wheatley family lived. He remained there until after Phillis Wheatley left on 8 May 1773 for London.

Delile returned briefly to Newport (August 1773–February 1774) before coming back to Boston to teach Latin and French. By 1774 he had "for these two Years past…taught in Boston, Cambridge, Providence, and Newport" (*Massachusetts Gazette*, 24 February 1774). Delile quickly seized the opportunity to associate his new Boston academy with the publicity surrounding the recent arrival from London of Phillis Wheatley's *Poems*. He closes his announcement of his new academy by celebrating what Wheatley has achieved, despite lacking the advantages of the classical Greek poets Pindar and Sappho:

Four Lines in Latin Verse to be put under the Frontispiece of PHILLIS's Performances, by Benevolence for the Poet, and Regard for the Subscribers.

> *Pyndarum* formant studium, labor, arsque poetam;
>   Pro *sapphone*, puer carmina fecit amor;
> Divitiae, tempus, regio; illis cuncta faverunt;
>   *Phillidis* ingenium numina sola creant.

[Study, labor, and skill form the poet Pindar;
The boy Cupid made songs for Sappho;
Wealth, opportunity, country; all these favored them;
Only divinity creates the genius of Phillis.] [my translation]

                                        Boston, 24 February 1774.

Wheatley's surviving poetry and prose writings suggest that she probably had at most only "small Latin and less Greek." All of Wheatley's classical allusions were available in English in contemporaneous mythographies, such as the anonymously published two-volume *An Universal, Historical, Geographic, Chronological and Poetical Dictionary* (London, 1703); the translation of Antoine Banier's four-volume *The Mythology and Fables of the Ancients, Explain'd from History* (London, 1739–40); Samuel Boyse, *A New Pantheon: or, Fabulous History of the Heathen Gods, Heroes, Goddesses, &c.*... (London, 1753; republished 1758, 1760?, 1771, 1772); and the four-volume *A New and Complete Dictionary of Arts and Sciences* (London, 1754), published by a "Society of Gentlemen."

[29f] To the Publick.

Archibald Bell also used the address "To the Publick" that prefaces Wheatley's *Poems* in his London newspaper advertisements for her book during September 1773. The book added the attestation of Boston worthies. The Honourable ("The Hon.") names on the list were members of the governing council of the colony of Massachusetts, followed by the gentlemen ("Esq;"), ministers who were Doctors of Divinity ("D.D."), and other clergymen. In retrospect, the signers seem to be an improbable combination of religious denominations, political positions, and views on slavery. But in 1772 those categories had not yet become as divisive as they soon would be. Many of the signers were related to each other by blood or marriage. Henry Louis Gates, Jr., imagines how an oral examination of Wheatley to determine whether she was capable of writing the poems might have been conducted. Rather than considering Phillis Wheatley's "examination" to have been an actual event, Gates, *The Trials*, conceives it as an allegorical trial symbolizing the practice of requiring white authentication of black authorship. (Henry Louis Gates, Jr., *The Trials of Phillis Wheatley: America's First Black Poet and Her Encounters with the Founding Fathers* [New York: Basic Books, 2003].) But besides being very unlikely, such an examination would have been unnecessary. Most of the men named in the "Attestation" had demonstrable direct as well as indirect ties to Phillis Wheatley herself. They already had ample evidence of her abilities. By 1773 many of them were also either the recipients, addressees, or subjects of her writings. Phillis Wheatley was the nexus linking these disparate men to each other.

The "Attestation" includes the politically and socially most powerful and eminent men in the colony. Thomas Hutchinson (1711–80) was Governor of Massachusetts from 1771 to 1774, when he fled to England in the face of rising colonial opposition. Lieutenant-Governor Andrew Oliver (1706–74) was Hutchinson's brother-in-law. Wheatley wrote an elegy dated 24 March 1773 on the death of Oliver's wife that was first published in her *Poems* [29pp]. She had also earlier written poems on the deaths of Thomas Hubbard's son-in-law and daughter [16], [26]. John Erving (1728–1816) was a prominent Boston merchant, whose daughter married James Bowdoin (1726–90), a politician and statesman (he became Governor of Massachusetts in 1785, and Bowdoin College would be named after him). Bowdoin was probably the author of "A REBUS. By I.B." [29rr], the only poem by another author that Wheatley includes in her *Poems*. Wheatley would later address her unpublished "On the Capture of General Lee" to Bowdoin [51]. Bowdoin's sister was married to James Pitts (1710–76). Joseph Green (1705?–1780) was a merchant (distiller), as well as a poet who owned one of the largest personal libraries in Boston. He may have been the "Mr. Green" who reportedly vetted Wheatley's elegy on Whitefield before it was published in 1770 [14]. Harrison Gray (1711?–1794), an important merchant, was actively opposed to slavery. John Hancock (1736–93), another important merchant, and one of Boston's major slave owners, is most famous for his signature on the *Declaration of Independence*. Richard Cary (1717–90) wrote letters praising Phillis Wheatley to the Countess of Huntingdon on 25 May 1772, 3 April, and 3 May 1773. Wheatley carried a letter from him to the Countess on her trip to England.

The most popular and influential clergymen representing a range of denominations in Boston also signed the "Attestation." Charles Chauncy, the minister of the First Unitarian Church and a writer on religious subjects, opposed the emotional style of Whitefield's preaching. Chauncy had given Wheatley a copy of Reverend Dr. Thomas Amory's *Daily Devotion Assisted and Recommended, in Four Sermons* in October 1772 [29jj]. Ebenezer Pemberton was minister of the Congregationalist New Brick Church in the North End. When he published his sermon in London in 1771 on the death of Whitefield, Pemberton appended to it Wheatley's previously published elegy. Andrew Eliot (1718–78), minister of the Congregationalist New North Church, was an outspoken opponent of slavery. John Moorhead (1703–73), minister of the Federal Street Presbyterian Church, was either the owner or employer of Scipio Moorhead [29oo]. John Moorhead's wife, Sarah (1712–74), a well-known Boston art teacher, may have instructed Scipio Moorhead. Wheatley would publish an elegy addressed to Reverend Moorhead's daughter on the death of her father in December 1773 [cf. 36]. Samuel Cooper (1725–83) had baptized Wheatley in 1771. She published an elegy on his death in 1784 [56]. Reverend Samuel Mather (1706–85), the minister of the Tenth Congregationalist Church, was the son of Reverend Cotton Mather (1663–1728), the son-in-law of Governor Hutchinson, and the cousin of Reverend Mather Byles (1707–88). Byles (1707–88), a Congregationalist minister, was the nephew of Cotton Mather. Byles owned a very significant colonial library of more than three thousand volumes, and was well known as a wit and poet. He published *Poems on Several Occasions. By Mr. Byles* in Boston in 1744, but despite the similarity in titles, his *Poems* and Wheatley's volume have little distinctive in common in terms of content, arrangement, versification, and quality.

[29g] To Maecenas.

Not included in the 1772 "Proposals" [18]. Probably composed between April and June 1773.

Wheatley follows the classical tradition of opening her collected works with a poem addressed to a patron. By appropriately acknowledging the patron's support, Wheatley loosely imitates works by the Roman poets Horace (65–8 BCE) and Virgil (70–19 BCE). Horace begins his *Odes, Epodes, Satires,* and *Epistles* with poems addressed to Maecenas (d. 8 BCE), an extremely wealthy and politically powerful friend and patron. Virgil also dedicates his *Georgics* to Maecenas. By the eighteenth century, Maecenas had long been the archetype of the patron of poets. Although both John Wheatley and Mather Byles have been suggested as Wheatley's "Maecenas," there is no evidence that either man sponsored the publication of her *Poems*.

The reference to "*Thames*" in line 48 clearly suggests that the patron addressed is English. An appropriate and likely candidate for Wheatley's "Maecenas" is the Countess of Huntingdon, to whom Wheatley dedicates her volume. "Maecenas" is explicitly gendered male only in the poem's concluding stanza, when the poem's speaker addresses him as "great Sir," and solicits "paternal rays" of protection. The closing request that "Maecenas" "defend my lays" echoes the hope that Wheatley expresses in her 27 June 1773 letter to the Countess that through her patronage "my feeble efforts will be shielded from the severe trials of unpitying Criticism" [30]. As an aristocratic widow, Huntingdon had virtually all the authority and power of a man. With no classical models of female patrons available to her, Wheatley's decision to address the Countess in the guise of a male would be understandable, and a fitting way for her to celebrate her relationship with Huntingdon.

Like most eighteenth-century writers lacking a formal education, Wheatley most probably knew the second-century BCE Greek epic poems the *Iliad* and *Odyssey*, attributed to Homer, through the translations of Alexander Pope, and the *Aeneid*, a Latin epic poem by Virgil, through the translation by John Dryden (1631–1700). "To Maecenas" enables Wheatley to claim a place in the Western literary tradition, which, as she notes, has always included Africans. The position of "To Maecenas" in *Poems*, as well as its content, phrasing, and allusions, are all designed to demonstrate that Wheatley is familiar with the tradition, and to alert her readers that she intends to appropriate that tradition.

Wheatley's note that the classical Roman playwright Terence (195/185–159 BCE) had been born in Africa implies that he was of sub-Saharan birth. Doing so allows her to implicitly draw further parallels between his life and hers. Although Terence's ethnonym, Afer, indicates that he had been born in Africa, his birthplace was probably in North Africa, most likely in the area of either modern-day Tunisia or Libya. Terence was brought as a slave to Rome, where his owner had him educated and was so impressed by his talents that he set him free. The speaker in Wheatley's poem challenges the assumption that "partial [i.e., biased] grace" granted poetic inspiration to Terence "alone of *Afric*'s sable race."

Wheatley's invocation of her African predecessor marks a turning point in the poem. Humility in the face of the epic achievements of Homer and Virgil had earlier rendered the speaker mute. The precedent set by the African Terence inspires the African speaker in "To Maecenas" to "snatch a laurel" (l. 46) as well from her own eminent patron.

52–3:1-6 "beneath the myrtle shade": may echo the phrase "underneath a Myrtle Shade" in the introductory ode, "To Maecenas," in the frequently reprinted translation of the works of Horace: *The Odes, Satyrs, and Epistles of Horace. Done into English by Mr.* [Thomas] *Creech* (London, 1684; reprinted 1711, 1720, 1730, &c.). Citing several sources who report that Maecenas composed poems "seated beneath the cool shades of his green spreading trees" (54), Henri Richer (1685–1748) notes in *The Life of Maecenas: with Critical and Historical Notes. Written in French by M. Richer, Translated by R[alph] Schomberg, M.D.* (London: 1748, 2nd ed. 1766), 51: "MAECENAS not only protected the literati, he was himself a man of great learning, and a judicious writer, both in prose and in verse."

53:7 *"Homer"*: Wheatley appears to acknowledge the advice that Pope gives to aspiring poets in *An Essay on Criticism* (London, 1711):

> *You* then whose Judgment the right Course wou'd steer,
> Know well each ANCIENT'S proper *Character*,
> …
>
> Be *Homer*'s Works your *Study*, and *Delight*,
> Read them by Day, and meditate by Night,
> …
>
> And let your *Comment* be the *Mantuan Muse* [i.e., Virgil].
>
> (ll. 118–19, 124–5, 129; emphases in original)

53:7 "circumfus'd": spread everywhere.

53:15–16 The diction and alternating rhythm of these lines demonstrate that Wheatley acknowledges and affirms Pope's dictum in *An Essay on Criticism* that "The *Sound* must seem an *Eccho* to the *Sense*" (l. 365; emphases in original).

53:17–20 Wheatley alludes to the opening of Pope's translation of *Iliad* xvi, in which Achilles' close friend Patroclus asks Achilles for permission to wear Achilles' armor and aid the Greeks against the Trojans.

53:19 "Prone": leaning forward.

53:20 *"Pelides"*: one of the epithets often applied to Achilles because he was the son of Peleus, king of Phthia.

53:21 "Great *Maro*": The full Latin name of Virgil, who was born near Mantua, was Publius Vergilius Maro Mantuanus.

53:22 "The *Nine*": The nine Muses were the daughters of Zeus, king of the Greek gods, and Mnemosyne (Memory), who as mother of the muses inspired the arts and literature: Calliope (epic poetry), Clio (history), Euterpe (flute-play-ing), Terpsichore (lyric poetry and dancing, especially choral), Erato (lyric poetry), Melpomene (tragedy), Thalia (comedy), Polyhymnia (hymns and pantomime), and Urania (astronomy). One of the Muses' sacred residences was Helicon, a mountain in southwestern Boeotia.

53:28 "surprise;": Edition 1 ends "surprize;"

53:29 "grov'ling mind": repeated in "To a Lady on Her Coming to North-America with Her Son" [29dd], line 1. Wheatley's frequent use of the humil-ity topos in her writings is a particularly appropriate rhetorical strategy for an enslaved adolescent female author.

53:37 "happier *Terence*": the second-century BCE Roman playwright's cognomen, Afer, means *the African*.

54:46 "I'll snatch a laurel from thine honour'd head": The laurel symbolizes dis-tinction or eminence in society and politics, as well as in the arts. The phrase "snatch a laurel" appears in at least seven works published before 1773, including Thomas Gilbert, *A Panegyric on a Court* (London, 1739) and Francis Coventry, *The History of Pompey the Little, or the Life and Adventures of a Lap-Dog* (London, 5th ed. 1773). Wheatley may also be alluding to Pope's observation in *An Essay on Criticism* that great poets may ignore the rules "And *snatch* a *Grace* beyond the Reach of Art" (l. 155; emphases in original). Wheatley may, moreover, refer to Maecenas' reputation as a poet, as well as a patron, noted above.

54:49 "*Naiads*": Naiads, or nymphs, were mythological young female figures who inhabited and animated various places of nature.

54:50 "*Phoebus*": Phoebus Apollo, god of the sun, and leader of the Muses, espe-cially in music and poetry.

54:51 "*Aurora*": the goddess of the dawn.

54:53 "*Parnassus*": another Greek mountain, site of the Castalian fountain sacred to the Muses, as well as to Phoebus Apollo.

[29h] On Virtue.

Included in the 1772 "Proposals" [18], dated 1766. Published 1773.

The first of the "moral" poems referred to in the title of Wheatley's *Poems*. "On Virtue" is one of the very few poems in the volume not written in rhymed couplets. Unlike Wheatley's other surviving poems composed in the 1760s, which use the simple declarative mood and excessively end-stopped final couplet, the lines in this allegorical poem flow syntactically smoothly into one another from its opening. "On Virtue" is also more theologically profound than her earlier manuscripts. Though seemingly an imitation of a classical pagan celebration of virtue, wisdom, chastity, greatness, and goodness, "On Virtue" concludes by leading Wheatley's readers to recognize that classical ethics are insufficient to achieve the immortality, "enthron'd with Cherubs," that Christianity alone offers.

[29i] To the University of Cambridge, in New-England.

Included in the 1772 "Proposals" [18], dated 1767. Published 1773.

Cf. an earlier variant version [6].

Confident that "the muses" will "assist my pen," Wheatley's persona asserts her authority as one who has "left my native shore | The land of errors, and *Egyptian* gloom" and "those dark abodes," and who has known "sin, that baneful evil to the soul," and rejected it to embrace the "Father of mercy." From a position of moral superiority gained through experience she speaks as an "*Ethiop*" to warn her implicitly complacent students—"Ye pupils"—to "Improve your privileges while they stay." Audaciously, the teenaged, enslaved, self-educated, female, and formerly pagan poet of African descent assumes a voice that transcends the "privileges" of those who are reputedly her superiors in age, status, abilities, authority, race, and gender.

[29j] To the King's Most Excellent Majesty. 1768.

Included in the 1772 "Proposals" [18], dated 1768. Published 1773. Cf. the earlier variant version [9].

Comparison of the manuscript draft and published versions of Wheatley's "To the King's Most Excellent Majesty" reveals how much her artistry had developed in just five years. Wheatley's repositioning of the occasion of the poem—the repeal of the Stamp Act—from the title to a footnote renders her praise for the King greater and less contingent upon one event. The improvements in concision, diction, metaphor, syntax, and versification are striking. Seventeen lines have been reduced to fifteen. Even more than the draft, the published version celebrates the King as a paternal figure ("Rule thou in peace, our father, and our lord!") who has freed his children from the tyranny of Parliament and the politicians in his ministry. Wheatley perfects the incomplete first line in the draft by addressing the King as "dread Sire." Wheatley's choice of "dread," which means both feared and revered, allows her to delete the references in [9] to "great wars" (3) and "france" (7) while enhancing rather than diminishing her recognition of the King's authority and power. The choice also enables her to delete the clumsy line five in the draft. The common association of the adjective "dread" with both monarchs and deities anticipates Wheatley's transition from her opening address to the King to her imperative call in line twelve: "Great God, direct, and guard him from on high." "Brows" humanizes the King by conveying emotional connotations lacking in the draft version's "head" (2). Perhaps most tellingly, by deleting the last two lines of the draft with their reference to war-making, Wheatley, an enslaved person of African descent, emphatically concludes her poem with a not-so-subtle reminder that not only taxed colonists, i.e., "subjects," should be liberated, from chattel as well as metaphorical slavery.

[29k] On being brought from Africa to America.

Included in the 1772 "Proposals" [18], dated 1768. Published 1773.

"On being brought from Africa to America" has been called "the most reviled poem in African American literature" (Gates 71). The poem's notoriety understandably, but unfairly, derives from Wheatley's apparent endorsement of contemporaneous theological justifications for the transatlantic slave trade.

Modern critics have accused Wheatley, or at least the primary voice in her poem, of rejecting her African heritage and engaging in racial self-hatred. But such critics confuse accommodation with appropriation. Like many later authors of African descent, Wheatley repeatedly appropriates the values of Christianity to judge and find wanting hypocritical self-styled Christians of European descent. Theologically, the speaker's captivity in Africa proves to have been a fortunate fall that has enabled her now enlightened soul to rise from its former "benighted" condition to embrace Christianity. Physical slavery paradoxically leads to the spiritual freedom offered to the servants, or slaves, of Christ.

Wheatley's position is completely consistent with a belief in an omniscient and benevolent deity. But that belief does not necessarily imply that she either accepts or endorses slavery. In "On being brought from Africa to America" Wheatley expresses the common eighteenth-century equation of darkness with evil and sin, an equation whose origins probably lie in primordial human fears of nocturnal creatures, a fear that continues to be exploited in horror fiction and film. But by the eighteenth century the equation had taken on racist implications. Seeking a religious justification for their own economic self-interest, despite the absence of any biblical foundation whatsoever for their claim, defenders of the enslavement of Africans since the middle of the fifteenth century increasingly embraced the notion that in Genesis 4:1–16 and 20–7 God cursed the descendants of Cain and/or Ham with black skin. Defenders of slavery argued that sub-Saharan Africans, as the alleged descendants of Cain and/or Ham, were cursed with a dark complexion and destined to slavery. Hence, by the late eighteenth century blackness and slavery were often synonymous in pro-slavery discourse.

Wheatley may, however, be subverting conventional equations of blackness with evil and whiteness with good. The imperative "Remember" in the final couplet may not be addressed solely to Christians. Perhaps we should not read the couplet as "Remember, *Christians*, [that] *Negros*, black as *Cain*, | May be refin'd, and join th' angelic train." In an alternative reading, the "Father of mercy" may also redeem Wheatley's readers who are not among the "Some [who] view our sable race with scornful eye," but who "Remember [that], *Christians*, *Negros*, black as *Cain*, | May be refin'd, and join th' angelic train." Blackness in the second reading, still associated with sin, is more clearly metaphoric than phenotypic. Anyone can be as "black as Cain" in sin.

[29l] On the Death of the Rev. Dr. Sewell.

Included in the 1772 "Proposals" [18], dated 1769. Published 1773. Cf. the variants [11], [11a], [11b].

[29m] On the Death of the Rev. Mr. George Whitefield. 1770.

Included in the 1772 "Proposals" [18], dated 1770. Published 1770.

Whereas Wheatley addresses the political as well as religious relationships between Whitefield and the American colonists in the variant version that she published in Boston in 1770 [14], [29m] omits the earlier politically provocative lines 15–22 for London readers in 1773. Her addition of the transitional line eleven creates one of the rare triplets found in her poems.

[29n] On the Death of a young Lady of Five Years of Age.

Included in the 1772 "Proposals" [18], dated 1770. Published 1773.

John Wesley published a variant version in London in the December 1781 issue of his *Arminian Magazine*.

[29o] On the Death of a young Gentleman.

Included in the 1772 "Proposals" [18], undated. Published 1773.

The *Arminian Magazine* published a variant version in London in December 1781.

[29p] To a Lady on the Death of her Husband.

Included in the 1772 "Proposals" [18], undated. Written 1771, published 1771.

Cf. the variant version [16].

[29q] Goliath of Gath.

Included in the 1772 "Proposals" [18]. Written 1772?, published 1773.

Wheatley's inclusion of the epyllion "Goliath of Gath" in her *Poems* acknowledges epic poetry as the most esteemed and challenging poetic genre, and the Bible as the most prestigious source of narrative subjects. She may have written the poem in response to Mather Byles's earlier, more conventional, paraphrase of 1 Samuel 17 in his "Goliath's [*sic*] Defeat," in *Poems on Several Occasions* (Boston, 1744). Wheatley's title masks her epyllion's true hero, David. As an enslaved black woman poet entering the commercial publishing market, Wheatley was understandably drawn to a story that revealed true strength underlying apparent weakness, and that demonstrated confidence beneath professed diffidence. Unlike the overly masculine "monster" Goliath, "[o]f fierce Deportment, and gigantic frame," who mistakenly relies on his own physical strength, Wheatley's David is a relatively feminized hero, a "stripling," "in youthful bloom," who has "left the flow'ry meads, | And soft recesses of the sylvan shades," and who relies on faith in God for his moral strength. Wheatley may even have been consciously writing within the tradition of associating powerful women with David traceable to the Renaissance iconography surrounding Queen Elizabeth.

64:76 "*Eliab*": David's eldest brother.
68:204 "the son of *Ner*": Saul's cousin and general, Abner.

[29r] Thoughts on the Works of Providence.

Not included in the 1772 "Proposals" [18]. Written 1772–3, published 1773.
The *Arminian Magazine* published a variant version in London in December 1781.

68:12 "vast machine": a phrase commonly used in philosophical and religious
poems to refer to the created world; cf. John Ogilvie (1732–1813), *Providence.
An Allegorical Poem. In Three Books* (London, 1764), l. 865.
70:63 "Shall day to day, and night to night conspire": cf. Psalm 19:2 (*King James
Version*) "Day unto day uttereth speech, and night unto night sheweth
knowledge."
70:82 "diffus'd abroad": a phrase commonly used in religious poetry in relation to
God's light, love, or glory; cf. Isaac Watts (1674–1748), *Horae Lyricae: Poems,
Chiefly of the Lyric Kind* (London, 1706), 29.
70:88 "*Fancy*'s queen in giddy triumph reigns": cf. the reference by Mark Akenside
(1721–70) to fancy's "giddy empire," in *The Pleasures of the Imagination*
(London, 1744), Book 3, line 70. "Giddy": inconstant, mutable.

[29s] To a Lady on the Death of Three Relations.

Not included in the 1772 "Proposals" [18]. Undated, published 1773.

[29t] To a Clergyman on the Death of his Lady.

Not included in the 1772 "Proposals" [18]. Written 1772, published 1772.
Cf. the variant versions [22, 22a].

[29u] An Hymn to the Morning.

Not included in the 1772 "Proposals" [18]. Undated, published 1773.
Antecedents to Wheatley's aubade—a poem appropriate to the dawn or early
morning—include William Dawson (1704–52), "Hymn to the Morning," in *Poems
on Several Occasions* (London, 1736); Mary Leapor (1722–46), "An Hymn to the
Morning," in *Poems upon Several Occasions. By the Late Mrs. Leapor* (London, 1751).

[29v] An Hymn to the Evening.

Not included in the 1772 "Proposals" [18]. Undated, published 1773.
As her title indicates, Wheatley's hymn is a contribution to the tradition of
earlier neoclassical and secular "Odes to Evening," including the often-republished
ones by William Collins (1721–59), 1747, and Joseph Warton (1722–1800), 1749,
as well as those by the more obscure William Woty (1731?–1791), 1761, and John
Ogilvie (1732–1813), 1764.

[29w] Isaiah lxiii. 1–8.

Not included in the 1772 "Proposals" [18]. Undated, published 1773.

Who *is* this that cometh from Edom, with dyed garments from Bozrah? this *that is* glorious in his apparel, travelling in the greatness of his strength? I that speak in righteousness, mighty to save.

2 Wherefore *art thou* red in thine apparel, and thy garments like him that treadeth in the winevat?

3 I have trodden the winepress alone; and of the people *there was* none with me: for I will tread them in mine anger, and trample them in my fury; and their blood shall be sprinkled upon my garments, and I will stain all my raiment.

4 For the day of vengeance *is* in mine heart, and the year of my redeemed is come.

5 And I looked, and *there was* none to help; and I wondered that *there was* none to uphold: therefore mine own arm brought salvation unto me; and my fury, it upheld me.

6 And I will tread down the people in mine anger, and make them drunk in my fury, and I will bring down their strength to the earth.

7 I will mention the lovingkindnesses of the LORD, *and* the praises of the LORD, according to all that the LORD hath bestowed on us, and the great goodness toward the house of Israel, which he hath bestowed on them according to his mercies, and according to the multitude of his lovingkindnesses.

8 For he said, Surely they *are* my people, children *that* will not lie: so he was their Saviour. (Isaiah 63:1–8, *King James Version*)

75:2 *"Idumea"*: another name for Edom.
75:3 *"Bozrah"*: Edom's strongly fortified capital.
76:25 Cf. Alexander Pope, *Rape of the Lock* (1714), 3:155: Then flash'd the living Lightnings from her Eyes.
76:27 *"Zion"*: Jeusalem.

[29x] On Recollection.

Not included in the 1772 "Proposals" [18]. Written late 1771, published 1772.

See the variant version [18]. The *Gentleman's Magazine* for September 1773 (43: 456) reprinted the more concise [29x], probably as part of the advertising campaign for Wheatley's 1773 *Poems*.

[29y] On Imagination.

Not included in the 1772 "Proposals" [18]. Undated, published 1773.

The *Arminian Magazine* published a variant version in London in December 1784.
Title: As Mark Akenside does in *The Pleasures of the Imagination*, Wheatley uses *Imagination* and *Fancy* interchangeably to refer to the creative faculty. Akenside

refers to *fancy* twenty-two times in the poem, but to *imagination* only four
times. He equates *fancy* and *imagination* in his note on page 100. Cf. the defin-
ition by Samuel Johnson (1709–84) in his *Dictionary of the English Language*
(London, 1755): "Imagination. 1. Fancy; the power of forming ideal pictures;
the power of representing things absent to one's self or others."

78:11 "silken fetters": cf. Akenside, *The Pleasures of the Imagination*, Book 2, line
562: "The silken fetters of delicious ease."

78:21 "There in one view we grasp the mighty whole": cf. Edward Young (1683–
1765), *A Poem on the Last Day* (London, 1713), 24: "The Muse is wont in
Narrow Bounds to sing, | To *Teach the Swain*, or *Celebrate the King*: | I grasp
the Whole, no more to Parts confin'd, | I lift my Voice, and sing to *Humankind*:
| I sing to Men and Angels; Angels joyn, | While such the Theme, their
sacred Songs with mine."

78:27 "*Flora*": goddess of the spring and flowers.

78:29 "*Sylvanus*": god of forests, fields, and herding.

79:43 "*Tithon*": Tithonus, mortal lover of Aurora.

[29z] A Funeral Poem on the Death of C.E. an Infant of Twelve Months.

Not included in the 1772 "Proposals" [18]. Undated, published 1773. Cf. the earlier variant [24].

[29aa] To Captain H—D, of the 65th Regiment.

Not included in the 1772 "Proposals" [18]. Undated, published 1773.

Robinson, *Phillis Wheatley and Her Writings*, 273, identifies "H—d" as Captain
John Hanfield, a member of the British regiment sent in 1769 to pacify anti-British
sentiment in Boston.

[29bb] To the Right Honourable William, Earl of Dartmouth, His Majesty's Principal Secretary of State for North-America, &c.

Not included in the 1772 "Proposals" [18]. Written October 1772, published 1773.
Cf. [25].

81:3 "genial": generative.

[29cc] Ode to Neptune. On Mrs. W—'s Voyage to England.

Not included in the 1772 "Proposals" [18]. Written 1772, published 1773.

J.L. Bell plausibly suggests that Wheatley's "Mrs. W—" refers to Susanna
Wooldridge, wife of Thomas Wooldridge [cf. 25]. (http://boston1775.blogspot.
com/2015/08/phillis-wheatley-and-susanna-wooldridge.html.)

82:2 "*AE'lus*": Aeolus, god of the winds.

*[29dd] To a Lady on her coming to North-America with her Son,
for the Recovery of her Health.*

Included in the 1772 "Proposals" [18], undated. Published 1773.

83:1 "grov'ling mind": cf. "To Maecenas" [29g], line 29, and note.
83:5 *"Goddess"*: Venus.

*[29ee] To a Lady on her remarkable Preservation in an
Hurricane in North-Carolina.*

Included in the 1772 "Proposals" [18], undated. Published 1773.
The most recent devastating hurricane to hit North Carolina before the publication of Wheatley's "Proposals" in February 1772 occurred in 1769. The 19 October 1769 issue of the *New York Chronicle* printed an "Extract of a letter from Newbern in North Carolina, September 24ᵗʰ, 1769," in which the author gives a detailed description of some of "the horrors of this hurricane" during the "so terrible a night" of 7 September 1769. The same hurricane is probably referred to in the 26 March 1770 issue of the *Massachusetts Gazette and the Boston Post-Boy and Advertiser*, which reprints a 3 January notice from London mentioning that "the late Hurricane in North-Carolina" has raised the price of tar.

84:5 *"Boreas"*: the north wind.
84:6 *"Nereids"*: nymph daughters of Nereus, Homer's "old man" of the sea.

*[29ff] To a Lady and her Children, on the Death of her
Son and their Brother.*

Included in the 1772 "Proposals" [18] as "To Mrs. Boylston and Children on the Death of Her Son and Their Brother." Undated. Published 1773.

*[29gg] To a Gentleman and Lady on the Death of the Lady's Brother
and Sister, and a Child of the Name Avis, aged one Year.*

Included in the 1772 "Proposals" [18] as "To *James Sullivan*, Esq; and Lady on the Death of her Brother and Sister, and a Child, *Avis*, Aged 12 Months." Undated. Published 1773.
The "Gentleman" was James Sullivan (1744–1808). He was a lawyer, and a future Governor of Massachusetts (1807–8). He married Mehitable ("Hetty") Odiorne (1748–86), daughter of William and Avis (Adams) Odiorne of Durham, Maine, on 22 February 1768. James Sullivan, the first president of the Massachusetts Historical Society, was an admirer of George Whitefield, and an early supporter of resistance to British rule. Avis Sullivan was born on 8 October 1770, and died on 16 October 1771.

86:5 "the offspring of six thousand years": According to the calculations of James
Ussher (1581–1656), archbishop of Armargh, Ireland, the earth had been created in 4004 BC, approximately six thousand years before 1772.

[29hh] On the Death of Dr. Samuel Marshall. 1771.

Included in the 1772 "Proposals" [18]. Written and published 1771.
   See the variant versions [17, 17a].

[29ii] To a Gentleman on his Voyage to Great-Britain
for the Recovery of his Health.

Not included in the 1772 "Proposals" [18]. Published 1773.
   Daniel Ricketson, *The History of New Bedford* (New Bedford, 1858), 262, iden-
tifies the gentleman as Joseph Rotch, Jr. Cf. [29]. On 22 March 1773 the *Boston
Evening-Post* reported his death in England.

88:1 "gay *Elysian* scenes": Elysium, or the Elysian Fields, in Greek mythology
was the paradise in the afterlife where the souls of the heroic and the virtuous
rested.

[29jj] To the Rev. Dr. Thomas Amory on reading his Sermons on Daily
Devotion, in which that Duty is recommended and assisted.

Not included in the 1772 "Proposals" [18]. Written 1772, published 1773.
   The Presbyterian minister Reverend Thomas Amory (1701–74) wrote on religious subjects. On 14 October 1772, Reverend Charles Chauncy gave Wheatley a
copy of Amory's *Daily Devotion Assisted and Recommended, in Four Sermons*, 2nd
ed. (London, 1770; reprinted Boston, 1772). On 26 March 1774, Wheatley gave
the book, as well as a copy of John Lathrop's *The Importance of Early Piety* (Boston,
1771), to her young friend, and Susanna Wheatley's grandnephew, Thomas
Wallcut (1758–1840). On Wallcut, cf. [45].

[29kk] On the Death of J.C. an Infant.

Not included in the 1772 "Proposals" [18]. Undated, published 1773.
   The *Arminian Magazine* published a variant version in London in November
1784.

[29ll] An Hymn to Humanity. To S.P.G. Esq;

Not included in the 1772 "Proposals" [18]. Undated, published 1773.
   A variant version in the Special Collections Department of the Robert
W. Woodruff Library at Emory University, dated 12 December 1773, identifies
"S.P.G." as "S.P. Gallowy Esq: who corrected some Poetic Essays of the Authoress."

I thank Professor Julian D. Mason, Jr. for bringing the Emory variant to my attention, and I am very grateful to both him and Dr. Randall K. Burkett, African
American Studies Bibliographer for the Robert W. Woodruff Library, for sharing
their thoughts about the documents with me. The present edition does not include
the variant because it is not in Wheatley's hand. It would be a unique instance of
Wheatley having subsequently revised a work that originally appeared in her 1773
Poems.

92:23 "Their G—!": "Their G—y!" in Edition 1.

[29mm] To the Honourable T.H. Esq; on the Death of his Daughter.

Not included in the 1772 "Proposals" [18]. Published January 1773 in Boston.
     Cf. the variant poem and note on the death of Thomas Hubbard's daughter,
Mrs. Thankfull Leonard [26].

[29nn] Niobe in Distress for her Children slain by Apollo, from
Ovid's Metamorphoses, Book VI. and from a view of the Painting
of Mr. Richard Wilson.

Not included in the 1772 "Proposals" [18]. Undated, published 1773.
     Wheatley's poem is an ekphrasis—a verbal description of an actual or imaginary
material work of art. The British painter Richard Wilson (1714–82), best known
for his landscapes, based several works on the tale of Niobe and her children.
Wilson's *The Destruction of Niobe's Children* (1760), formerly owned by William
Augustus, Duke of Cumberland (1721–65), is now at the Yale Center for British
Art. Wheatley may have seen the engraving by William Woollett (1745–85) after
Wilson's painting before she went to England. Or she may have first seen either
one of Wilson's Niobe paintings, or (more likely) an engraving after it, when she
was in London. If the latter, Wheatley must have written "Niobe in Distress"
while she was in England during the summer of 1773.
     Wheatley's "Niobe" exemplifies the way she balances biblical subjects with
classical ones in *Poems*. "Niobe" is almost exactly equal in length to "Goliath of
Gath," the only other epyllion in the volume. But whereas Wheatley implicitly
likens her poetic persona to the central figure of David in "Goliath," in "Niobe"
she implicitly contrasts her persona with that of its protagonist. Wheatley charac-
teristically creates a humble persona—"Muse! lend thy aid, nor let me sue in vain,
| Tho' last and meanest of the rhyming train!" (ll. 7–8)—to paraphrase Ovid's tale
of an arrogant mother whose "love too vehement hastens to destroy | Each bloom-
ing maid, and each celestial boy" (ll. 35–6). By doing so she contrasts God's
providence demonstrated in "Goliath of Gath," and the consolations of
Christianity found in her elegies, with the arbitrariness of pagan deities.
     Ovid composed his unconventional fifteen-book epic, *Metamorphoses*, around
CE 8. According to the myth, Niobe married Amphion, king of Thebes, which

Cadmus had founded. Niobe is so excessively proud of their seven sons and seven daughters that she foolishly disparages the Titaness Leto (Latona), daughter of Coeus and the Titaness Phoebe, for having only two children, the twin gods Apollo ("the *Delian* god," l. 166) and Artemis (or Diana, or Phoebe). Their father, Zeus (Jove), has an oracle at Dodona. Apollo and Artemis were born on Mount Cynthus on the island of Delos. Niobe's arrogance is hereditary: her father was Tantalus, who was condemned to eternal torment in Tarturus for having tried to deceive the gods into eating his own son, Niobe's brother. Having heard Niobe's comment on Latona, the prophetess Manto, daughter of the prophet Tiresias ("*Tiresia*," l. 39), advises the Theban women to offer sacrifices to Latona and her children to implore them for forgiveness. Niobe interrupts the sacrifice by again bragging of her and her children's superiority to Latona and her offspring, even remarking that she has so many children that were a few to die she would still have more than Latona. Latona orders Apollo and Artemis to kill all the sons and daughters of Niobe as punishment for her hubris. Stupefied by woe, Niobe gradually transforms into eternally weeping stone.

Wheatley's relatively sympathetic treatment of Niobe was not unprecedented. The anonymously published *A New Translation of Ovid's Metamorphoses into English Prose, as near the Original as the Different Idioms of the Latin and English Languages Will Allow. With the Latin Text and Order of Construction on the Same Page; and Critical, Historical, Geographical, and Classical Notes, in English, from the Best Commentators, both Ancient and Modern; beside a great Number of Notes entirely New. For the Use of Schools as well as of Private Gentlemen* (London, 1748; 3rd ed. 1759) asks the reader of the tale of Niobe, "Is it possible to represent a more compleat [*sic*] Scene of Misery and Woe? What Richness and Luxuriance of Imagination must a Poet possess, who could bring together such a Crowd of the most distressing Circumstances?" (218).

94:10 "*Phrygian*": The kingdom of Phrygia was located in Anatolia, part of modern-day Turkey.

94:10 "beautiful in woe": Wheatley's use of this striking phrase to end a line is anticipated by Walter Harte (1709–74), *Poems on Several Occasions* (London, 1727, 1739), 155; William Thompson (1712?–1766?), *Winter, an Ode: to a Friend. A Translation from the Latin....* London, 1747), 9; and Myles Cooper (1737–85), *Poems on Several Occasions* (Oxford, 1761), 341.

94:11 "*Maeonia*": Lydia, in western Anatolia.

94:14 "*Tantalus*": legendary king of Sipylus, son of the Olympian god Jove (Zeus), and father of Niobe and her brother, Pelops. Tantalus tried to trick the gods into eating the flesh of his own son, Niobe's brother, when he was one of the first mortals permitted to dine with the gods. He consequently suffers exemplary eternal punishment in Tartarus, where food and drink are forever just beyond his reach. Ovid (and Wheatley) hint that Niobe's arrogance is hereditary.

94:15 *"Dodonean Jove"*: Dodona, the sanctuary of Jove, considered the oldest Greek oracle.

94:17 *"Atlas"*: Niobe's grandfather, who supports the pillars that separate heaven and earth.

94:21 *"Amphion"*: He played his lyre to charm stones to form the walls around Thebes.

95:33 *"Aurora"*: the goddess of morning.

95:58 "Like heav'nly *Venus"*: Wheatley compares Niobe to the Olympian goddess of love in terms of beauty, though she does not say that she is equally divine.

96:75 *"Titaness"*: The Titans were the gods of the generation before the Olympians

96:78 "pitying *Delos"*: the island on which the Olympian gods Apollo and Artemis were born.

96:84 *"Latona* pay;": Edition 1 ends *"Latona* pay?"

96:90 *"Cynthus'* summit": birthplace on Delos of Apollo and Artemis.

96:105 *"Phoebe"*: another name for Artemis, goddess of the moon.

98:166 "the *Delian* god": Apollo, god of the sun.

99:213–24 "This Verse to the End is the Work of another Hand": Wheatley's note. William H. Robinson, *Phillis Wheatley and Her Writings* (New York: Garland, 1984), 274, believes that these lines were "probably the work of Mary Wheatley."

[2900] To S.M. a young African Painter, on Seeing his Works.

Not included in the 1772 "Proposals" [18]. Undated, published 1773.

The *Arminian Magazine* published a variant version in London in April 1784.

"S.M.": a manuscript note, not in Phillis Wheatley's hand, in a copy of *Poems* at the American Antiquarian Society identifies him as "Scipio Moorhead—Negro Servent to the Revd Mr. Moorhead of Boston, whose Genius inclined him that way." Cf. [29a].

Wheatley employs the ekphrastic context of viewing the works of "S.M." to affirm the Horatian dictum in *Ars Poetica*, "Ut pictura poesis"—"as is painting, so is poetry." She ultimately elevates poetry over painting, "For nobler themes demand a nobler strain, | And purer language on th' ethereal plain" (ll. 31–2).

100:18 "Celestial *Salem"*: the heavenly Jerusalem.

100:29 *"Damon's* tender sighs": Damon is a common name for love-struck shepherds in pastoral poems, e.g., in Virgil's *Eclogue* 8, and in Pope's pastoral "Spring."

[29pp] To His Honour the Lieutenant-Governor, on the
Death of his Lady. March 24, 1773.

Not included in the 1772 "Proposals" [18]. A manuscript copy, not in Phillis Wheatley's hand, is in the Massachusetts Historical Society (Oliver Family Papers).

Mary Sanford Oliver (1713–73), wife of Lieutenant-Governor Andrew Oliver, died on 17 March 1773.

101:9 "refulgent": radiant, shining brightly. Compare Akenside, *Pleasures of the Imagination*, Book 1, lines 329–30: "as Venus, when she stood | Effulgent on the pearly car."

101:24 "heav'n's high concave": a common phrase in eighteenth-century poems, e.g., William Whitehead (1715–85), *An Essay on Ridicule* (London, 1743); Marco Girolamo Vida (*c*.1485–1566), *Scacchia, ludus: a Poem on the Game of Chess* (Dublin, 1750); Francis Fawkes (1720–77), "On the Death of the Right Honourable the Earl of Uxbridge," in *Original Poems and Translations* (London, 1761); William Falconer (1732–69), *The Shipwreck. A Poem* (London, 1762); Mary Latter (1725–77), *The Siege of Jerusalem, by Titus Vespasian; a Tragedy* (London, 1763); Joseph Partridge (1724–96), *The Anti-Atheist, a Didactic Poem* (Manchester, 1766); Melchior de Polignac (1661–1742?), *A Translation of Anti-Lucretius. By George Canning of the Middle Temple* (London, 1766).

[29qq] A Farewel to America. To Mrs. S.W.

Not included in the 1772 "Proposals" [18]. Written and published May 1773.

See also the variant versions of this poem [28], [28a].

"Mrs. S.W." most likely refers to Susanna Wheatley. Handwritten notes in the American Antiquarian Society's copy of Wheatley's *Poems* incorrectly identify "Mrs. S.W." as Susannah Wright.

Wheatley uncharacteristically uses the ballad stanza form, alternating iambic tetrameter and trimeter lines rhyming abcb, to address Susanna Wheatley.

102:4 "tempt": to attempt.
102:14 "crystal": clear, transparent.
103:29 "Health": Hygeia, Greek goddess of good health.
103:31 *"Hebe's* mantle": Hebe was the Greek goddess of eternal youth.
103:36 "around.": Edition 1 ends "around,".
104:46 "train": followers, attendants.

[29rr] A Rebus, by I.B.

Not included in the 1772 "Proposals" [18]. Written and published 1773.

Mason (110) very plausibly suggests that James Bowdoin was the "I.B." who wrote the rebus. Wheatley includes a poem by someone else as the occasion for her response.

[29ss] An Answer to the Rebus, by the Author of these Poems.

Not included in the 1772 "Proposals" [18]. Written and published 1773.

Wheatley explains the riddle with the words "*Quail*," "*Unicorn*," "*Emerald*," "*Boston*," "*Euphorbus*," and "*C[hatha]m*," whose initial letters spell out the answer: Quebec.

105:4 Cf. Numbers 11:32-33.

105:13 "*Euphorbus* of the *Dardan* line": Wheatley refers to the incident in the *Iliad* when the Greek leader Menelaus kills Euphorbus, an ally of Troy, for having wounded Patroclus, who had borrowed Achilles' armor (see note to Wheatley's "To Maecenas"). The adulterous relationship between Menelaus' wife Helen and the Trojan prince Paris led to the Trojan War.

105:16 "*C—m*": William Pitt (1708–78), Earl of Chatham, had been prime minister during the Seven Years' War (1756–63), known in North America as the French and Indian War. He was perceived as being sympathetic to the colonists' cause. Pitt received credit for the decisive British military victories in 1759, especially at Quebec, which led to the Peace of Paris in 1763.

[30] Letter to the Countess of Huntingdon (27 June 1773)

Manuscript in Huntingdon Papers at the Cheshunt Foundation, Cambridge, United Kingdom (A3/5/4).

Huntingdon had been interested in Phillis Wheatley at least since receiving her eulogy on the death of Whitefield [15]. On 30 April 1773, Susanna Wheatley wrote the Countess that Phillis was coming to England with Nathaniel Wheatley on the advice of her doctors and asked Huntingdon to advise them when they arrived. Phillis brought with her a letter of introduction from Carey:

This will be deliver'd Your Ladiship by Phillis the Christian Poetess, whose behavior in England I Wish may be as Exemplary, as its been in Boston. This appears remarkable for her Humility, Modesty and Spiritual Mindedness. [I] hope she will continue an ornament to the Christian Name and Profession, as she grows older and has more experience. I doubt not her Writings will run more in an Evangelicall Strain. I think your Ladiship will be pleas'd with her. (Manuscript in Huntingdon Papers at the Cheshunt Foundation, Cambridge, United Kingdom: A3/5/8.)

Phillis was not able to deliver Carey's letter in person, however, because the ailing Countess had retired to her home in Talgarth, South Wales, where in 1768 she had established a college at Trevecca to teach ministers the doctrine of her Connexion.

[31] Letter to the Countess of Huntingdon (17 July 1773)

Manuscript in Huntingdon Papers at the Cheshunt Foundation, Cambridge, United Kingdom (A3/5/5).

Wheatley's comment that "the Ship is certainly to Sail next Thurs[day on] which I must return to America" suggests that the timing of her return was not dependent upon any news that she may have received that her mistress in Boston was ill, but rather on the fact that Calef's cargo was loaded in time for him to cross the Atlantic before the height of the hurricane season.

"Your Brother" probably refers to James Albert Ukawsaw Gronniosaw (1710?–1775), whose *A Narrative of the Most Remarkable Particulars in the Life of James Albert Ukawsaw Gronniosaw, an African Prince, as Related by Himself* (Bath, 1772) was dedicated to the Countess of Huntingdon. Her clergyman cousin, Reverend Walter Shirley (1725–86), wrote the Preface to Gronniosaw's *Narrative*.

[32] "Ocean"

Manuscript at Collection of the Smithsonian National Museum of African American History and Culture, object number 2023.82.1. Included in Wheatley's 1779 "Proposals" [55].

Many of the classical allusions in "Ocean" are identified in the notes on "To Maecenas" [29g].

107:17 "mighty Sire of Ocean": Neptune.

107:18 adapted from Pope's translation of Homer's *Iliad*, which Wheatley acquired in London.

108:24 "Syb's, Eurus, Boreas": the south, east, and north winds, respectively.

108:27 "Eolus": Aeolus, god of the winds.

108:31–2 an allusion to the Greek myth in which Zeus, disguised as a snow-white bull, tricks the maiden Europa into getting on his back so that he can take her across the sea to Crete. There he transforms himself into an eagle and rapes her.

108:44 "pluto's dreary shore": Pluto, or Hades, was the god of the underworld, land of the dead.

108:55 "Iscarius": perhaps Wheatley's combination of the names Judas Iscariot, betrayer of Jesus, and Icarus (Icarius), who fell into the sea when the wax holding his artificial wings melted because he flew too close to the sun. Or perhaps Wheatley's "Iscarius" is simply a misspelling of Icarius.

[33] Letter to David Wooster (18 October 1773)

Manuscript at the Massachusetts Historical Society (Hugh Upham Clark Collection).

This extremely significant letter tells us that Phillis Wheatley gained her freedom sometime between her return to Boston from London on 13 September and the date of this letter, 18 October 1773. David Wooster was a prosperous merchant in New Haven, who held several judicial and administrative positions there, including that of collector of customs. He was a Yale graduate (1738), who in 1746 married Mary Clap, the eldest daughter of Yale College president Thomas Clap. Wooster was appointed colonel of Connecticut's Second Regiment in 1756, during the Seven Years' War. In 1778 Wheatley enclosed a poem on Wooster's death in battle in a letter that she sent to his widow [53].

Wheatley tells Wooster that during the "no more than 6 weeks" she was in England she had toured much of greater eighteenth-century London—from

Westminster in the west to the City of London in the east, Greenwich in the south, and Sadler's Wells in the north. She saw the Observatory, Park, and Royal Hospital for Seamen in Greenwich, as well as the Tower of London and Westminster Abbey. Almost all the places she visited were (and still are) included in standard tour guides to London, such as the *Companion to Every Place of Curiosity and Entertainment in and about London and Westminster*, the third edition of which was published in London in 1772.

Phillis arrived in London just after the fashionable season, which ended on 4 June, George III's birthday. Consequently, the Drury Lane and Covent Garden theaters were closed. But less reputable venues were available and understandably dazzled the young girl from the colonies who had never before seen a performance on stage. Wheatley attended the light entertainment at Sadler's Wells, where "various pleasing and surprising Performances in LADDER DANCING" as well as the "new Entertainment of Music and Dancing, call'd VINEYARD REVELS; Or, HARLEQUIN BACCHANAL," were staged during her time in London. (*Public Advertiser*, 1 July 1773.) Among the "too many things and Places to trouble" Wooster with "in a Letter" may have been a performance of the musical comedy *The Padlock* by Charles Dibdin (1745–1814), which was playing at the Hay-Market theater while she was in town. Dibdin performed in blackface the role of Mungo, the wily servant-hero of the play, the most famous comic black figure in eighteenth-century drama.

Cox's Museum was located next to present-day Admiralty Arch. James Cox (*c.*1723–1800), a jeweler, opened his museum at the beginning of 1772. It was the talk of the town for the next three years because of its precious jewels, metals, and curios designed by such artists as Joseph Nollekens (1737–1823) and Johann Zoffany (1733–1810). Its contents were valued at the astounding sum of £197,000, equivalent to approximately £16 million or $26.4 million in today's money. Someone other than Phillis presumably paid the 10 shillings, 6 pence (equivalent today to about £40 or $66) for her admission ticket to Cox's Museum, as well as the smaller fees to see the paintings displayed in the great hall of the Royal Hospital in Greenwich, and the charge to visit the Tower of London, with its collections of armor, jewels, and animals from all over the world.

Of the people Phillis Wheatley met in London, Benjamin Franklin is today the best known. He had been representing the colonial interests of Pennsylvania, Georgia, New Jersey, and Massachusetts in London since July 1757 and would return to America in 1775. He visited Wheatley on 7 July 1773 and offered her his services at the prompting of Jonathan Williams (1719–96), his nephew-in-law in Boston. Phillis's owners had encouraged Williams to mention Phillis in his letters to his uncle. Franklin's slave, Peter, probably accompanied him on his visit.

But among the "friends" that Phillis tells Wooster she made in London, the one who was probably the most consequential in her own life was Granville Sharp (1735–1813). Almost exactly a year before she met Sharp, he had procured a judgment from the King's Bench that anyone in her condition—an enslaved person brought from the colonies to England—could not legally be forced to return to the colonies as a slave. The ruling was widely reported in colonial newspapers before Phillis sailed to London. She and Sharp certainly would have discussed its significance and relevance to her own situation.

For many of the people Phillis Wheatley met while she was in London, a pious, enslaved, teenaged, female poet of African descent from the colonies probably seemed as much a curiosity as anything they would have paid to see in Cox's Museum or the Tower. Even aristocrats treated her like an exotic visiting celebrity. She had initiated a correspondence with William Legge, 2nd Earl of Dartmouth, in 1772, when she sent him her poem celebrating his appointment as Secretary of State for North America [25]. John Kirkman (1741–80), a silk merchant, was an alderman of the City of London from 1768 to 1780. Lord Lincoln, a courtesy title for Henry Fiennes Pelham Clinton (1750–78), was a Member of Parliament for Aldborough, 1772–4, and a supporter of the North ministry. He was styled Lord Lincoln because he was the eldest son of Henry Fiennes Pelham Clinton (1720–94), whose highest title had been the 9th Earl of Lincoln until he succeeded his uncle Thomas Pelham-Holles (1693–1768) in 1768 as 2nd Duke of Newcastle. Dr. Daniel Solander (1736–82) was a Swedish-born botanist who accompanied Sir Joseph Banks (1743–1820) as a researcher in the South Pacific, 1768–71, aboard the *Endeavor*, commanded by Captain James Cook (1728–79). Solander, who became keeper of the natural history collections in the British Museum in March 1773, was probably the person who invited Phillis Wheatley to the Museum, which allowed very few members of the public to view its collections of natural history, antiquities, manuscripts, and books. A search by Carole Holden, Head of American Collections at the British Library, of the archives of the British Museum and the papers of Daniel Solander in the British Library found no references to Phillis Wheatley (private correspondence 16 and 17 August 2010).

Others whom Phillis mentions having met in London include Israel Mauduit (1708–87), who had represented the royal governor of Massachusetts, Thomas Hutchinson, as his private agent in London since 1771. Mauduit had assisted his brother Jasper (1697–1772) when Jasper was the agent representing Massachusetts (1762–5). Israel published both *A Short View of the History of the Colony of Massachusetts* (London, 1769) and *A Short View of the History of the New England Colonies* in London in 1769. In 1773 Ezekiel Russell reprinted a Boston edition of Israel Mauduit's *The Case of the Dissenting Ministers*, an argument supporting greater religious tolerance that was first published in London in 1772. In 1774 Mauduit joined Alexander Wedderburn (1733–1805), the British solicitor-general, in defending Governor Hutchinson against Benjamin Franklin's attempt to have him removed from office. Mauduit defended British interests in *Considerations on the American War. Addressed to the People of England* (London, 1776). Brook Watson (1735–1807), a future Lord Mayor of London, was a prominent London merchant who had spent much of his youth in Boston and Nova Scotia before returning to London in 1759. His loss of a leg to a shark in Havana in 1749 would become the subject of a famous and controversial painting by John Singleton Copley (1738–1815) in 1778. Dr. Thomas Gibbons was a dissenting minister who taught rhetoric at the Mile End Academy. He published *Juvenalia: Poems on Various Subjects of*

Devotion and Virtue (London, 1750), and a Latin poem on the death of Whitefield in 1771. Gibbons, a member of the social and religious circles of Dartmouth and the Countess of Huntingdon, met Reverend Samson Occom in London in 1766. Gibbons recorded his meeting with Wheatley on Thursday, 15 July 1773: "Was visited this Morning by Phillis Wheatley a Negro young Woman from Boston in New England A Person of fine Genius, and very becoming Behaviour." ("The Diary of Rev. Dr. Thomas Gibbons, 1749–1785," Dr. Williams's Library.) "Lady Cavendish" probably refers to Lady Sarah Cavendish (1740–1807), wife (née Bradshaw) of Sir Henry Cavendish, 2nd Baronet (1732–1804). Cavendish was an Irish politician who represented the ("rotten") borough of Lostwithiel in Cornwall in the House of Commons in Westminster between 1768 and 1774. "Lady Carteret Webb" probably refers to the wife (née Smith) of lawyer Philip Carteret Webb, Esq. (1736?–1793). Mary (Reynolds) Palmer (1716–94) was the sister of the famous painter Sir Joshua Reynolds (1723–92).

Wheatley neglects to tell Wooster that she spent part of her time in London at the home of John Thornton. She corresponded with Thornton before and after her trip to London (cf. [20]). Thornton later told a friend that "Phillis the African Girl...was lately from Boston & staid with me about a Week." (Cambridge University Library: John Thornton to Rev. William Richardson, 2 June 1774 [Thornton Family Papers, GB 012 MS. Add. 7826].) Thornton was the half-brother of Hannah Wilberforce (d. 1788), the aunt of the future abolitionist William Wilberforce (1759–1833). (Wheatley's unpublished second volume of writings was to include a letter to Hannah Wilberforce, another admirer of George Whitefield.) Wheatley also met the ailing statesman and man of letters Baron George Lyttelton (1709–73), who died the month after she sailed back to Boston. Nor does Wheatley mention planning to meet King George III. According to Margaretta Matilda Odell, great-grandniece of Susanna Wheatley, and Wheatley's first biographer, Phillis was to have been presented to the King, but her mistress's illness intervened.

The books that Wheatley names, and their known present-day locations, include: Alexander Pope, translation of Homer's *Iliad* (Dartmouth College), translation of Homer's *Odyssey* and the nine volumes of his own works (University of North Carolina at Charlotte); Tobias Smollett (1721–71), translation of Cervantes's *Don Quixote* (volume two is in the Schomburg Center for Research in Black Culture of the New York Public Library); John Milton (1608–74), *Paradise Lost* (Houghton Library, Harvard University); Samuel Butler (1612–80), *Hudibras*; John Gay (1685–1732), *Fables*. Wheatley does not mention that Granville Sharp also gave her a copy of his *Remarks on Several Very Important Prophecies, in Five Parts* (London, 1768), now at the Essex Institute, Salem, Massachusetts.

In addition to the books that Wheatley acquired in London, on 24 September 1774, soon after she returned to Boston, Mary Eveleigh (1754–1837) of South Carolina gave her the four-volume *Complete Works in Verse and Prose* of William Shenstone (1714–63), the last two volumes of which are at the Schomburg Center of the New York Public Library. The copy of *Poems* that Wheatley gave Eveleigh in exchange, perhaps in person in New England, is now in Duke University's rare book collection.

Once Phillis mentions her freedom, gained "at the desire of my friends in England," she turns to pragmatic affairs. Wheatley tells Wooster that she shrewdly has taken out an extra insurance policy by sending a copy of her manumission papers to Israel Mauduit in London. She is clear about her motives for having done so. "The Instrument is drawn, so as to secure me and my property from the hands of the Exectutrs [executors], administrators, &c. of my master, and secure whatsoever Should be given me as my Own. A Copy is Sent to Isra. Mauduit Esq.ʳ F.R.S. [Fellow of the Royal Society]." Phillis apparently already had property, besides her own person, to protect, and she clearly expected to acquire more, all of which she sought to keep out of the hands of John Wheatley and his heirs.

Phillis signifies her transition from slavery to freedom with a new paragraph. Her "short Sketch" reveals her transformation from an enslaved adolescent girl from the colonies astonished at being treated as a celebrity by the rich, famous, and powerful members of society in the capital of the British Empire, into a savvy businesswoman. The transition is reflected in the shift from the predominately passive voice she uses in the first two paragraphs to the active voice in the last. Rather than emphasizing what her "friends" had done for her in England, in her last paragraph she stresses what she is doing for herself now that she is back in Boston, and "upon my own footing." She seeks Wooster's help in selling copies of her book, informing him that she has taken the precaution to protect her profits so that "whatever I get by this is entirely mine": "If any[one] should be so ungenerous as to reprint them [without my permission] the Genuine Copy may be known, for it is sign'd in my own handwriting."

[34] Letter to Obour Tanner (30 October 1773)

Manuscript at the Massachusetts Historical Society (Miscellaneous Bound Manuscripts).

The "young man" referred to in the postscript may be John Peters (1746?– 1801), Phillis Wheatley's future husband. Wheatley's "asthma" persisted through the winter. She writes to Reverend Samuel Hopkins on 9 February 1774 that she has been "much indispos'd by the return of my Asthmatic complaint" [38]. And she writes Tanner on 21 March 1774, "I have been unwell the greater Part of the winter, but am much better as the Spring approaches" [40]. Wheatley never says how she was treated for her "complaint." If Wheatley followed the advice of Benjamin Rush (1745–1813), with whom we know she corresponded at some point, the treatment was certainly not what would be recommended today. Rush advises in *A Dissertation on the Spasmodic Asthma of Children* (London, 1770), which first appeared in the *Pennsylvania Gazette*, "1. *Bleeding* . . . A physician should always be directed by the age, sex, habit of body, and state of the pulse of his patient. The season of the year likewise, as well as the nature of the weather, should influence him considerably with regard to the use of his lancet. . . . 2. *Vomits*. Our chief dependence should be placed on these. They may be given at all times of the disorder." (Rush, 19, emphases in original.) Wheatley's "Asthmatic complaint" probably afflicted her for the rest of her life, and may have been the cause of her death on 5 December 1784.

112:2 "Complaisant": accommodating.

[35] Letter to John Thornton (1 December 1773)

Manuscript in National Records of Scotland, Edinburgh (GD26/13/663/4).

Jane, Henry, and Robert were John Thornton's children. Mrs. Wilberforce, John Thornton's half-sister, was the aunt of the abolitionist William Wilberforce. See [36] on Reverend Moorhead.

[36] An Elegy, To Miss. Mary Moorhead, on the Death of her Father, The Rev. Mr. John Moorhead.

Broadside published 15 December 1773. Not included in Wheatley's 1779 "Proposals" [55].

The Presbyterian minister John Moorhead died on 6 December 1773. His obituary in the 13 December issue of the *Boston Post Boy* attributes to him many of the qualities Wheatley mentions in her poem, and describes his death: "Nature had blessed him with a hale constitution, which he assiduously cultivated and preserved until two or three years since, when a disorder cruel in its nature seized him, and although it did not confine him for any great space of time, yet its repeated attacks wasted and destroyed his health, and finally put a period to his usefulness and life." Wheatley's elegy on Moorhead's death differs notably from her earlier elegies. It stresses the effect of "the afflicting Providence" (l. 76) felt by those he left behind, rather than the theme of Christian consolation that pervades the previous poems. Several reasons may account for the somber treatment of death here. She probably knew the Moorhead family far better than she did most of the other subjects of her elegies. She frequently saw Reverend Moorhead. For example, Moorhead visited John Wheatley almost daily during the five weeks he was unable to leave his bed unassisted after a fall in spring 1773. Furthermore, Susanna's declining health and Phillis's own languishing illness during the winter of 1773–4 may have made the progress of Moorhead's death feel all too familiar.

114:5 "Shade": spirit, ghost.

114:11 "deplore": lament (Johnson, *Dictionary*).

114:22 "Like great *Elijah*": refers to 2 Kings 2:11, when the prophet "Elijah went up by a whirlwind into heaven."

115:41 "Tremendous Doom": "the final Judgment" (l. 39).

115:42 "Tophet": "fire place" in Hebrew, the site where children were burned alive as sacrifices to Molech. See 2 Kings 23:10; Jeremiah 7:31 ff., 19:6, 13 ff.

115:51–2 refers to the cross—"the Tree"—on which Christ—"th' incarnate Deity"— was crucified.

115:58 "Like MOSES' Serpent in the Desert wild": the brazen serpent that Moses fashioned in the wilderness at the command of God to cure anyone who looked upon it who had been bitten by a snake (Numbers 21:8–9).

115:66 "To Him whose Spirit had inspir'd his Lays": Moorhead also wrote poetry.

116:76 "Own the afflicting Providence, divine": acknowledge the afflictive dispensations of Providence intended to humble the believer, and to test his or her faith. See Deuteronomy 8:1–2.

[37] Letter from John Thornton to Phillis Wheatley, c.February 1774

John Thornton holograph copy at National Records of Scotland of a letter he sent to Wheatley (GD26/13/663/7).

[38] Letter to the Reverend Samuel Hopkins (9 February 1774)

Manuscript at the Historical Society of Pennsylvania (Simon Gratz Collection, Box 7/Case 10, Folder 36). First printed 9 May 1839 in the *Pennsylvania Freeman*, a weekly abolitionist newspaper published by John Greenleaf Whittier (1807–92).

The "two Negro men" Wheatley mentions were Bristol Yamma (1744?–94) and John Quamine (1743?–79). Wheatley probably heard Hopkins when he preached at Old South Church in Boston in 1769. Hopkins had been minister of the First Congregationalist Church in Newport, Rhode Island, since 11 April 1770 (cf. [21]). His familiarity with the transatlantic slave trade, one of the foundations of Newport's prosperity, prompted him to become one of New England's most outspoken abolitionists. Hopkins and Reverend Ezra Stiles (1727–95), pastor of the Second Congregationalist Church in Newport (and a slave owner), circulated a petition during the summer and fall of 1773, first in manuscript and later in print, soliciting funds to be used to train Yamma and Quamine (or Quamino) at what is now Princeton University to become Christian missionaries to Africa. Both men had been enslaved in the 1750s on the Gold Coast of Africa (present-day Ghana) and brought to Newport, where they had recently bought their freedom with money from a winning lottery ticket. They were keen to be sent back to their homeland. As Wheatley's 9 February 1774 letter to Hopkins [38] indicates, he had sent her a copy of the solicitation.

Hopkins and Ezra Stiles subsequently published a circular entitled *To the Public* (Newport, Rhode Island), dated 10 April 1776. *To the Public* is a progress report of the success Stiles and Hopkins have had in raising funds in America and Britain, as well as in having trained Yamma and Quamine for their mission to Africa. That mission was never accomplished because the American Revolution intervened. Quamine did not survive the war. He died in 1779 while serving on a privateer he had joined in hopes of gaining the money needed to buy his wife's freedom.

Thornton was not the first to suggest that Wheatley be sent to Africa as a Christian missionary. Occom had asked Susanna Wheatley on 5 March 1771,

"Pray Madam, what harm would it be to Send Phillis to her Native Country as a Female Preacher to her kindred, you know Quaker Women are alow'd to preach, and why not others in an Extraordinary Case" (Brooks, ed., *The Collected Writings of Samson Occom*, 97). Though we do not know whether Phillis was ever told of Occom's idea, she rejected Thornton's request politely but firmly, and with good reason, on 30 October 1774 (cf. [44]).

"the precious crumbs": cf. Matthew 15:27.
"the divine royal Psalmist": King David; see Psalm 68.

[39] Letter to Samson Occom (11 February 1774)

Published in the *Connecticut Gazette; and the Universal Intelligencer*, 11 March 1774. On Occom, cf. [29e]. Wheatley's most direct attack on slavery was subsequently reprinted in 1774 in the *Connecticut Gazette* (11 March), *Boston Evening Post* (21 March), *Essex Gazette* (22 and 29 March), *Boston Post-Boy* (22 March), *Boston News-Letter* (24 March), *Massachusetts Spy* (24 March), *Providence Gazette* (26 March), *Essex Journal and Merrimack Packet* (30 March), *Connecticut Journal* (1 April), *Newport Mercury* (11 April), as well as in the *Nova Scotia Gazette and Weekly Chronicle* (3 May).

[40] Letter to Obour Tanner (21 March 1774)

Manuscript at the Massachusetts Historical Society (Miscellaneous Bound Manuscripts).
Susanna Wheatley died 3 March 1774, aged 65.

[41] Letter to John Thornton (29 March 1774)

Manuscript in National Records of Scotland, Edinburgh (GD26/13/663/5).
Wheatley is replying to Thornton's response to her letter of 1 December 1773 [35].

[42] Letter to Obour Tanner (6 May 1774)

Manuscript at the Massachusetts Historical Society (Miscellaneous Bound Manuscripts).
Mr. Pemberton may be the Reverend Ebenezer Pemberton who attested to the authenticity of Wheatley's *Poems* (cf. [29f]). The 25 April to 2 May 1774 issue of the *Boston Post-Boy* reports that "Capt. White arrived here last Monday, and on Tuesday [26 April] Capt. [Robert] Calef, from London." Calef conducted trade between Boston and London for Phillis Wheatley's owners. He brought the 300 copies of the second edition of her *Poems* from London to Boston aboard the *London Packet*, the same vessel on which he had taken Phillis from Boston to and from London in 1773.

[43] Letter to Reverend Samuel Hopkins (6 May 1774)

Manuscript in the Chamberlin Collection, Boston Public Library (Ch A.6.20).

Philip Quaque (1741?–1816), son of an African ruler, had been brought in 1754 from Cape Coast, Africa (present-day Ghana), to England to be educated at the expense of the Anglican Society for the Propagation of the Gospel. The bishop of London ordained him an Anglican priest in 1765. After marrying an Englishwoman, Quaque was appointed "Missionary, Catechist and Schoolmaster to the Negroes on the Gold Coast in Africa." Except for a brief period in 1784–5, when he returned to England to arrange for his children's education, he spent the rest of his life trying to pursue his mission at Cape Coast Castle, with very limited success. Hopkins and Quaque conducted a transatlantic correspondence during the mid-1770s. (Vincent Carretta and Ty M. Reese, eds., *The Life and Letters of Philip Quaque, the First African Anglican Missionary*. Athens, GA: University of Georgia Press, 2010.) Quaque tracked down Quamine's family in Africa for Hopkins (cf. [38]).

In December 1773 Hopkins sent Quaque a copy of Wheatley's "*proposals, &c.*, supposing it will give you pleasure to see what a remarkable African appears in N. England. She has lately been to Europe, and was taken much notice of there. She will, I hope, be a means of promoting ye best interests of Africans" (Carretta and Reese, eds., *The Life and Letters of Philip Quaque*, 115). Through Hopkins, Quaque and Wheatley became the first authors of African descent to have their writings published together. Ezra Stiles and Hopkins included parts of two letters from Quaque to Hopkins, as well as an edited version of Wheatley's 9 February 1774 letter to Hopkins, in *To the Public*. Stiles and Hopkins quote Wheatley and Quaque to bear witness to the promising prospects and rewards of converting people of African descent on both sides of the Atlantic to Christianity.

The ninth edition of Thomas Salmon (1679–1767), *The Modern Gazeteer: or, a Short View of the Several Nations of the World* (London, 1746) was published in London in 1773.

[44] Letter to John Thornton, 30 October 1774

Manuscript at National Records of Scotland, Edinburgh (GD26/13/663/6).

"Anamaboe": the homeland of John Quamine (cf. [38]), located in present-day Ghana.

[45] Letter from Thomas Wallcut to Phillis Wheatley ### *(17 November 1774)*

Manuscript at Massachusetts Historical Society (Thomas Wallcut Papers, 1671–1866).

Thomas Wallcut was one of the earliest (and youngest) admirers of Wheatley's poetry. He was the youngest of the three sons of Elizabeth Wallcut (1721–1811), a close friend of John and Susanna Wheatley. Phillis actively promoted his education, initially corresponding with him through his mother, and soon directly. Cf.

"To the Rev. Dr. Thomas Amory on Reading His Sermons on Daily Devotion, in Which That Duty Is Recommended and Assisted" [29jj], note. On 30 January 1773, Elizabeth Wallcut sent Thomas manuscript copies of Wheatley's elegy on Sewell [11], and of her "To the University of Cambridge" [6]:

Dear Tomy

... And according to your Desire I have Sent you Dr Sewalls picture and the Verses on his Death Composd by phillis wheetly which with a piece She made on our Colledg She Sends as a present to you ... (Massachusetts Historical Society manuscript, Thomas Wallcut Papers, 1671–1866)

Thomas Wallcut subsequently became an author, an antiquarian, and a copier of documents.

[46] "[To a Gentleman of the Navy]"

Published in the *Royal American Magazine*, December 1774. Included in the 1779 "Proposals" [55] as "To Lieut. R— of the Royal Navy."

The "Gentleman" was John Prime Iron Rochfort (b. 1751). Born in Dublin, Ireland, the twenty-four-year-old Rochfort was rated, or ranked, an able seaman on the *Preston*, which sailed from England 6 May 1774 under the command of Captain John Robinson. Rochfort would be discharged from the *Preston* on 30 December 1775 to be promoted to lieutenant on the *Nautilus*.

Identifying Wheatley's "Greaves" (a phonetically accurate alternative spelling of "Graves") is very difficult because several relatives of Vice Admiral Samuel Graves (1713–87) served under him in the British fleet. For example, with Rochfort on the *Preston* was 3rd Lieutenant John Graves, a nephew of the vice admiral. One of John's brothers, Lieutenant Thomas Graves (1747?–1814), served on the *Lively* in the same fleet. Thomas Graves may have inspired Wheatley's thoughts of "pleasing Gambia" in her "Reply" [47]. He had served as a lieutenant on the *Shannon* off the coast of Gambia in 1765.

127:11 "Achaian": Greek.
127:19 "Albion": Britain.
127:33 "Cerulean": sky-blue.

"The Answer"

John Prime Iron Rochfort's anonymous response to Wheatley's poem [46] appeared in the same December 1774 issue of the *Royal American Magazine*. "The Answer" is not included in Wheatley's 1779 "Proposals" [55]:

The Answer

Celestial muse! sublimest of the nine,
Assist my song, and dictate every line:
Inspire me once, nor with imperfect lays,
To sing this great, this lovely virgins praise:
But yet, alas! what tribute can I bring,   5
WH—TL—Y but smiles, whilst I thus faintly sing,

Behold with reverence, and with joy adore;
The lovely daughter of the Affric shore,
Where every grace, and every virtue join,
That kindles friendship and makes love divine;   10
In hue as diff'rent as in souls above;
The rest of mortals who in vain have strove,
Th' immortal wreathe, the muse's gift to share,
Which heav'n reserv'd for this angelic fair.

Blest be the guilded shore, the happy land,   15
Where spring and autumn gently hand in hand;
O'er shady forests that scarce know a bound,
In vivid blaze alternately dance round:
Where cancers torrid heat the soul inspires;
With strains divine and true poetic fires;   20
(Far from the reach of Hudson's chilly bay)
Where cheerful phoebus makes all nature gay;
Where sweet refreshing breezes gently fan;
The flow'ry path, the ever verdent lawn,
The artless grottos, and the soft retreats;   25
"At once the lover and the muse's seats."
Where nature taught, (tho' strange it is to tell,)
Her flowing pencil Europe to excell.
Britania's glory long hath fill'd the skies;
Whilst other nations, tho' with envious eyes,   30
Have view'd her growing greatness, and the rules,
That's long been taught in her untainted schools:
Where great Sir Isaac! whose immortal name;
Still shines the brightest on the seat of fame;
By ways and methods never known before;   35
The sacred depth of nature did explore:
And like a God, on philosophic wings;
Rode with the planets thro' their circling rings:

Surveying nature with a curious eye,
And viewing other systems in the sky.   40

    Where nature's bard with true poetic lays,
The pristine state of paradise displays,
And with a genius that's but very rare
Describes the first the only happy pair
That in terrestial mansions ever reign'd,   45
View'd hapiness now lost, and now regain'd,
Unravel'd all the battles of the Gods,
And view'd old night below the antipodes.
On his imperious throne, with awful sway,
Commanding regions yet unknown today,   50

    Or where those lofty bards have dwelt so long,
That ravish'd Europe with their heavenly song,

    But now this blissful clime, this happy land,
That all the neighbouring nations did command;
Whose royal navy neptunes waves did sweep,   55
Reign'd Prince alone, and sov'reign of the deep:
No more can boast, but of the power to kill,
By force of arms, or diabolic skill.
For softer strains we quickly must repair
To Wheatly's song, for Wheatly is the fair;   60
That has the art, which art could ne'er acquire:
To dress each sentence with seraphic fire.

    Her wondrous virtues I could ne'er express!
To paint her charms, would only make them less.
                December 2nd. 1774.

208:15 "guilded shore": the western coast of Africa.
208:19 "cancers torrid heat": Africa, under the zodiacal sign of Cancer.
208:26 adapted from Alexander Pope, *Windsor Forest* (London, 1713), line 2: "At once the Monarch's and the Muse's Seats."
208:33 "great Sir Isaac": Sir Isaac Newton (1642–1727), English mathematician, scientist, and religious writer.
208:41 "nature's bard": John Milton, English epic poet, author of *Paradise Lost* (1667).
208:42 "The pristine state of paradise": the Garden of Eden before the fall of Adam and Eve recounted in *Paradise Lost*.
208:53 "this happy land": England.

[47] "Philis's [sic] Reply to the Answer in our last by the
Gentleman in the Navy"

Published in the *Royal American Magazine*, January 1775. Included in Wheatley's 1779 "Proposals" [55] as "To the same."

128:16 "At British Homer's and Sir Isaac's feet": at the feet of Milton and Newton.

128:22 "pleasing Gambia on my soul returns": Both Rochfort and Wheatley use poetic diction to depict Africa as "display'd" in a "painting" of a golden age, where winter never comes, and sin is nowhere to be found. They are engaged in a traditional classical competition of corresponding pastoral poems, with neither attempting to convey accurate cultural, geographical, or historical information. Certainly the transatlantic slave trade that brought Wheatley from Africa to Boston has no place in either Rochfort's or Wheatley's depiction of Africa. Her poem is at least as conventionally pastoral and idealized as Rochfort's, and gives no evidence whatsoever that she is describing an actual place or time, or speaking from personal experience.

Wheatley may mention "Gambia" because "Greaves" had been there. The equation of Rochfort's "guilded shore" and Wheatley's "Gambia" may be traced back to the reference to "Gambia's golden shore" by John Singleton (fl. 1760s) in *A General Description of the West-Indian Islands* (Barbados: Printed by George Esmand and William Walker, for the Author, 1766), Book 2, line 49. An abridged version was published the following year under the title *A Description of the West-Indies, A Poem, in Four Books* (London: Printed for T. Becket, the corner of the Adelphi in the Strand, 1767). Singleton, Rochfort, and Wheatley may all confuse Gambia with the Gold Coast of Africa. Senegal and Gambia had been idealized in descriptions of Africa since at least 1759, when Michel Adanson (1727–1806), *Histoire Naturelle du Sénégal* was published in London as *A Voyage to Senegal, the Isle of Goree, and the River Gambia. By M. Adanson, ... Translated from the French. With Notes by an English Gentleman, who Resided some Time in that Country* (London: Printed for J. Nourse, and W. Johnston [*sic*], 1759). Anthony Benezet's quotation of Adanson's Edenic description of Senegambia in his *Some Historical Account of Guinea*, first published in Philadelphia in 1771, made the account widely available to later opponents of the transatlantic slave trade and slavery.

[48] "To His Excellency General Washington"

Published in the *Virginia Gazette* on 30 March 1776. Included in the 1779 "Proposals" [55].

Wheatley enclosed this poem in a letter to Washington (1732–99) dated 26 October 1775. Washington responded from Cambridge on 28 February 1776 [50].

Washington sent Wheatley's poem and her letter to his former secretary, Colonel
Joseph Reed (1741–85), on 10 February 1776, telling him,

I recollect nothing else worth giving you the trouble of, unless you can be amused
by reading a Letter and Poem addressed to me by Mrs or Miss Phillis Wheatley—
In searching over a parcel of Papers the other day, in order to destroy such as were
useless, I brought it to light again—at first, With a view of doing justice to her
poetical Genius, I had a great Mind to publish the Poem, but not knowing whether
it might not be considered rather as a mark of my own vanity than a Compliment
to her I laid it aside till I came across it again in the manner just mentioned. (*The
Papers of George Washington*, Revolutionary War Series, vol. 3, *1 January 1776–31
March 1776*, ed. Philander D. Chase. Charlottesville: University Press of Virginia,
1988, 286–91)

Reed apparently took Washington's hint and sent the poem and letter with his
own headnote to the editors of the *Virginia Gazette*. Thomas Paine (1737–1809)
republished them in the April 1776 issue of his *Pennsylvania Magazine or American
Monthly Museum* 2.

130:2 "Columbia's scenes of glorious toils": the American colonists' recent military victories against British forces. Wheatley's use of *Columbia* here, and
again in *Liberty and Peace* in 1784, enlists her as an early participant in the
contemporaneous discussion of what to call the American colonies united in
rebellion against Great Britain. Both poems anticipate the evolution of the
thirteen loosely confederated separate colonies into the single nation codified
by the *Constitution* in 1787. Samuel Johnson may have been the first to use the
neo-Latin toponym *Columbia* as a synonym for *America*, in his "Reports of the
Debates of the Senate in Lilliput," in the *Gentleman's Magazine* 8 (June 1738).
Earlier in 1775 than the date of Wheatley's letter to Washington that accompanied her poem, Mercy Otis Warren (1728–1814), celebrates the opposition
of *Columbia* to *Britannia* in her dramatic farce, *The Group, as lately Acted*. The
identification of Columbia with America, however, was still infrequent enough
in 1780 that Charles Henry Wharton (1748–1833) felt the need to clarify the
identification with a footnote in his *A Poetical Epistle to His Excellency George
Washington, Esq.* (Annapolis, MD, 1779). And on 14 February 1782, *Thomas's
Massachusetts Spy or, The Worcester Gazette* (Worcester, MA) reprinted a letter from a correspondent to the *Pennsylvania Journal* on the subject: "I observe
with great pleasure in many modern publications, the United States distinguished by the name of *Columbia*.... For the future let the free citizen of our
infant republicks be known by the name of *Columbians*, and let our language
(instead of bearing the name of our proud and vengeful enemies) be called the
Columbian language.... The dignity and habits of independence can only be
acquired by a total emancipation of our country from the fashions and manners
of Great-Britain."

130:10 "binds": corrected to *bind* when Wheatley quotes herself in 1784 in *Liberty and Peace, A Poem*, line 4 [57].

130:30 "When Gallic powers Columbia's fury found": probably refers to the "fury" that French forces and their Indian allies—"Gallic powers"—experienced at the hands of the British and colonial American forces during the Seven Years' War. France and the American colonies rebelling against Britain did not sign The Treaty of Alliance until 5 February 1778.

[49] Letter to Obour Tanner, 14 February 1776

Manuscript in private hands.

On (John) Quamine, cf. p. 203, [38]. Cato Coggeshall, Zingo (Stevens), Tanner, and Quamine belonged to Phillis Wheatley's network of enslaved as well as free people of African descent based in Rhode Island. They were members in Newport of either Reverend Samuel Hopkins' First Congregational Church, or Reverend Ezra Stiles' Second Congregational Church. Wheatley refers to them in [21] as "so many of my Nation, seeking with eagerness the way to true felicity." Cato Coggeshall, a distiller, was owned by Nathaniel "Deacon" Coggeshall. Zingo, a stonemason, had been enslaved to John Stevens II, who freed him in his will in 1774. In 1780, Zingo was a cofounder in Newport of the Free African Union Society, the first African American benevolent society.

[50] Letter from George Washington to Phillis Wheatley, 28 February 1776

Manuscript in George Washington Papers at the Library of Congress, Series 3: Varick Transcripts, 1775–85.

[51] "On the Capture of General Lee"

Manuscript at Bowdoin College library, dated 30 December 1776 (Bowdoin Family Collection M15.2.3, Box 1, Folder 84a). Included in the 1779 "Proposals" [55]. Not published.

Wheatley's poem is an imagined dialogue between a patriotic Major General Charles Lee (1732–82) and his oppressive British captors. Wheatley probably knew that Lee had been with Washington in Cambridge during the siege of Boston. But she apparently was unaware that Lee was frequently reprimanded for insubordination, and aggressively sought to replace Washington as commander-in-chief of the Continental army. Lee may even have become disloyal to the American cause after the British captured him in Morristown, New Jersey, on 13 December 1776, the occasion for Wheatley's poem. He was released early in 1778 as part of a prisoner exchange. Lee's behavior during the Battle of Monmouth, New Jersey, on 28 June 1778, caused him to be court-martialed for insubordination, convicted, and suspended from duty for a year. When he failed to get Congress to overturn his conviction, he publicly attacked Washington's character. Wheatley's poem was not published until the late nineteenth century, probably because Bowdoin knew how greatly it misrepresents Lee's relationship with Washington.

[52] Letter to Obour Tanner, 29 May 1778

Manuscript at the Massachusetts Historical Society (Miscellaneous Bound Manuscripts).

[53] "On the Death of General Wooster"

Manuscript at the Massachusetts Historical Society (Hugh Upham Clark Collection). Included in the 1779 "Proposals."

A New Haven, Connecticut, merchant, Major General David Wooster died on 2 May 1777, having been mortally wounded by the British. Wheatley sent the letter and poem to Wooster's widow, Mary, on 15 July 1778. Cf, [22], note; [33], note.

Wheatley uses ventriloquism here to express her opposition to slavery through Wooster's imagined dying prayer.

"a martyr in the Cause": cf. "martyr for the cause" [13].

[54] Letter to Obour Tanner, 10 May 1779

Manuscript at the Massachusetts Historical Society (Miscellaneous Bound Manuscripts).

[55] Proposals (30 October 1779)

Published in the *Boston Evening Post and General Advertiser*, 30 October, 6 November, and 27 November, 1779. James White (1755?–1824) and Thomas Adams (1757?–99), the printers of the *Boston Evening Post and General Advertiser*, may have been chosen as potential publishers of the proposed second volume because they had recently published the sermon that Reverend John Lathrop delivered at the funeral of his wife, Mary Wheatley Lathrop (*Consolation for mourners, from the doctrine of a resurrection, and the future happiness of believers. A discourse occasioned by the death of Mrs. Mary Lathrop, who departed this life 24th September, 1778. Aged 35. Delivered the Lord's Day after the funeral. By her afflicted consort, John Lathrop. A.M. Pastor of the Second Church in Boston. Published at the desire of many who heard it, and the particular acquaintance of the deceased* [Boston, 1778]).

Versions of seven of the thirty-three poems, which are not listed in chronological order in the "Proposals," are known to exist: [51], [48], [53], [46], [47], [32], [59]. The recipients of most of the letters listed can be identified with a high degree of probability: (1) William Legge, Earl of Dartmouth; (2) Reverend Timothy Pitkin; (3) Thomas Wallcut; (4) Thomas Hubbard; (5) Benjamin Rush; (7, 12, 13) Selina Hastings, Countess of Huntingdon; (8) Israel Mauduit; (9) perhaps Hannah Wilberforce; (11) perhaps Susanna Wheatley.

[56]

AN ELEGY, SACRED TO THE MEMORY OF THAT GREAT DIVINE, THE REVEREND AND LEARNED DR. SAMUEL COOPER, *Who departed this Life December* 29, 1783, AETATIS 59.

BY PHILLIS PETERS. BOSTON: *Printed and Sold by E. Russell, in Essex-Street, near Liberty-Pole,* M,DCC,LXXXIV.

To the CHURCH *and* CONGREGATION *assembling in Brattle-Street, the following,* ELEGY, *Sacred to the* MEMORY *of their late Reverend and Worthy* PASTOR, *Dr.* SAMUEL COOPER, *is, with the greatest Sympathy, most respectfully inscribed by their Obedient,*

Humble Servant,

PHILLIS PETERS.

BOSTON, Jan. 1784.

An eight-page pamphlet apparently published soon after 2 January 1784. Appended to the pamphlet is William Billings (1746–1800), "Words for a funeral anthem. Taken from the following scriptures; and set to Musick by Mr. Billings. And performed at the Funeral of the Reverend Dr. Samuel Cooper, on Friday, Jan. 2, 1784." Billings's anthem had been advertised separately before Ezekiel Russell published it together with Wheatley's poem following Cooper's funeral. Billings is often considered the father of American choral hymn music. His *New-England Psalm-Singer: or, American Chorister* (Boston: Printed by [Benjamin] Edes [1732–1803] and [John] Gill [1732–85], 1770) was the first published collection of American music.

The *Continental Journal, and Weekly Advertiser* (Boston) on 1 January 1784 was one of the first periodicals to report that prior to his death on 29 December 1783, Reverend Samuel Cooper "had been confined to his Chamber with a Disorder of the lethargick Kind for upwards of six Weeks." Hence, Phillis Wheatley Peters may have drafted her elegy in anticipation of Cooper's death, as she had done with "On the Death of the Rev. Dr. *Sewell,* when sick, 1765—" in mistaken anticipation of Reverend Joseph Sewall's death in 1765 [18].

Samuel Cooper was the only minister of the Brattle Street Congregationalist Church from 1747 until his death. He received his BA and MA from Harvard (1743, 1746), another MA from Yale (1750), and his doctor of divinity in 1767 from the University of Edinburgh. Cooper became an overseer of Harvard in 1746, and a member of its corporation in 1767. In 1774 he chose to remain the pastor of the church in Brattle Street rather than accept the presidency of Harvard. A lengthy obituary on 22 January 1784 in the *Independent Chronicle and the Universal Advertiser* (Boston) describes Cooper as an eloquent, learned, and passionate preacher of moderate Congregationalist theology. It also notes his "fame for literary accomplishments," and that he was "an active member of the society for propagating the gospel among the aboriginals of America." Cooper opposed British rule during the American Revolution. Like Phillis Wheatley, he fled Boston during the British occupation in 1775, and returned after they evacuated in 1776.

Cooper baptized Phillis Wheatley in Old South Church on 18 August 1771. He was one of the men who authenticated her *Poems* [29f]. In lines 40–4 of her elegy Wheatley acknowledges Cooper's support of her literary efforts.

A manuscript copy of Wheatley's elegy at the Massachusetts Historical Society (Smith-Carter Family Papers, 1669–1880) probably postdates the printed copy: the manuscript is not in Wheatley's hand, and her name is misspelled on it.

[57]

LIBERTY AND PEACE, A POEM. *By* PHILLIS PETERS. BOSTON*:* *Printed by* WARDEN *and* RUSSELL, *At Their Office in Marlborough-Street.* M,DCC,LXXXIV [1784].

The four-page pamphlet is a celebration of the Peace of Paris that Congress ratified in January 1784. Not surprisingly given its subject, the poem exudes joy and optimism. The tone is even somewhat self-congratulatory. In her description of "Freedom" Phillis Wheatley Peters self-referentially quotes from her earlier poem to Washington. *Liberty and Peace, a Poem* is quite similar in subject matter and tone to Reverend John Lathrop's *A Discourse on the Peace; Preached on the Day of Public Thanksgiving, November 25, 1784. By John Lathrop, A.M. Pastor of the Second Church in Boston* (Boston: Printed by Peter Edes [1756–1840], in State-Street, MDCCLXXXIV [1784]). Consequently, rather than having been published at the beginning of 1784, Phillis's poem may have been, as Lathrop's sermon was, occasioned by Governor John Hancock's *Proclamation* published on 28 October 1784 calling for a day of thanksgiving on 25 November 1784. The celebratory and optimistic nature of *Liberty and Peace*, however, is so inconsistent with the dire personal and economic situation of Phillis and John Peters near the end of 1784 that an earlier publication date in the year seems more likely.

141:3–4 quoted directly from lines 9–10 of Wheatley's poem to Washington [48]. 142:37 *"Hibernia"*: Latin name for Ireland.

[58] Wheatley's Final Proposal (September 1784)

The Boston Magazine, September 1784. Cf. [59].

[59] To Mr. and Mrs.—, on the Death of their Infant Son.

Published with [58] in the September 1784 issue of the *Boston Magazine*. The use of Phillis Wheatley Peters's maiden name, albeit misspelled, suggests a composition date before her marriage on 26 November 1778. Mason (179) suggests that this is the poem "To P.N.S. & Lady on the death of their infant son" included in Wheatley's 1779 "Proposals." It may also be a variant of "To a Gentleman and Lady on the Death of their Son, aged 9 Months" listed in her 1772 "Proposals" [cf. 18]. Joseph Greenleaf (1720–1810) and Edmund Freeman (1764–1807) were the printers/publishers of the *Boston Magazine*.

INDEX OF TITLES OF POEMS

INDEX OF FIRST LINES OF POEMS

GENERAL INDEX TO INTRODUCTION AND EXPLANATORY NOTES